THE LIFE OF UNA MARSON
1905–65

MANCHESTER
UNIVERSITY PRESS

THE LIFE OF
UNA MARSON
1905–65

Delia Jarrett-Macauley

MANCHESTER
UNIVERSITY PRESS
MANCHESTER AND NEW YORK

distributed exclusively in the USA by St. Martin's Press

Published by Manchester University Press
Oxford Road, Manchester M13 9NR, UK
and Room 400, 175 Fifth Avenue, New York, NY 10010, USA

Distributed exclusively in the USA by
St. Martin's Press, Inc., 175 Fifth Avenue, New York, NY 10010, USA

Distributed exclusively in Canada by
UBC Press, University of British Columbia, 6344 Memorial Road, Vancouver, BC, Canada V6T 1Z2

British Library Cataloguing-in-Publication Data
A catalogue record is available from the British Library

Library of Congress Cataloging-in-Publication Data
Jarret-Macauley, Delia, 1958–
    The biography of Una Marson / Delia Jarrett-Macauley.
        p.   cm.
    Includes bibliographical references (p.) and index.
    ISBN 0–7190–5284–x (cl)
        1. Marson, Una.   2. Women authors, English—20th century—Biography.
    3. Jamaicans—England—London—History—20th century.
    4. Jamaicans—Great Britain—Biography.   5. Feminists—Great Britain—
    Biography.   I. Title.
    PR6025.A695Z73   1998
    821'.912—dc21
    [B]   97–4355

ISBN 0 7190 5284 x *hardback*

First published 1998

01   00   99   98   10   9   8   7   6   5   4   3   2   1

Typeset in Charter
by Northern Phototypesetting Co. Ltd, Bolton
Printed in Great Britain
by Redwood Books, Trowbridge

Contents

The illustrations appear between chapters 6 and 7 – pp. 57–67

Preface

Born in 1905 in rural Jamaica, the wayward youngest daughter of a stern Baptist parson, Una Marson became an internationally famous feminist, activist and writer. After a privileged but painful adolescence, she established herself in early 1920s Jamaica as a pioneering journalist, playwright and poet. Weary with the constraints of the imitative colonial world and the restrictions on young women, she travelled to London in 1932, but life in England proved to be a bitter disappointment in many ways. It was hard to find lodgings, a job and even places to socialise, but Una became integrated into black social and political circles. In Europe Una Marson associated with leading black figures including Haile Selassie, travelling with him to Geneva in 1935; the African-American star Paul Robeson; and visiting African leaders.

As the first black British feminist to speak out against racism and sexism in Britain, Una Marson emerges as a significant forerunner to contemporary black feminists operating within Euro-American contexts as well as to those who are concerned with debates on 'Third World' feminism as an autonomous, home-grown ideology and praxis, since much of her work concerned women of African origin in their own countries.

Her literary contacts were as broad as her talents: she was befriended by Winifred Holtby, nurtured by James Weldon Johnson and, as a BBC producer during the Second World War, she worked alongside George Orwell. So while Una Marson steps out of post-colonial literary history as 'the first major woman poet of the Caribbean and as a forerunner of contemporary black British women writers',[1] she is unusual for her relations with mainstream British writers long before black women's literature had earned the cachet it enjoys today. And her literary life is a reminder that better-known Caribbean male authors, such as V. S. Naipaul and George Lamming, 'imitated' her experience of 'exile' in 1950s and 1960s London.

Una grew intellectually by travelling extensively and crossing multiple boundaries; she refused to allow the constraints of 'race', gender or sexuality to limit her politics or her creative vision. She brought issues of gender into male-dominated nationalist politics, racialised white mainstream feminist thinking and creolised conservative Jamaican theatre; she moved definitions to serve people.

Una Marson has rarely been researched and discussed in either black literary, feminist or political contexts. The notable exceptions are an essay by literary critic Erika Smilowitz, 'Una Marson – a Woman Before her Time' (*Jamaica Journal*, May 1983), which has become the chief source on Marson and the basis of such other rare articles as Honor Ford Smith's work on *Pocomania*, Marson's third play, under the title *Una Marson: Black Nationalist and Feminist Writer* (Sistren, 1986), and some of Una Marson's literary work considered in 'Women in Jamaican literature 1900–1950' by Rhonda Cobham-Sander (extract from unpublished Ph.D. thesis, University of St Andrews, 1982).

Although the Institute of Jamaica holds Una Marson's papers, the collection is very small. It contains few unpublished manuscripts, only three letters, no notebooks, diaries or pictures. In January 1989 Erika Smilowitz wrote to me and advised me against visiting Jamaica:

> I'm not sure a trip to Jamaica is really worth your time. The Institute didn't have much – I suspect all the important material was in the box that got thrown out [by a family friend, Jenny Gaffe]. Mrs Gaffe may not be willing to see you, but one never knows.

Thankfully, Jenny Gaffe did see me, as did numerous other friends, colleagues and fellow writers of Una Marson; together they provided me with a substantial body of additional material, which enabled me to develop a fuller picture of her life and personality, having already constructed a chronology using newspaper articles from the 1920s to 1965.

From her early radical journalism in *The Cosmopolitan* to her last article published in the *Gleaner* in 1965, she expressed her views in a voice that was authoritative, passionate and iconoclastic. She frequently wrote about the ills at the heart of women's lives, partly because she knew sorrow, loneliness and romantic disappointment. She also wrote about women's political rights, culture, literature and social issues.

Una Marson is a major figure in twentieth-century feminist, black and literary histories. Her story arcs towards untouched visions for black people and for women, and confronts the complexities of 'identity' in the modern world. And yet it has been erased because it is alternative, and discredited because it is critical. So often, even now, black women of Una's stature appear only as token women in black texts or as token blacks in feminist ones. Where their contributions are noted, they might be represented as superwomen – separate from their peers.

This first biography presents the woman from her birth in colonial Jamaica to her death sixty years later. It places Una within a broad historical context, revealing the men and women and the social forces which shaped her life and perhaps our own. And it draws on Una Marson's personal letters and the testimony of friends and associates worldwide – from Israel, Jamaica, the USA and Europe – to show the unselfish, spontaneous and determined, yet tragically vulnerable and depressive woman behind the public image.

Delia Jarrett-Macauley

NOTE

1   'Introduction', in R. Cobham-Sander and Merle Collins, *Watchers and Seekers* (London, Women's Press, 1987).

Acknowledgements

I am deeply indebted to all the individuals whose words appear in this book and to many others whose good wishes are here in spirit because they gave me insight, encouragement and their precious time. In particular, I thank all the friends and former colleagues of Una Marson who answered my letters and shared their knowledge of her career with me. I am indebted to the many libraries and other institutions mentioned in the notes and bibliography for allowing me access to their collections and for carrying out diligent searches on my behalf. In particular, I thank the National Library of Jamaica; the Gleaner Company Limited, Kingston, Jamaica; the Library of the University of West Indies; the Yale Collection of American Literature, Beinecke Rare Book and Manuscript Library, Yale University; Jewel Sims Okala for the James Weldon Johnson archive; the Chicago Historical Society for the Claude A. Barnett papers; the BBC Written Archives Centre; the British Library; University College London Library and the George Orwell Archive; the University of Reading; Kingston upon Hull Central Library; the Winifred Holtby Archives; Rhodes House Library, Oxford; Angus Library, Regent's Park College, Oxford; Public Record Office, London; London School of Economics Library; Fawcett Library, Guildhall, London; United Nations Library, Geneva; Mills Memorial Library, McMaster University, Hamilton, Ontario; and Milli Kutuphane, Ankara, Turkey.

Mina Ben-Zwi, Ursula Larsen and the late Egon Larsen, Mona Macmillan and Erica Koch have all shared letters and photographs without which my picture of Una Marson would have been much dimmer: I thank them. Elena Lappin, Mehmet Ali Dikerdem, Rainer Lotz and Kamau Brathwaite all secured materials from overseas on my behalf – I thank them for helping me stalk Una Marson.

I am grateful to academics whose critical and sensitive readings of drafts of this work helped me: Lyn Innes, Stewart Brown, John Thieme and Louis James. I thank Marike Sherwood, Hakim Adi and Catherine Hall for their responses to my work and for sharing their own. Many friends, especially Debbie Licorish, Deborah Cheney and Juliette Verhoeven, have successfully turned my anxieties about writing into bearable calm: I thank them all.

I have had a supportive editor in Matthew Frost at Manchester University Press. He gave his blessing to this work at a time when my own faith had faltered. I am also grateful to Gemma Marren, Stephanie Sloan and other staff at Manchester University Press.

I thank here the many people known and unknown to me who have helped to construct the movements to which Una's life was committed.

Finally, this book and I owe much to many years of gentle support from my friends, socialist-feminist writer Sheila Rowbotham and Nigel Pollitt.

I

'Parson's Baby'

SHE was born on 6 February 1905, the youngest child of the Reverend Solomon Isaac and Ada Marson. Her arrival was promptly heralded with not one but two names. The people of Sharon village, her birthplace in rural Jamaica, simply called her 'Parson's Baby', while her father later registered her, on 24 March, as Una Maud Victoria Marson. Both names stuck. When, in her early forties, Una Marson returned to the village after many years overseas, old women from her father's former church hugged her, calling out 'Parson's Baby', even then.[1]

Una's earliest memory was of the Sharon Mission House where she was born. It belonged to the local Baptist church of which her father was minister, and it housed the twelve Marson family members. For several decades this house, a two-storey wooden structure, remained a landmark against the Sharon sky until, one day in the mid-1960s, it was razed to the ground, burying in its discarded timbers the conversations of generations of Baptist parsons and their families: the Browns, the Houses, the Marsons and the DaCostas. Carried away too were any childhood notebooks, pictures and letters that might have furnished intimate details of Una's first years. The grounds, however, are undisturbed. A long drive running up to the house from a wide gate still slips round to the rear where tall, deep-brown-barked trees of the coffee patch loom, casting a shadow. There, among the white, frilly springtime blossoms the Marson children had played, camouflaged and concealed from their parents.

The Marsons' home was comfortable, dignified and spacious, though the nine children had to share bedrooms. Una, being the youngest, slept in the nursery, a light and airy room, decorated with pictures and flowers. Her mother, Ada, had a sewing room where she made and mended their clothes; and downstairs in his large study, 'lined with heavily bound books'[2] and littered with Baptist church magazines and circulars, the Reverend Marson worked. In this house Una Maud Marson spent the first ten years of her life.[3]

There was no shortage of people to nurture the little Una Maud. Rosalind Mullings, her maternal grandmother, a tall olive-skinned woman, was still alive in 1905 and helped to raise all the Marson children. Rosalind's father had been an Irishman who came to Jamaica in the early 1800s and settled, possibly near the village of Burnt Ground in the north of the island, where Rosalind was born. As an adult Una Marson warmed to the Irish and when she was in London in the 1940s would seek out a favourite London tea-room where she might hum along to the mellifluous tunes of 'Come Back to Erin', 'The Mountain of Mourne' or 'Danny Boy'. But, apart from such flimsy longings, she never showed any enduring interest in unearthing this European strain. She turned instead to Africa: this, she felt, was her true ancestral home, the land of her father's forefathers.[4]

Solomon Marson headed a large household consisting of his devoted and devout wife, Ada, and their six children: Edith, Ethel, Ruby, Ewart, another son whose name is unknown, Una's grandmother, and Una. There were also three adopted children, who probably came from local, semi-destitute families, and four servants, one of whom was nicknamed Old Cookie and 'swore she'd been a pickney [child] when slavery was abolished' in 1834.[5] There is no evidence that Una maintained contact in later life with her siblings apart from Edith and Ethel.

Solomon Isaac Marson, Una's father, came from a family of moderately successful peasants in Brown's Town, a village in St Ann, a parish in the north of Jamaica. The Brown's Town Marsons belonged to that class of smallholders whose modest cultivations included tall breadfruit trees, coffee and citrus, yams, sweet potatoes and small green cabbages. They had chickens running about, a pig, one or two goats tethered to the house and a cow tended by the family. They also had fighting spirit. When Solomon Marson was born in 1858 the smallholders of his parish were enduring a terrible drought which was to last three years, burning their crops and leaving them near to destitution. In desperation they petitioned Queen Victoria: 'we are compelled to rent from the large proprietors ... the rent must be paid in advance.' But so harsh was the response to this plea that the seeds for political and religious uprising were sown in more Jamaican minds:

of this the famous Morant Bay Rebellion of 1865 was an inevitable outcome.

Throughout his early life Solomon Marson learnt a respect for hard work and religious faith, values that stayed with him all his life. He trained as an elementary school teacher at Mico Training College in Kingston and became known as a formidable teacher, ruling with the command of a general the small schoolroom with its makeshift blackboard and holes for ventilation. In the typical late nineteenth-century village school, a little wooden world, the voices of twelve children could be heard, reciting their tables, poems or dates with a handful of books, slates or copybooks at hand.

Solomon Marson was on school holiday in Montego Bay when he decided to join the Church. His own pastor was George Henderson, whose account *Goodness and Mercy: a Tale of a Hundred Years* tells of how several of his parishioners, bright keen young men, volunteered for the ministry during his time at that parish.[6] Solomon Marson was one of those 'recommended by the Church and accepted by the Managing Committee of Calabar', the Baptist training college in Kingston.[7]

Montego Bay, a popular coastal resort from the early nineteenth century, was a receptacle for new ideas from North America. Ships frequently travelled for Jamaica from US eastern ports such as Wilmington, Savannah, Charles and Boston, and trade in molasses and rum was welcomed by the North American colonies. But of greater importance to the professional development of Solomon Marson was the American religious influence imported by loyalist families who, at the outbreak of the American War of Independence, had transferred to Jamaica. Some of them were slave owners whose slaves were drawn to missionary zeal, as in the case of George Lisle, who began to preach, later set up a chapel in Kingston and appealed to the Baptist Missionary Society in London for support. But there were other pioneering missionaries in the Montego Bay area, including the famous Thomas Burchill and the dynamic William Knibb. It is little wonder then that it was a Montego Bay holiday which prompted Solomon Marson too to quit teaching for the ministry. This career conversion advanced in 1886 when he enrolled at Calabar Baptist Theological College, and he was ordained two years later.

When Solomon Marson first as a student preacher visited Sharon village, near the market town of Santa Cruz in the centre of the parish of St Elizabeth, he already had a mature and forceful presence. The Sharon 'station', established in 1872, was then a little more than ten

years old. In the *Missionary Herald* of 1 August 1875 it was reported
that at Santa Cruz:

> A piece of land was given by a resident in the locality on which a sub-
> stantial rustic chapel has been built. A church has been formed, which
> consists of forty-nine members and twenty-five inquirers. A day-school
> has been opened, and a Sunday school is in full work. But inasmuch as
> the distance betwixt Wallingford and Santa Cruz is so great (eighteen
> miles), with a wide, and sometimes impassable lagoon betwixt them,
> the latter station has been placed under the care of the Rev. W. N.
> Brown, who will make Santa Cruz his headquarters, and, as an agent
> of the Jamaica Baptist Missionary Society, will work the populous and
> destitute outlying districts.[8]

By 1876 the church had a small congregation of fifty-eight members.
It was not, however, until the Reverend George House, an English missionary associated with Calabar Baptist College, took over the church
that its numbers increased substantially. When Solomon Marson visited Sharon, George House had died, and the leaderless congregation,
impressed by his charismatic preaching, invited him to become their
pastor. By the time of Una's birth in spring 1905, Solomon Marson's
authority across the entire parish was unassailable, and the Marson
family, who had already lived at the Mission House for seventeen
years, had become a part of the landscape.

Life in the Marson household centred on the parson's work whether
he was at the Mission House or not. Una adored her father and missed
him when he was away. On first Sundays the Reverend Marson was
always at home and would preach his 'vital and dynamic' sermons to
the Sharon congregation.[9] Una used to sit with her family in the front
pew and gaze up 'spellbound', but usually had to stay home, recite her
Golden Passage set every week at Sunday School, and read from the
Bible. Other Sundays, when the parson was away, were more hectic.
Then the coachman would drive Solomon Marson in the buggy to his
various outstations, scattered across the St Elizabeth countryside at
Burnt Savannah, Wallingford or Nightingale Grove. But all Sundays
were long days with an 'early communion here, a morning service
there, a celebration following and an evening service in a third place,
to say nothing of Sunday School, interviewing parishioners in the
vestry and meetings of church committees'.[10] Una formed the impression that 'Papa never had a moment to spare on Sundays'.

The Reverend Marson's work was not restricted to Sunday preaching. Like every other Jamaican pastor he was frequently called upon to

do the work of magistrate and solicitor in settling disputes about property among his parishioners, to act as domestic adviser in family councils, as physician to the sick, as government agent in the management of day schools, and in the work of parochial and government boards. Solomon Marson also sat on the General Committee of his former college, Calabar, in Kingston and advised local schools too.[11] His executive responsibilities were considerable, but then so were the rewards.

In comparison with most other Jamaicans the Marsons were fairly well off. In later life Una was to write about her family's modest lifestyle in a way that suggested that the Marsons had struggled to make ends meet. 'Mama and Papa brought up nine of us on manna from heaven', she wrote to George Orwell in 1949, while revisiting the old house at Sharon. What the family did not possess, however, was cash for luxuries, savings for a rainy day or easy access to moneyed people. But neither did they have to fill their hours with unpleasant chores. There was always someone to wash, starch and iron their clothes, dust and polish the wooden floors the St Elizabeth way, with the scooped-out coconut brush, make ginger beer, kola wine or orange wine; someone to shop, make beds and tuck the children in at night.

For his pains Solomon Marson earned a good salary of around £90 a year: the Jamaica Baptist Missionary Society gave £20 and the remainder came from the ticket system, dues collected from full church members, whose responsibility it was to provide the minister with a reasonably stable income, if he was worth it. Solomon was; he could pull in the crowds.[12] And since the house and buggy were both free, a servant's wage no more than 1s a week, and you could buy a whole line of fish for 6d, or get six or seven good bananas for a quattie (quarter of a sixpence, 1½d) – if you were smart at market – the Marson budget was ample.[13]

Una worshipped her father, and was jubilant when from time to time the parson took her in the buggy with him to other stations or when she was allowed to read the theological books in his study. Yet such occasions were rare, and Una's veneration only emphasised the closer relationship she longed for in vain and which, as an adult, she struggled to recreate with other men. Solomon Marson so dominated her life that, even at her memorial service in the parish in August 1965, he was recalled as a 'renowned Baptist clergyman, a man whose dominating personality was felt not only in Santa Cruz where he laboured in the ministry, but throughout St. Elizabeth'.[14] Una loved him and feared him. In her plays, *At What a Price* (1931) and *Pocomania* (1938), the less attractive aspects of the dominant father's personality were most visible. In the latter the 'stern', inflexible Baptist deacon, who is frequently absent, holds all the power: 'I am her father and I have more experience than you have. I say that under no circumstances must she go. Good night.'[15]

The most free and enjoyable times in Una's childhood were those she spent in the company of visitors. 'Old Cookie' not only prepared all the family meals but, for special occasions, had lengthy discussions about menus with Ada Marson. Meals were often elaborate: when, for example, local dignitaries called, or English ministers came to preach at Sharon, they feasted on roasted pig, cooked until 'he was as brown as a biscuit and presented at table with a lettuce in his mouth, looking as though he were about to take off'.[16] Parishioners came in for rose-tea parties with Ada Marson, and relatives occasionally came to stay. Una enjoyed the periodic arrival of guests at Sharon and would eagerly await the familiar sound of horses neighing in the yard as the double buggy stopped outside the Marson residence. Then running down to welcome friends she would be 'thrilled at the shininess of the harness, the sleekness of the horses and the elegance of their guests, sitting in the buggy with what looked to us like shawls over their knees'.[17]

Una's favourite visitor was Solomon's younger cousin, Angie. She was one of his few living relatives and a close family friend besides. Cousin Angie was 'inordinately proud' of Solomon's career, Una wrote in late middle age, and deeply fond of his wife and children, on all of whom she lavished presents and affectionate pampering. Every year she visited once or twice, staying for a few weeks at a time and travelling from her home in Top Road, Brown's Town, in the mail and passenger mule-drawn coach from Balaclava to Santa Cruz. A single woman of independent means, Angie owned 'a little cloth store and would always bring us material for dresses. This was chosen with great care as to patterns and colour. And of course, there was a tie for Cousin Sol.'[18]

This Brown's Town relative also brought a much-needed vigour, love and affection to the female members of the Marson household. No less dignified or devout than Una's mother, Cousin Angie emerges strongly as the most spirited and tender person in Una's slender memoir. 'During her stay, she was often busy with my mother. Great was her joy when Cousin Sol agreed that Miss Ada could buy a Singer sewing machine from the agent and put away the little dock stitch which had been our companion for so long.'[19]

Una warmed to her older cousin, not just for her material gifts but because she brought news, gossip and conversation into the house. Late at night Angie would sit with Una's parents recounting stories about church members and relatives in Brown's Town, some of whom Solomon had not seen for years. She also made time for her youngest cousins and would tell them bedtime stories and even ghost stories 'and we were not a bit frightened'. Up on the nursery wall was a picture of some children with pigeons and the words beneath read, 'Be kindly affectioned to one another', a maxim which Una remembered Angie pointing to as she kissed them goodnight.

Angie died after a short illness in May 1964, when she was ninety-three years old. Throughout her long life she remained close to Una, although they didn't see one another for years at a stretch. On her return visits home, Una stayed with her and noted how differences in their attitudes had surfaced over the years. For instance Angie was taken aback that Una should visit the market on her own to buy fish and then cook for herself, when there was a maid there to do it for her.

In summer 1964 Una penned a short sketch of her Cousin Angie in which she described her as 'one of the rare and significant daughters of the land' and 'of a type not uncommon in Jamaica'. Angie had come to represent for Una the good old values of 'Christian faithfulness' and 'quiet dignity'. She described how, in her nineties, Angie

> Complained about the poor quality of domestic help and though a niece lived with her, she insisted on cooking the very little she ate and doing her own washing and ironing. She had set hours for all her chores and kept rigidly to them. She read her Bible everyday and knelt down to pray even though her knees hurt.[20]

This gushing adulation for her older relative comes from a Una who longed for a Jamaica which would retrieve some of the values she had known as a girl. She was by that time reluctant to admit that she too had changed, and altered her ways and principles, preferring to stand as representative of 'old Jamaican values' to the newly independent country in 1962.

The lovely portrait of Cousin Angie has an idyllic quality about it which diminishes the truth it may contain – Mother is not such a dear. Nowhere does Ada Marson, Una's mother, receive such attention. In fact she is barely present in the historical record. Depicted in occasional thumb-nail sketches in the prose of a consistently adoring Una, she is making her children's clothes, hearing them recite passages from the Bible or discussing menus with the cook. She is only just there. Yet Una Marson sighed and wept over her mother, expressing an unambivalent grief, as in 'My Mother', first published in *The Cosmopolitan* in December 1929:

My Mother

Oh! my Mother, my Mother, I hear the bells ring,
And the glad Christmas carols the dear children sing;
But my thoughts turn to you and the teardrops will start,
For I miss your sweet presence to comfort my heart.

Oh! my Mother, my Mother, can you hear me call?
Can you see the heartache, the tears as they fall?
I know that Christ sees them, but Mother of mine
It is so hard without you, sweet Mother Divine.

Una's poetic Mother, the passive, self-immolating, loving figure, fails to ring true when set against the factual accounts of Ada Marson. Jenny DaCosta, a long-term family friend, remembers her as 'a proper and dignified woman. She was extremely devout, well-mannered and correct. ... The eldest daughter, Edith, took after her in appearance and manner, both were tall and fair-skinned ... Una was quite different. .... She was very down to earth and wasn't a bit like them.'[21]

Ada was genteel convention personified: virtuous and chaste, mentally and physically corseted. It was only Una, her youngest daughter, who would make the generation gap distinct: her modernity would be traceable in her sexual curiosity, her idiosyncratic dress, her inglorious needlecraft and her years in 'exile'. Una's lack of affinity with Ada and Edith Marson, which Jenny DaCosta pinpointed, can also be noticed in other areas. All her life Una's physical appearance was a source of conflict and pain. She was conscious of her dark skin even after she found, in adult life, that there was beauty in blackness. In Jamaica fair skin was and is associated with beauty, charm and womanliness. It is only a small step from this notion to the idea that black also equates with dullness, stupidity and likely failure. Una never felt she was quite as clever as her fairer, elder sisters. The prevailing atmosphere of well-assured femininity in which Una grew up challenged her immature self-esteem. Una also insinuated that there was more parental discipline at Sharon than maternal love: 'We had to learn to sit nicely, to close doors quietly, to refrain from shouting in the house and quarrelling with one another as children are sometimes apt to do.'[22]

Perhaps the most striking illustration of Una's emotional distance from her mother is her erroneous assertion that Ada Marson died while Una was at school. It is tempting to conclude from this inaccurate statement that in her imagination Una wished herself free of maternal control from her early adolescence. Or more likely that Ada Marson had so emotionally absented herself from her daughter's life that Una felt like a motherless child. In her plays mothers are either dead or weak. In *At What a Price* the mother, an ineffectual figure, hides behind her dominant husband, mouthing inanities which her daughter, the heroine, a plucky young woman about to leave home for Kingston, overhears:

> Mary Maitland: And we always looked forward so much to the holidays. It seems but yesterday she left for her first term at school.
> James Maitland: Don't worry your dear old head. Ruth is a Maitland, her head is screwed on right and she has had the advantages of a good education and home training. We have done our part.[23]

In many families there is one member whose perceptions, temperament and talents seem to separate them from the whole; among the Marsons the odd one out was Una. Her elder sisters were secure in their close resemblance to their mother and accepted her conventional ways, but for Una, the Parson's Baby, this adult feminine world often seemed alien and inaccessible. As an adult she vacillated between shyness and anger at pretty, cultured femininity, and prised herself out of its narrowness. But she was born female and was never totally free of feminine conventions although her lifestyle was more like a man's. She was her father's daughter-son. Over the years it is as if Una became, like her father in his study, an individual outside the feminine sphere to which Ada, Edith and Ethel belonged. She was very much like her father, both physically and in other ways. Perhaps this enabled her to live an independent life as sons of robust fathers are said to live. What she lacked was real confidence, a quality which is born of affection in childhood; neither of her parents gave her quite enough of this.

And yet a bare account of Una Marson's life would read as a manual on courageous womanhood. From a mixture of circumstance, pride, ambition and a sense of conviction, she determined her own life. Some of these qualities can be traced to those early years in St Elizabeth, the parish which Una always treasured and to which, when she reached her nadir, she would return. Here as a girl Una loved to ramble, grubbing her shoes on St Elizabeth's stubborn red soils. Her sisters taught her the names of all the local flowers on their early morning walks, which sometimes turned into botany walks:

> interrupted every few yards as we stopped to pick up wild flowers, admire and examine them. If no one mentioned the word Easter, we knew of its approach, for on the banks of the road (and we always called them banks or bank-sides), in place of the Fee-Fee, Kiss me quick Blue bell, Spanish Needle and Morning Glory we were greeted with red lily buds; and as Easter came closer masses of red lilies. Without any exaggeration we gathered them in hundreds. Very seldom did we find white lilies growing wild but we cultivated these in our garden along with lilies of the valley and tube roses.[24]

And on most days they proffered pretty blooms to their mother on their return. Every season had its flower. Christmas bowed down to the flaming red poinsettia; Harvest Festival welcomed whatever a pickney could gather – bunched bouquets of wild blossoms, two or three orchids off the rocks. Perhaps, if you asked nicely, your neighbours would spare you something from their garden.

Una's childhood was vigorously physical and sensual. While her father was away at his church meetings, the house might be filled with feminine voices reciting favourite verses and humming the melodies of Marson ditties. All the Marson women and girls were talented in the literary and performing arts. Ada, their mother, was an accomplished organist and frequently played for church services, a skill particularly admired in a parson's wife and encouraged in parson's daughters. Ethel, whose greatest hobby was always music, also learnt to play well. She and Edith brought home sheets of school music: glees they had learnt, carols, voice duets and religious piano solos like 'Jesu, Joy of Man's Desiring' and love songs, such as 'Before I Love', 'The Last of Love' and similar songs of painful love, all of which added to Una's store of sounds and themes from adult life. In time she too started to play the piano. Although the instrument itself did not mean as much to her as it did to her sisters, Una filled up on the goodness of creative activity – the discipline, the freedom and the pleasure. Her first piano pieces, now housed among her papers in Jamaica, included *First Lessons in Bach*, though she later graduated to Schubert's songs and Beethoven and Mozart sonatas before eventually mastering the organ as well. One or two people remember her playing for occasional services at Coke Street Methodist Church in Kingston in the late 1940s.[25]

The children were sometimes able to go to Kingston, the capital about ninety miles away, where music could be purchased from Astley

Clerk's store known as Cowen's Music Rooms, and here they heard chamber music, a slither of the island's cultural life beyond the realms of rural Santa Cruz.

Their favourite activity was reading. Edith and Ethel, precocious readers from an early age, introduced Una to poetry, which she later nominated 'the chief delight of our childhood days'.[26] She and her sisters whiled away the hours making up tunes and singing them to poems they had learnt, many of them verses which were popular in England at the time like:

> You must wake and call me early, call me early, Mother dear,
> Tomorrow'll be the happiest day of all the glad New Year,
> Of all the glad New Year, Mother, the maddest merriest day,
> For I'm to be Queen of the May, Mother, I'm to be Queen o' the May.

They also sang along to:

> Elaine the Fair, Elaine the lovable
> Elaine the lily maid of Astolat.

This childhood enthusiasm for English poetry was less remarkable than it would be today; the Marson girls, like their peers, had no thought of this being a 'foreign literature'. American classics also had shelf space in their home. Even before she attended school, at the age of ten, Una had read 'Longfellow's collected works from cover to cover, knew yards of *Hiawatha*, *Evangeline* and *Tales of a Wayside Inn*, *Paul Revere* and *Barbara Fritchie* as well as Emerson's *Essays*',[27] books which her father had in his study. Freed from his inhibiting presence, Una liked to browse at the parson's heavy-backed books: Dr Fosdick's sermons, and other religious texts or Baptist church histories like *Men of Backbone* by the Reverend C. A. Wilson.[28] In one of these Una was 'thrilled to see photographs of some of those men who had visited my home'.[29] But the religious text which captured her imagination most vigorously was the tale of Latimer and Ridley. With a 'glow of pride', she had read and reread this text: 'as the flames shot up around him and he, smiling, thrust his hand into it, saying; "Be of good cheer, Brother Ridley, for we shall this day light such a fire in England that shall never be put out."'[30]

On rare occasions Una was allowed to venture further afield. The first journey Una remembered, and with pleasure, was a solo trip to Lacovia which she made at seven years of age. Lacovia was a small, picturesque St Elizabeth village, sandwiched between Santa Cruz and the wide-sweeping Black River. In 1912 Lacovia was on the brink of making huge profits from its logwood estates, which flourished during the First World War when the unusually high demand for logwood's russet dye vacuumed up supplies. Then pyramids of logwood stacked on boats could be seen travelling towards the prosperous Black River port, destined for the European theatres of war. It is a glorious stretch of land, where the 'Road to Lacovia', as A. L. Hendricks has described it, is 'a long, forbidding road, a narrow / hard aisle of asphalt under / a high gothic arch of bamboos'.[31] St Elizabeth, a hard parish to work, is a land of various tableaux: corn is grown on the savannahs; there are beautiful horses, brood mares and studs; coffee, sugar and tobacco and the famous logwood.

Una's account of this holiday, written in 1964, reveals more about her own personality and attitudes than about the people and places she describes. She marvelled at this rich landscape, the wealth of its people, and relished the memory of the women selling cashew nuts whose voices would ring out with the legendary, whimsical 'Cobie to be sure' when asked where they came from. And they would turn their heads and laugh, thinking of the money they had made from their trade.

Succulent sweet cassavas, pumpkins, breadfruit and yams also grew in abundance in the swampy soils bordering the river. Sugar estates and cattle rearing too provided the landowners with easy money and the working people with jobs. Most of the land from the low hills down to Maggotty Falls, about eight miles away, belonged to wealthy 'barons' and it was to the hearth of one of these that Una had been invited.

Once safely across the precarious bridge situated near the centre of the village, the young tourist took in Lacovia's few sights: Tomlinsons Dry Goods Store, a couple of little groceries, a bar, a school and St Thomas's Anglican church. Then she made her way to the home of the Hutchinsons, friends of the family and her hosts. The *paterfamilias*, generally referred to simply as J.C., was a robust, cigar-smoking business gent, 'quite black and good-looking' by Una's standards, 'with a ready smile and quick eyes. ... Always immaculately dressed, he invariably wore a gold chain which kept his large gold watch in his pocket.'[32] His wife was by contrast a diminutive, sparrow-like creature, 'very active' and of dark brown complexion. Their three adult children lived with them.

The Hutchinsons, the local gentry, owned several houses on the estate. Una's entire visit was not spent in the company of the rich. She records her experiences with some of the farm hands and servants on the estate, speaks vaguely of 'wonderful memories' and of 'picnics with them around the beautiful blazing kilns and catching bangers in the large horse pond on the property', but fails to provide individualised portraits of them. In Una's memoir they are nameless, colourless figures whose chief virtues she describes as 'respect' and' 'honesty of labour', placed at the back of her pretty tableau.

Stratification within Jamaican society mirrored its English Edwardian model as closely as a multi-racial colonial country could. Una Marson's upbringing was strictly middle-class. It is not surprising that in her attempts, many of them successful, to improve conditions for the working class she often encountered those who accused her, sometimes unfairly, of not understanding working-class life, aspirations or problems. It is true that her upbringing was shaped more by nineteenth-century philanthropy than by social deprivation. It is equally true that in spite of her upbringing she achieved more in concrete terms in social welfare for Jamaicans than many of her younger, professionally trained peers.

Reacting to the view that the Jamaican working class had always been the oppressed majority, Una writes defensively: 'I can't remember the miserable, hateful oppressed and despised, starving, filthy-mouthed labourer about whom I have read so much. A few there must have been for this was no Paradise, but I never met them.' Neither did she meet any of the 'gentlemen of means' who came to Belmont as dinner guests of J.C. during her stay.

A middle-class child and already an inveterate observer of social class distinctions, Una was aware of the limitations of her father's social standing. 'Though my father was a great friend of J.C.'s, he was never invited to dine with him', she noted, and added, with some sadness, 'I suppose he could not fit in with the talk, cigars and the excellent wines and spirits.'

She too did not fit, but she found a way, as she would many times in the future, to be a part of the elegant world and watch the main action of the moment:

> Coming from a poor Baptist Mission House, I could not but notice the elegance around. ... For 2 or 3 days previous, to the dinner, there was great activity ... The boiling of hams, the roasting of pigs, the cleaning of silver and the polishing of all the brass and furniture in the house. The carpets were taken up, sunned and cleaned ... Boxes of liquor came

in. At last the hour came for carriages to roll up. Assisted by her daughter, the lady of the house received the guests. Alas, I had to go to bed at 7.30 as usual. But I was not going to sleep; not on your life. I lay awake a long time, listening to the loud talk and laughter. I had never heard such laughter before. I crept out of bed, opened the door just a little and put myself in a strategic position where I could see the table without anyone seeing me, except they came very close. What I saw amazed me ... I had never seen such a huge table, the very white damask cloth competing for glamour with the silver cutlery and the cut glass jugs. The light was very bright. J.C. must have had a Delco Plant or specially imported lamps. My memory may not serve me right, but I think there was a chandelier.

The servants came in and out swiftly and efficiently with the dishes. J.C. carved the pig and at the other end of the table was turkey and ham. I was suddenly startled by someone coming towards me. I rushed into bed just in time as one of the maids came in with a tray on which there were many delicacies which I greatly enjoyed. I crept back later to my stand to watch coffee being served. After this the men went with the host to the smoking lounge and the ladies to the sitting room. I tried to sleep for I had to be up at 7 for my riding lesson with William.

NOTES

1 Una Marson to George Orwell, 2 April 1949, George Orwell, University College Archive, London.
2 'Talking it Over', broadcast 11 July 1940, Una Marson, Home Service, BBC written archives, Caversham.
3 These details come from interviews with Jenny DaCosta and the current (1990) parson's wife at Sharon, Santa Cruz.
4 'Cousin Angie', *Daily Gleaner*, 9 July 1964, p. 3.
5 *Ibid.*
6 The preface notes that Henderson 'came from the land of missionary pioneers, the Baptists and the Moravians who in the days of slavery and after slavery endured scorn and insults'.
7 George Henderson, *Goodness and Mercy: a Tale of a Hundred Years* (Kingston, Jamaica, Gleaner Company, 1931), p. 141.
8 *Missionary Herald*, 1 August 1875. See also the annual report of the Jamaica Baptist Missionary Society for 1876.
9 'Cousin Angie', p. 3.
10 Frank Cundall, *Handbook of Jamaica* (Kingston, Jamaica, Institute of Jamaica, 1922).
11 For Calabar see Calabar papers, Angus Library Oxford. W1/19 P. Williams (1872). A letter dated 18 February 1901 with minutes attached gives details of a meeting attended by Solomon Marson.
12 General information from W. A. Tucker, *Glorious Liberty* (London, 1914), p. 47.

13 Prices used here come from interviews with Aimee Webster, novels of Claude McKay (*Banana Bottom* (London, Pluto Press, 1986)) and Herbert G. Lisser (*Jane's Career* (London, Heinemann, 1972)). For details of the ticket system see *Glorious Liberty*, p. 49.

14 'Una Marson's Memorial Service in St Elizabeth', *Daily Gleaner*, 11 August 1965, p. 11. Over five hundred people packed into the hall at St Elizabeth Technical High School for the service.

15 'Pocomania', Act 3 Scene 1. Unpublished manuscript in Una Marson papers, Box 1944B, National Library of Jamaica.

16 'Lacovia: Cobie to be Sure', *Daily Gleaner*, 2 July 1964, p. 3.

17 *Ibid.*

18 'Cousin Angie', p. 3.

19 *Ibid.*

20 *Ibid.*

21 Jenny DaCosta interviewed by the author, Kingston, Jamaica, May 1989.

22 'Cousin Angie', p. 3.

23 'At What a Price', Act 1 Scene 1, pp. 3 4. Unpublished playscript in the British Library, London.

24 'Consider the Lilies', no date, Una Marson papers, Box 1944B, National Library of Jamaica.

25 Connie Mark interviewed by the author, London, July 1990. See also Una Marson papers at the National Library of Jamaica for copies of music sheets, some of which are marked Hampton School.

26 'Talking it Over'.

27 'How I Discovered America', no date, Una Marson papers, Box 1944B, National Library of Jamaica.

28 'Wanted: Writers and Publishers', *Public Opinion*, 12 June 1937, p. 6.

29 *Ibid.*

30 'Unsung Heroes', *Public Opinion*, 30 October 1937, p. 12.

31 A. L. Hendricks, 'Road to Lacovia', in Pamela Mordecai and Grace Walker Gordon (eds), *Sunsong 2* (London and Kingston, Jamaica, Longman Caribbean, 1987), p. 54.

32 This and all subsequent quotations in this chapter from 'Lacovia: Cobie to be Sure', p. 3.

2

Hampton

MALVERN is an old, stately town in the parish of St Elizabeth. High in the Santa Cruz mountains, two thousand feet above sea level, Malvern lies in the embrace of Jamaica's finest climate, where ocean breezes drift inland, tempering the sun's heat. Attracted by the weather, better-off Jamaicans – successful traders and landowners – settled here around the turn of the century. The Calders, Farquarsons, Hendricks and Clakens were among the wealthy families who came to occupy the superb residences lining the town's streets. The area to which these families seemed to lay siege was bounded to the north, south and west by a scholastic trinity – the Bethlehem Training College, Munro College and, of closer concern to Una, Hampton High School.

In the autumn term of 1915, ten-year-old Una joined Hampton High as a boarder. This was a fee-paying establishment for the daughters of the colony's upper middle class whose budgets did not quite run to sending them to England. However, towards the end of the First World War, Hampton, according to Una, was 'overcrowded with girls who normally would have been sent abroad to school'.[1] From this and other related comments it seems that Una Marson resented her schoolmates and was irked by their increased numbers. Hamptonians came mostly from moneyed white and creole families, owners of luxurious properties and 'noisy Ford cars'.[2] She, as a member of the educated black middle classes, suffered the adverse distinction of being of both modest and highly competent stock.

From the late 1920s to the 1950s Una was to compose several versions of her Hampton years in poetry and prose: 'To Hampton' was the first, in 1930, and a newspaper article entitled 'Are Our Secondary Schools Snob Centres?' appeared in the *Daily Gleaner* around 1950.

These revealed different, though not necessarily conflicting, attitudes towards her *alma mater* and its pupils. Una's perception of Hampton and her ability to write critically about it developed with time. As a young single woman embarking on a career in Jamaica, she tended to eulogy, perhaps for her own comfort. 'To Hampton' was pure educational nostalgia:

> Sweet Hampton – fairest school of all the Isle,
> Where happily I sojourned for a while
> And passed those happy years so free from pain,
> What would I give to dwell with thee again
> ...
> Thou dearest school of all my youthful days
> Oh that the muse would grant me voice to praise
> Thy charms, thy rare delights, thy bowers of ease
> Which often made e'en Latin verbs to please.
>
> For when at last the day's full tasks were done,
> Each afternoon, long ere the set of sun,
> We gladly clamoured out and gathered round
> To tennis, hockey, games or chat profound.[3]

There is a considerable gap between what Una Marson implies here and the more detached, anecdotal assessment published nearly thirty years later, in the *Daily Gleaner*. This later account coincides with the recollections and perceptions of others who would readily testify that Hampton was indeed a 'snob centre'. Common to both sets of recollections, however, is Una's respect for the consistently sound teaching she received. Hampton, a girls' school founded in the 1860s, was renowned for its academic excellence. After it was transferred from its original site at Mount Sion in 1894, its role steadily increased. Una's elder sisters, Edith and Ethel, were among its distinguished alumni, though Ruby, who was not as gifted, attended Westwood Girls School.

Today Hampton, a multi-racial establishment of over two hundred girls and twenty-five staff, still enjoys a favourable reputation as a leading girls' school. But in 1913 there were only sixty Hamptonians, five classrooms and a staff of ten women teachers. Half the teachers were English women, the others were Jamaicans. All of them had received their university education in England with the exception of Miss Lucas, the music teacher, who trained at the Paris Conservatoire. The school was governed by a board of trustees: professional men and local dignitaries including three ministers of religion, one of whom was the Reverend Solomon Marson. Once a month they met at Malvern to decide school policy and, no doubt, once a year discussed the applications for scholarships.

In 1915 Una won a Free Foundationers Scholarship which took care of the fees: £45 a year for tuition and board, according to the prospectus for 1913. With considerable coaching from Edith and Ethel, she passed tests in the three Rs, Geography and the Old and New Testaments. But in spite of this commendable achievement, this clever but under-confident girl still had the axe swinging above her head. The prospectus forewarned that foundationers were 'expected to maintain a reasonable standard of proficiency' – a threat evidently used, abused and relished by the headmistress, Miss Barrows, whom Una called the 'terror of small children'. The foundationers, mostly black girls like Una, were 'tortured by Maud Marion who never missed an opportunity to make them stand before the whole school for a berating for any minor misdemeanour. They were continually reminded that they were getting their education free.'[4]

Miss Maud Marion Barrows, head of ten years' standing, a self-possessed tyrant and classics graduate of London university, was licensed to browbeat her pupils at will, and especially disliked them when they were ill: 'Health was important and we were made to feel that it was a crime to be ill. When an epidemic like chicken-pox hit the school, Maud Marion stormed and ranted and told us we were guttersnipes and the worst school in the world.'[5]

With the benefit of hindsight and after a lifetime of experience of social work, journalism and broadcasting, which might have toned down her first impressions, Una felt that Miss Barrows's most positive attribute was to have repudiated feminine frailty in her pupils. She 'somehow got it across to her girls that if they were not prepared to make a real contribution to the world, they might as well be dead'. This uncompromising vigour seems to have had the desired effect on Una: it 'toughened me up'.[6]

Hardly ever in Una's writing did she ascribe blame to an individual. She tended instead to depersonalise her anger and frustration and to speak in non-specific terms of unkindnesses, thoughtlessness or misunderstanding. She did not maintain this guise of Christian virtue for Maud Barrows. The directness of this account of Miss Barrows therefore suggests that Una had suffered several humiliating encounters with the headmistress, to which the 1950 *Daily Gleaner* article was her considered response. But Maud Barrows was not the only guilty party.

Una was deeply unhappy because as a dark-skinned scholarship girl she was made to feel inadequate and unacceptable by the posh majority who knew and enjoyed the privilege of 'whiteness': 'Let it be said also that the 20 or so really dark girls were snubbed by some white and near white girls.'[7]

Hampton offered everything an English young lady needed: elocution, deportment, refined conversation, gardening, concerts and musical appreciation. Even the school ghost, Boxer, was a noble Englishman. His mother, one Lady Boxer, had owned the main building and now her son, who had suffered a limp, could be heard hobbling about the northern central section of the school in the dead of night! But in case some *obeah* (witchcraft) man's spell might violate these dreaming damsels, their nine low-ceilinged dormitories were signposted in the classical tradition: *Parnassus, Olympus, Areopolis* and *Forum*; or from London's West End: *Strand, Kingsway, Long Acre, Piccadilly* and *Charing Cross*.

So very many thousands of miles from London's drizzle or the shimmering heat of Athens, Jamaican girls like Una received an English public-school education. To assist them Hampton boasted a well-stocked library of textbooks on English literature, English history, English geography and even English flowers. There were a dozen music rooms for the practice of classical music, the singing of glees and playing of violins. Indeed, both indoors and out, school was palatial. Hockey pitches stretched out along one side, tennis courts along another; shaded nooks for girlish gossip and quiet places for serious study, the simulated English garden around the English school. Into these gardens Una, whose favourite subject was English literature, would wander with her poetry books, posing for the world to see. The curriculum demanded regular study of modern and classical literature. Every term Hampton's girls studied at least two literary texts; like English pupils of her generation she was reared on Palgrave's *Golden Treasury* and Wordsworth's *Lyrical Ballads*, which she enjoyed so much that, as exam time approached, she would rise at dawn, put on her blue pleated skirt and shining brown shoes and walk up and down the long driveway, learning more lines than required. During all her six years at school she was enchanted by Wordsworth and found, without fully realising it then, some codes to live by:

The world is too much with us; late and soon,
Getting and spending, we lay waste our powers;

Little we see in Nature that is ours;
We have given our hearts away, a sordid boon!

She vowed 'to cast my lot in with Wordsworth ... I agreed with him, that I would not have the world too much with me, I would not set out to be a good wage earner, but enjoy plain living and high thinking and be one of nature's children'.[8]

The guiding ethos of the education Una received at Hampton is evidenced in a self-conscious emphasis on the virtues of the co-ordinated teaching of Latin, French and English. For the school's governors, writing in the 1911 edition of the prospectus, the reason for the inclusion of the classics, public-school style, was clear: 'We owe to the Romans our laws and many of the foundations of our civilisation and it is by the study of Latin that we help to continue that stability which marks the British Empire today.'

Taken as a whole Una's school work was unremarkable. Unlike her elder sisters, she did not thrive at Hampton. One reason why Una performed only moderately was the death of her father, in 1915. He was fifty-seven. Solomon Marson had worked at Sharon for nearly thirty years. When he died the family had to leave their home in Sharon; at a stroke they lost their social standing and financial security. When re-evoking his death in her later writings, Una dealt briefly and gingerly with her loss and dismay: 'This meant the breaking up of our home. Three of us had gone to Hampton, one to Westwood and one to Calabar. We were growing up fast and so we moved to Kingston where two of Mother's sisters had long since settled. For us, it was the end of an era and the beginning of another. ... '[9]

This new era opened when Una, aged eleven, was entering early adolescence. Without having time and space to grieve her loss, Una seemed to absorb the pain and resent the cruelty of her fate.

It was a wrench from childhood and a cruel start in an unfriendly place. It is not known whether the bereft teenager had to go through the humiliating experience of returning to the Sharon Mission House to pack her belongings. It is clear, though, that Solomon Marson's death taught Una how to live independently without the financial and emotional backing of men. She would never rely on her elder brothers or overtly express a need for dependency on male support. As a woman she was never a homemaker, not even for herself. She relished the semi-nomadic existence: never a permanent home, but a 'room of her own' and suitcases always half-packed. Like a gypsy, she put her trust in impermanence.

Life at Hampton could be pleasurable. The maids knew how to woo a smile from their small charges by bringing them sweets from Malvern's Clacken Produce Shop; Una loved such childish intrigue. As a senior she attended dances, concerts and parties on Saturday nights to which neighbouring schools, Munro Boys and Bethlehem Girls College, came. She was also allowed into Malvern with friends and sometimes called on Miss Russell, a retired American nurse living at Mount Ida, where she had founded an International Rest Centre which was adorned with a stained glass window depicting the black and white keys of a piano, the motto for inter-racial harmony coined by West African teacher and activist Aggrey of Achimota. This image impressed Una. The struggle for racial harmony, not separation or revolution, was to preoccupy her for years to come.

In the fifth form Una followed the commercial skills option, provided for 'girls who expect to help their fathers in their business affairs or seek secretarial posts', but, having passed the Oxford and Cambridge Board's Lower Certificate (Letters) in 1921, she did not attempt the Higher Certificate and further education was never an option. She seems to have suffered from comparison with her older, more academic sisters who seemed 'clever and so in favour with Maud Marion'. Edith, according to the school chronicle, had left Hampton in summer 1911. She would have been an excellent university undergraduate, but the West Indies had no university and without parental backing there was no chance of an education abroad. Ethel, a few years younger than Edith but as articulate and conscientious, had sailed through her Higher Local Certificate, Class 2 Honours for Latin and French, with a distinction in Latin, in March 1912. She had also picked up form prizes for Arithmetic and for her Higher Certificate (Letters) in 1914. Ethel had every reason to be confident of a fruitful career, unlike her little sister, Una, who was perpetually filled with doubts.

Una left Hampton in the summer of 1922, along with seven other girls. But before leaving she faced a passing-out interview with Maud Barrows. Judging from her sketch written around 1950, when Maud Barrows was dead, this encounter did nothing to enhance her fragile self-esteem:

> She asked me what I planned to do. I told her that as my father was dead and I wanted to help my mother, I should probably study stenography and get a secretarial job.
>
> She was very angry. 'Only fools learn shorthand', she said, 'Why can't you take up teaching as your sisters have done?'

> I trembled. I just knew I couldn't teach and had no idea of any other career.[10]

And thus, Una's formal education ended.

NOTES

1 'Are Our Secondary Schools Snob Centres?', no date, Una Marson papers, Box 1944B, National Library of Jamaica.
2 'Malvern: the Glory has Departed', *Daily Gleaner*, 29 August 1964, p. 3.
3 'To Hampton', *Tropic Reveries* (Kingston, Jamaica, 1930), p. 69.
4 'Are Our Secondary Schools Snob Centres?'.
5 *Ibid.*
6 *Ibid.*
7 *Ibid.*
8 'Talking it Over', broadcast 11 July 1940, Home Service, Una Marson, BBC written archives, Caversham.
9 'Cousin Angie', *Daily Gleaner*, 9 July 1964, pp. 1–3.
10 'Are Our Secondary Schools Snob Centres?'

3

To Kingston

THE 1920s came to Jamaica in the shape of economic downturn: ragged migrant workers tramping back from Panama, some dying on the way; nervous young domestics hunting for a shilling-a-week jobs with well-to-do Kingston families; and bored young city slickers constantly craving new entertainments.

In 1922 Una's Santa Cruz days were over. Like both her sisters and her mother who had been living in Kingston since Solomon Marson died, she left the scene of her girlhood and made for the city, the capital and commercial centre ninety miles away, which was to be her home for the next decade. Kingston seemed to offer hope and prosperity to many rural-born Jamaicans. And Una was no exception. Santa Cruz was to become more than a charming memory, but now it was associated with her father's sudden death, the family's unpredictable social situation and her own very mediocre academic performance. And the idyll of West Indian village life, of slow change amid dreaming mountains and warm heavy-scented breeze, was but an idyll. For many years there had been unrest among the Jamaican peasantry. Farming was hard. Sometimes a drought came, parched their fields and withered the crops to a burnt yellow, or heavy rains would fall, washing away the soil and leeching the goodness out of their provisions; or, worse still, a hurricane could come and blow their livelihood away.

The country girl was becoming a city woman. But even in Kingston the openings available to young educated black women were few and unenticing. Ex-Hamptonians who were not immediately groomed for the marriage market worked as teachers, governesses, musicians or nurses; a handful, like Ethel Marson, became civil servants. But since neither Una's will nor her talents led her in those directions, social work, which had attracted increasing numbers of middle-class women volunteers since the turn of the century, enabled her to use her hard-won secretarial skills without, for the time being, transgressing any of the limits imposed upon her class and gender. Her first job was with the Salvation Army, based at 96 Orange Street, where it had a spacious hall and training garrison in which the West Indian Warriors, clad in long white suits, congregated before going to work in the community, visiting prisons, probationers and women in need. Una started to meet the island's social workers through her congenial colleagues Major Barrell, the Divisional Commander, a cheerful little man who played the concertina superbly, and his wife.[1] She also discovered to her dismay that, although slavery had ended more than ninety years before, the masses were still very poor, under-privileged and illiterate. Since the late 1880s many hundreds of thousands of Jamaicans had migrated to Cuba in search of a better living: many of the men laboured in construction of the Havana to Santiago Central Highway, while women worked as domestics and nannies to Cuban bourgeoisie. But migration was only a temporary relief to Jamaican poverty. Many were now coming home:

> Many are starving, some have to tramp long distances to Santiago in order to embark for Kingston; numbers collapse on the march. Not long ago, a few Jamaicans travelling to Santiago by rail passed the bodies of 14 or 15 of their country men who had died of starvation, having tramped miles in the hope of reaching Santiago.

So wrote a Salvation Army officer in summer 1922.

After a year Una left the Salvation Army, but not social work. She took a job with the newly established YMCA at 76 Hanover Street (the Jamaica Hotel building it acquired in 1920). Her boss was the general secretary, a sporty Englishman, Edgar Baker Hallett, formerly a welfare organiser on the Amity Hall and Vere estates in Clarendon. Hallett was forty-three, much older than Una, but she found him 'an indefatigable worker' and could barely keep up with his energetic schedules. Nicknamed 'Skipper Hallett', he trained a water polo team and 'was a vigorous soccer player until an ailment in one hip forced his withdrawal, but his enthusiasm for aquatics was not deterred'.[2]

Still something of a playful teenager, she fitted in for several years with the great escapades on summer evenings, with weekend hiking up to Blue Mountain peak and amateur dramatics including her own fundraising initiative, a dramatisation of H. G. de Lisser's novel *Susan*

Proudleigh, in which popular drag artist Ernest Cupidon starred and Una herself made her theatrical debut. Una was coming into her early twenties, enjoying a protracted adolescence and the excitement of sportsmanship and competition:

> The YMCA was top in football, basket ball and water polo … I used to go to some of the matches and thought of myself as a sort of mascot. I remember once when I was unable to get off in time to go I rushed into the lobby when I saw John Mordecai [a club member] returning to ask the results. Before telling me he gave me a lecture which indicated that he was a very serious young man. 'Is it really of very great importance which side won' he asked, 'There are many far more serious things than that' he added. … I have never forgotten that incident.[3]

Una was pleased with city life. She lived on South Camp Road, sharing a house with her sister, the gentle Etty. Their home was a few minutes away from the Institute of Jamaica, the well-established literary and cultural centre, and, since no barbed wire fencing barricaded the common ground near their house, Una could wander along the narrow tracks into the green open spaces as far as Vineyard Pen a few miles away.

The centre of Kingston had clean and bright streets, numerous cars, and noisy trams passing along the wide thoroughfares. Away from the bustle of the business centre was Victoria Park, laid out with large beds of red and yellow canna in full bloom, poinciana trees ablaze with crimson blossoms like thick clusters of gold, and the trim of grass plots. It was quiet in the early mornings but by mid-morning smart office girls were picnicking and tourists strolling in the sunshine. Una liked to rise early and see the barefooted village women coming into town, their heads bound with brightly coloured bandannas, as they carried very large baskets laden with yellowish-red fruit of the mango to the market; and in downtown Kingston, a chequerboard of narrow lanes, she watched hawkers pass up and down crying their wares.[4] There was also Kingston's magnificent harbour, fringed with palms and looking out to the Caribbean Sea.

There were some urban pleasures to sample: music, English touring theatre companies and increasingly films, particularly after *The Jazz Singer* brought sound to the picture palace in 1926, and she always admired Bette Davis, Clive Brook, William Powell and Charlie Chaplin.[5] Nevertheless, Una was of a generation for whom Kingston, though colourful, seemed tedious and slow compared with the outside world they heard about. The recent Oxford law graduate Norman Manley spoke for them all when he said:

Few were interested in anything except the daily round of events; books and drama were barren gambits, music was worse. Though there were some lively men in the legislative council, politics locally were of little importance. The people seemed content and quiet. The economy was turgid. There was a general air of emptiness.[6]

It was one of the livelier members of the legislative council, the representative for St Ann, Dunbar T. Wint, a former schoolmaster, who helped Una to escape from the tedium of secretarial work, by giving her a job as assistant editor on his socio-political monthly journal, the *Jamaica Critic*, in January 1926, when she was nearly twenty-one. There Una began to learn how journalism worked, and picked up the rudiments of magazine publishing: writing, editing and proof-reading – skills which she was to use profitably and almost continuously for the rest of her life.

However, Wint was an anti-feminist who had argued in the 1918 debate on the emancipation of women – in Jamaica free persons of colour were granted full civil rights in 1830, but universal adult suffrage was not granted until 1944 – that constitutional reform was much more important and that the 'women of Jamaica have too much worries at home to worry over which persons should go and sit in a council where they are of little use'. Una had to bide her time. Under Wint's regime she had almost no room for creative freewheeling and had to restrict herself to supposedly 'feminine' subjects, not straying into social comment that was to become her hallmark. Thus in 'The Language of Flowers' of January 1928 she attempted to extend the commonplace lexicon of floral attributes – roses are for lovers – with some meanings of her own. Two months later 'Friendship', with self-conscious references to Cicero and Atticus, Wordsworth and Coleridge, as fine friends, and by implication the colonised readers as inherently unfriendly beings, appeared with flashes of moralising: 'In modern days we seem to have become so steeped in materialism that there is little or no time to spend in the development of the finer things of life, among them true and disinterested friendships. ... Friendship requires a total magnanimity and trust.'[7]

Though lively and companionable when she chose, Una had just one or two close friends and was essentially already a loner. 'Of course I knew Una Marson', many people exclaimed thirty years after her death, but few would claim intimate knowledge and unbroken friendship. Una's extended period of exile from Jamaica and her slightly secretive nature account in part for this. Her closest friend was Ethel, her sister, who remained the touchstone in her life of action and change. Ethel stayed in the same employment all her life, working for many years as secretary to the Deputy Director of Agriculture, George Goode, in the Civil Service. She was devoted to him and to their musical activities which they shared – the Diocesan Festival Choir and the fourteen-strong Kingston Glee Singers, both of which Goode conducted. Although Etty would always help out, emotionally and financially, with Una's ambitions, she was always a little apart from Una's fiery emotional core. In the words of their mutual friend, Philip Sherlock, a teacher and writer: 'Ethel was much more practical in a prosaic way than Una. Una felt more intensely.'[8]

Edith, the eldest sister, also felt intensely, but in a different way. Since leaving Hampton she had become a formidable schoolmistress, an active member of the radical professional association, the Jamaican Union of Teachers. Isobel Seaton, a family friend, recalls Edith 'quite disapproving of Una' and as 'strong and dictatorial'. She read feminist material and at the 1929 Jamaican Women's Teachers Conference presented a paper on 'Specialisation versus Generalisation' in which she took the line of liberal feminist philosopher John Stuart Mill, author of *On the Subjection of Women*, that women surpassed men in mental versatility, a quality which should be considered a female virtue.[9] By the time she was thirty-three, Edith Marson-Jones had her own establishment – Cardiff School, a secondary school with a junior division based at 38 Upper South Camp Road. She was also married to a Baptist parson, a Reverend Jones, but according to some close sources communing was not happy; there were no offspring.

Although Ethel was firmly on Una's side, she struggled to hold Edith's support and, though it is not certain, that of her own mother. Small but significant events occurred during these years, Una's early twenties, which left her feeling 'bodily' wrong. It is as though she were being 'framed' by society, set up to see herself in a bad light. She had a go at musical composition, writing a piano version of 'The Vagabond': her counterpoint was a little shaky, but the adjudicator wrote: 'Your musical ideas are very nice and in places distinctly pleasing.'[10] But when she tested her uncertain public presence in an elocution contest at the Ward Theatre, Esther Hyman (later Chapman), an English critic and journalist, made these acerbic comments about her performance:

> Miss Marson has a pleasant manner, and a nice clear voice; her intonation is good. She drops her voice too much at the end of lines and some of her pauses are too long.

By contrast occasionally she speaks too quickly. She displays great promise and properly trained, should do well. Her principal fault is the pronunciation of certain words, especially the vowel sound in words like 'there' and 'stairs' which she pronounces 'theere' and 'steers'. This, in my opinion, should have disqualified her for second prize. She is one of the few competitors with real stage personality.[11]

The *Critic* was also grudging in its exposure of Una. While most young women who were featured in the journal, under the heading 'Daughters of Jamaica', posed as smiling society belles in evening finery, Una's photo was given a small, mean space. Her picture, placed alongside her essay on flowers, revealed an insecure young woman, wearing a fashionable tubular dress, but looking distinctly ill at ease. And yet she was circumscribed by the ageless expectation that women should be judged on their appearance much more than on their character. Like the heroine of her first play, *At What a Price*, she looked as though she felt 'not good looking enough to be ornamental'. Was Una indeed such a frail innocent? Appearances were deceptive; for this same early play included an approving reference to Michael Arlen's *The Green Hat* (1924), a racy bestseller which dealt with daring subjects such as casual sex, adultery, VD and miscarriages while upholding 'good' moral behaviour – a pointer to the very duplicity which has made Una herself so intriguing. In the process of untangling the life of Una Marson it becomes clear that there is frequently a gap between the demure, public face and the determined, spirited soul. Perhaps, like Iris March, the heroine of Arlen's novel, Una Marson was a much misunderstood young woman.

On the face of it she was contradictory. At the age of twenty-three she was still composing childlike poems, some in the idiom of the nursery rhyme such as 'On the Death of a Mouse' which was influenced by Robert Burns's 'To the Field Mouse':

> Poor little Mousie
> Killed by a car
> Your Mother is wondering
> Just where you are.
>
> Not come for supper!
> Not come for tea!
> Poor little Mousie
> Cold as can be.[12]

But at the same time she was preparing to leave Hallet at the YMCA and abandon Wint at the *Critic* for her own platform.

NOTES

1 'Speech and Hearing for the Deaf', *Sunday Gleaner*, 18 February 1962, p. 13.

2 Sibthorpe Beckett, 'Edgar Baker – Skipper Hallett', a biographical outline in the possession of the author.

3 'Serving Each Other With Love', *Sunday Gleaner*, 12 February 1961, p. 15.

4 'Sojourn', *New Cosmopolitan*, February 1931.

5 'Cinema and Our Youth', *Public Opinion*, 10 March 1951, p. 10.

6 Philip Sherlock, *Norman Manley* (London, Macmillan, 1980), p. 64.

7 'Friendship', *Jamaica Critic*, vol. 3, no. 3, 1926, p. 31.

8 Philip Sherlock interviewed by the author, 22 February 1990, Kingston, Jamaica.

9 See Edith Marson-Jones's paper from the 1929 Jamaican Women Teachers Conference, 'Specialisation versus Generalisation' in Una Marson papers, Box 1944B, National Library of Jamaica.

10 Musical Competition Festival, number of competitor 586. November 1931, Una Marson papers, Box 1944A, National Library of Jamaica.

11 Esther Chapman, 'The Elocution Contest', *Saturday Review of Jamaica*, vol. 2, no. 35, 24 November 1928, p. 5.

12 'On the Death of a Mouse', *Tropic Reveries* (Kingston, Jamaica, 1930), p. 68.

4

The Cosmopolitan

Our ambition is to do all we can to encourage talented young people to express themselves freely … and our chief aim is to develop literary and other artistic talents in our island home.

WITH THIS seemingly uncontroversial debut editorial Una became Jamaica's first women editor-publisher. In 1928 she set up a magazine called *The Cosmopolitan*, having raised sufficient financial support from an astute businessman, Bowen, who was managing director of an insurance company of the same name. That spring Una was to declare in her new monthly: 'This is the age of woman: What man has done, women may do'. Contrary to what anybody would have suspected from just seeing her strolling around the city, Una had set out to transform the literary scene by airing feminist views, literary and cultural topics and a range of social issues in an unprecedented way. *The Cosmopolitan*, which appeared monthly from May 1928 until 1931, was not really cosmopolitan in its remit, its readership, its contributors or its advertisers. It was purely Jamaican. And it bore no relation to today's international glossy, save for the fact that it was about women empowering themselves. Una sought to rescue the secretary of slender means, the hard-working higgler (street vendor), the single mother and the unemployed domestic from cold national disregard. She published profiles of women musicians – the pianists Sybil and Noele Foster-Davis who with Miss Viera, the viola player, conducted the Studio of Kingston Music Academy – and reports of women's conferences, and found a way, long before the existence of a Jamaican women's movement, of expressing feminist ideals which are instantly recognisable today. In her belief that women's consciousness was as important as women's wage packets, Una acted as a hyphen between social and cultural values, and between contemporary Jamaican women and early English pioneers such as Josephine Butler, Florence Nightingale and Emily Davies whom she cited in her articles. And she was beginning to assert women's control over their own bodies against men's power of sexual ownership.

More and more she started to look like a thoroughly modern Miss Marson with her knee-length skirts, bobbed hair and cheeky bags. The fashions of the 1920s, a visible declaration of female emancipation, won her approval – the masculine Eton crop, the very short shingle and the dropped waist which suited her slender, thin frame.

> I have read with a great deal of amusement the various comments on the dress of the modern women in the daily 'Gleaner' and I confess that the controversy has given me food for thought.
>
> The poor modern woman! she is always being pitied by the eloquent strong old fashioned young men – and it has been said that pity is akin to love, so we are almost tempted to feel that we are even more beloved than our dear ancestors who now that they have passed to the great beyond continually have roses and flowery epitaphs placed above them by those who grieve and sigh 'never more shall we look upon their like again!'

Jamaica women, she went on, were always being unfairly criticised for 'our morals, our stupidity and our dress'; men made a fuss about whether they were powdered, rouged or not; but were women themselves taking advantage of the feminist gains which had been won?

> Do the women of Jamaica today form a strong body with a voice that can be distinctly heard from the platforms where service, progress, improvement and advancement are being preached? Will the voting be affected by the influence of women as it will be in England where over five million women have registered? I think that in Jamaica, in line with many other countries, the women outnumber the men, but where do we stand?
>
> Eighty years ago there were no business women in our metropolis, now, there must be nearly a thousand and what have we been able to do in comparison with our numbers. Is it right that we should be regarded as doing a job and no more. ... What is the thrill that we women get out of life? Is it leaving the office, a new dress (preferably longer now for the sake of poor Jamaican) a car, dancing – playing the fool, going to the theatre and making our own Whoopee!!!...
>
> Are we to bow to the demands of modern civilisation and become mere machines with our minds attuned to our business or relaxation?

A typically Jamaican situation arose for example when in April 1931 the 'Miss Jamaica' contest organisers selected, as was their habit, another blonde-haired, blue-eyed beauty to carry the national crown:

> Some amount of expense and disappointment could be saved numbers of dusky ladies who, year after year, enter the Beauty competition if the promoters of the contest would announce in the daily press that very dark or 'black beauties' will not be considered. ... There is a growing feeling that Miss Jamaica should be a type of girl who is more truly representative of the majority of Jamaicans.[1]

The masthead of *The Cosmopolitan*'s first few issues contained the curious inscription, 'A monthly magazine for the Business Youth of Jamaica and the Official Organ of the Stenographers' Association', a professional association of which Una had become secretary in 1928. An unspectacular part of Una's routine as secretary to the secretaries involved writing up their activities in the journal, and she was keenly tackling other women's employment issues, including low pay, lack of unionisation, and training. According to the 1943 census, between 1921 and 1943 the female labour force declined from 219,000 to 163,000, by far the majority of whom were involved in agriculture as 'unpaid family workers'; but in Kingston a sizeable number of typists, secretaries and domestics were in need of worker organisation. Since unionisation was itself illegal, since women were not conditioned to join worker organisations, and since the threat of unemployment was real, it was difficult to press a disparate group of workers to move away from defending their individual interests to a more concerted offensive against their employers. Una could see that most wouldn't renounce their precious evenings for business meetings. Her ground plan, inflexible to others' needs, went through no fundamental changes at first. Time and again she would sit in a half-empty community hall, with an invited guest speaker awaiting the arrival of recalcitrant stenographers. Time and again, she would rebuke them in the journal: 'it is important not to be selfish, we must work for the good of the majority', and so on. Una was no fool. In the end she learnt her lesson, and in her acceptance of the stenographers' apathy, she came nearer to understanding the miseries of voluntary leadership.

As the months rolled by, the realities of the business world could no longer be kept at bay. The Stenographers' Association, barely three months old when *The Cosmopolitan* was launched in May 1928, tottered for a year, slipped into senility and collapsed. Even as it closed, some members were confused about its goals. But it had not been in vain. One conspicuous achievement was that some stenographers gained employment as civil servants and as business managers with commercial companies.

Another major element of Una's *Cosmopolitan* life was to promote the writings of Jamaican poets, short story writers and would-be novelists at a time when local publication was a very, very rare event. Among the upper classes high fashion had a greater value than highbrow fiction, and the educated middle classes who cared for reading were perpetually ridiculed. They cosseted themselves in quaint literary groups, and focused their gaze, however hazy, upon the London literary scene. Occasionally London waved back. And these genteel men and women who were well versed in Shakespeare, the great Victorians – Tennyson, Swinburne and Kipling, the pedigree of Palgrave's *Golden Treasury* – produced verse which was the height of decorum, didacticism and 'poetic diction', rapt effusions at the wonder and beauty of Nature, lofty, sounding moralising and patriotic verses, and waited for the great literary moment.

The Jamaican Poetry League members were ecstatic when one Thursday afternoon in late January 1930 copies of the pioneering anthology of Jamaican poetry, Clare McFarlane's *Voices from Summerland*, published in London by the Merton Press, finally reached their hands. Three days later, on 26 January, a zealous literary correspondent, possibly a League member not declaring her or his interest, registered this 'historical event' in the *Daily Gleaner*, noting that 'it is ... likely to be of far-reaching import in the intellectual life of the country'. It was not. Of greater significance to the small band of anthologised colonial poets and their trickling of followers was the much-craved acknowledgement of the English literary world. All that was needed to nudge this publishing event into perfection was a few words of praise from an established English poet.

Rudyard Kipling was such a poet. He happened to be wintering in Jamaica when he received a copy of *Voices from Summerland*, bearing his initials engraved in silver on the top right-hand corner of the cover. His hastily written acknowledgement of this humbly proffered first edition, dispatched after he had embarked for Canada, was published in the League's 1930 review booklet:

> Will you please convey to your launch of the League my deep appreciation of their gift as well as my interest in the quality and character of the Anthology, there are few things to my mind more important and

fruitful than the expression of the poet's interest in the land of his birth or of his love, especially when that land is beyond the ordinary circle of things known to the outer world, that is why I am especially [?] in the poems dealing with Jamaican scenes and life.

In Jamaica there was little interest in the anthology: even the *Gleaner*'s reviewer, while saying it was 'quite good quality', admitted he couldn't comment further because 'we have not read all the poems'.[2]

The paucity of readers and critics, the lack of publishing houses and bookshops, the absence of writing fees or other stipends, all forced the Jamaica Poetry League, the literary clique to which Una belonged, to struggle, under-nourished, on its way. But Jamaican writers were no less fortunate than their Caribbean peers. 'Writing in Trinidad', the novelist V. S. Naipaul would ruefully observe, 'was an amateur activity. ... There were no magazines that paid; there were no established magazines; there was only The [Trinidad] Guardian.'[3]

While the contemporary London literary scene was blessed with a dozen small magazines and periodicals, West Indian writers could usually look only to national newspapers for occasional publication. Una's *Cosmopolitan* poets were mainly members of the Jamaica Poetry League, established in Kingston in 1923 as a branch of the Empire Poetry League: the elderly Astley Clerk, a musician and collector of Jamaican folk songs, whose Cowen's Music Rooms was their regular meeting place; the genial and well-liked Amy Bailey, who was to share in many of Una's social and cultural projects; Eva and Arthur Nicholas, brother and sister poets, nicknamed 'the Wordsworthian duo'; Mary Adella Wolcott, who under the pen name 'Tropica' had published *The Island of Sunshine* in New York in 1904; Albinia Catherine Hutton, daughter of Scottish poet William Shand Daniel; and Constance Hollar, author of *Flaming June* (1941). 'The baby of the league', Vivian Virtue, author of 'Wings of the Morning', became a close, long-term friend, along with Philip Sherlock, whose sensitive review of W. H. Davies appeared in an early issue.

This literary band was held together by a clever, though somewhat dour young man, Clare McFarlane, a civil servant who had set up the Jamaica Poetry League. McFarlane had some talent, but sadly it failed to catch fire and his long poems, *Beatrice* and *Daphne*, are 'heavy handedly moralistic and embarrassingly derivative verse'.[4] Yet he belonged to that part of colonial thinking which was keen to graft some notion of Jamaicanness on to English culture and did much to hearten other writers. Una owed her initial publishing achievements to his personal encouragement, but McFarlane's views as an anti-feminist and a critic who wrote in 1950 'I have turned my back on the Whitmans, the Eliots and the Pounds, the Audens ... as being for the most part innovators and purveyors of a spurious originality which, I predict will pass and be forgotten' were the exact opposite of hers.[5] In McFarlane's *Case for Polygamy* (1932), for instance, he proposed that in a Christian society like Jamaica where women outnumber men, the men should take two wives, thus permitting the women to stay at home and have babies.[6]

Una did not feel that marriage and family life were for everyone, and she rejected his anti-feminist moralist stance. She found herself at odds with her main literary allies because she was relating the specific oppression of women as a sex to marriage, family and religion, and argued that 'a living wage' not marriage was woman's prime need. But she found herself in a difficult position, both shocking to her elders and vulnerable to traditional reprisals. In her column 'Gentlemen: No Admittance – Ladies Only' of *The Cosmopolitan* she had published some anonymous poems proclaiming these new freedoms and a parody of Hamlet's speech, entitled 'To Wed or Not to Wed', in August 1929:

> To wed, or not to wed: that is the question:
> Whether 'tis nobler in the mind to suffer
> The fret and loneliness of spinsterhood
> Or to take arms against the single state
> And by marrying, end it?

Over the next decade the rift in their thinking only widened as Una became more assured and perhaps even less dependent on McFarlane's avuncular judgement. Many years later he was to describe her as 'modern', pointing out 'a new spiritual tone, an element of unrest and discontent, of uncertainty and questioning for which no earlier parallel can be found'[7] in Jamaican literature. With this assessment of Una's later poetry other critics have easily concurred.

In her twenties Una had the temperament for parodies, and unwittingly unleashed a round of iffy poems when she had a go at Kipling's 'If':

> If you can keep him true when all about you
> The girls are making eyes and being kind,
> If you can make him spend the evenings with you
> When fifty Jims and Jacks are on his mind;
> If you can wait and not be tired by waiting,

> Or when he comes at one, be calm and sleep
> And do not oversleep but early waking
> Smile o'er the tea cups, and ne'er think to weep.

One of the better masculine retorts in this battle of the sexes, with apologies to Kipling and Miss Marson, was 'VCP''s:

> If you can keep your head when all about you
> Are stacks and stacks of never-ending bills
> If you can bear to hear the author flout you
> Because you 'squeal' at these invited ills;
> If you can see the dress worn once and no more
> Discarded for the wardrobe of her maid,
> Or stand all day the stifling complex odour
> Of costly scents for which your money paid.[8]

Una also commented on social issues such as land irrigation. She tackled such subjects as street lighting for the city's main thoroughfares, many of which were gas-lit or completely dark; housing; and education. She called for cheap housing for domestics ('How can a servant pay rental from a wage of 4/-, 5/- 6/- per week?'), for separate leisure facilities for women and for the representation of women on boards and councils.

In her small, sparsely furnished office Una wrote some of her most trenchant articles. She argued for technical education and for the development of local industries. Everywhere she looked she saw stark social contrasts – planters with vast estates, luxurious cars and troops of servants, sipping cocktails at the bar of the Myrtle Bank Hotel; and impoverished labourers living in surroundings of dust, cardboard and hot zinc roofs. 'We have to set about to bring better times for Jamaica and Jamaicans', she wrote in an article about local industries. More than sixty per cent of the Jamaican labour force was in agriculture, so Una wrote about the small independent farmer, whose meagre lifestyle was little better than his enslaved forefather's:

> Anyone who has had the opportunity of travelling through even a few of the parishes of the island will have noticed the thousands of acres of land lying idle, and if it was at the time when guavas or oranges were in season, they would have seen much of these going to waste. We mention those particularly because so much could be done to make a real industry of preserves but there are many other fruit, Cheremelias, Roseapples, Jew Plums, Black berries, Cocoa plums and others which would also make wonderful jams and jellies. The guava jelly and dolce and orange marmalade are, however, the best known … and those

which have been sent to England or America ... attracted attention and created a demand.

... Is there any feasible reason why this industry could not be developed and protected?[9]

By 1929 the twenty-four-year-old Una was taking her country's future very seriously. She found Jamaican politicians boring. The Legislative Council was dominated by complacent old men, but there a middle-aged printer called Marcus Garvey whose politics were very exceptional. This short, statuesque figure with his dark suit and panama hat and his 'Back to Africa' cry had exploded upon the Jamaican political scene in her teens. The establishment hoped nothing would come of his movement, the Universal Negro Improvement Association, founded in Jamaica after the First World War; some hedged their bets with condescension, most decried his every word. But the number and barbarity of social abuses which Garvey exposed prompted Una to take him seriously:

the UNIA is out to help all negroes who will be helped and ... help is needed. The need that lies closest to our heart and is no doubt giving Mr Garvey some concern is the way in which our people live in such a large portion of a comparatively small city. To us it seems a farce to preach religion, race pride, morality and physical and mental fitness to people who chiefly through economic causes, live as many of them do, anything from 4 to 10 in one room. Now that the UNIA is progressing rapidly with its aims, ... our hopes are high that in conjunction with their spiritual and mental uplift this state of affairs will receive the attention of Mr Garvey.

The powers of leadership are given to few. Mr. M Garvey has these gifts. ... Mr Garvey's methods of helping [Jamaica] may not be methods that others would adopt. But the world is large enough for every man to work out his own individual ideas – and it is the spirit of love, sacrifice and devotion that must always be the dominant factor.[10]

This was, in many senses, a significant commentary: not only did Una, using the occasion of the UNIA anniversary, shrewdly dignify Garvey's message, but she also praised his method with vigour and commitment.[11]

The period immediately after the First World War had seen Garvey champion the cause of black servicemen whose contribution had been unacknowledged; woo Jamaicans to adopt a more positive self-image; and fight for unionisation – vast organisational schemes in commerce, art and politics. He inspired millions. Surrounding himself with artists at his Edelweiss Park house, he encouraged a radical cultural politics among black artists. But according to the *Jamaica Times* his proposals for – among much else – land reform, a university and a minimum wage 'would have commended themselves to the characters in Mr Wells' *Modern Utopia*'.[12] His activities were viewed as seditious; he was imprisoned and finally in 1935, disillusioned with Jamaica, he retreated to England where he died five years later.

The Cosmopolitan was in trouble. Sales had fallen off, advertisers – shy after the crisis caused by the Wall Street crash – were backing away and Una was under pressure to provide a 'more snappy' magazine with 'more society gossip'. She protested: 'We are aware, and too well aware of the fact that magazines of the standard to which we aspire are never "best sellers" though several times during the year just closed we disposed of our entire issues.'[13] What was chiefly harassing Una was the terrible workload and her own shortage of money – not only for her personal needs but for the books she was planning. She found help and support in the form of Aimee Webster, an articulate, creole graduate whose planter parents had given her a sheltered upbringing and who was now making her name on the *Jamaica Times*. Aimee came in as co-editor – 'We were the only contributors' – and shouldered half the financial burden. This was handy since Una had no real capital of her own and was still doing other jobs, including secretarial work for the Headmaster at Calabar Boys School.

In February 1931 a revamped magazine sporting a few external changes appeared on the shelves. The black and white cover had become tangerine orange, the format had shrunk, the masthead bore the promising title *The New Cosmopolitan*, and the two editors' names appeared. It was a congenial but short-lived arrangement. Just two months later, in April, Una drew her readers' attention to the situation:

> It is with a deep sense of regret that I make the announcement that the publication [of the *New Cosmopolitan*] is now postponed for an indefinite period. I say indefinite because I cannot foresee how long the present depression will last ... I very much regret having to do this but have no alternative.

Aimee too was to have some regrets. Una had been 'very pleasant to work with, a gifted and diligent co-editor, and far in advance of her time', but she 'believed the world owed her a handsome living and this delusion led her to many dishonesties', Aimee remembered with some bitterness years later.

On the plantation I had lived a very sheltered life and had not discovered this rascality before, which is a characteristic of all Jamaicans of all races. Una left to collect monies from advertisers and then used it to pay her personal bills, leaving me with the magazine's bills and she migrated soon after.[14]

This story has a cruel ring of truth. That 'rascality' tells how hurt Aimee was and that Una could be completely self-centred, not least when she had her eye on a new, more exciting project.

Besides, Christianity had taught her to be charitable towards the humble and the weak; but the rich, those who stood between her and her many unfulfilled ambitions, were different.

NOTES

1 *New Cosmopolitan*, April 1931.
2 *Daily Gleaner*, 28 January 1930.
3 Quoted in H. Swanzy, 'Literary Situation in Contemporary Caribbean', *Books Abroad*, summer 1955, pp. 266–74.
4 Lloyd W. Brown, *West Indian Poetry* (Oxford, Heinemann Educational Books, 1984), p. 30.
5 Clare McFarlane, 'In Defense of "A Treasury of Jamaican Poetry"', *Daily Gleaner*, 25 August 1950, p. 8.
6 McFarlane, *Case for Polygamy* (Kingston Jamaica, published by the author, 1932).
7 McFarlane, *A Literature in the Making* (Kingston, Jamaica, Pioneer Press, 1956).
8 'Local Poems', *The Cosmopolitan*, November 1929, p. 223.
9 'Local Industries', *The Cosmopolitan*, vol. 1, no. 5, September 1928, pp. 127–8.
10 'The UNIA', *The Cosmopolitan*, vol. 2, no.1, May 1929, p. 6.
11 When Marcus Garvey was living in London during the late 1930s, Una Marson was again in contact with him. She was by his side during his last year, 1940.
12 *Jamaica Times*, 8 February 1930.
13 'The Third Year', editorial, *The Cosmopolitan*, vol. 3, no. 1, May 1930, p. 5.
14 Aimee Webster interviewed by the author, May 1989, Kingston, Jamaica.

5

A voyage of heights and depths

ON A sunny morning in May 1989 Archie Lindo, a Jamaican journalist and photographer in his seventies, chatted about Una Marson's multi-faceted life and her feelings about love. He was puzzled by
the fact that, after a lifetime of being her friend, he could not say for
certain if she had ever been in love. He remembered that he had
wanted her. She was warm and funny and clever. He remembered
how passionately she had worked at *The Cosmopolitan*, to which he
had contributed, and how fiercely she had fought the stenographers'
cause. No longer hurt by the memory of her affable rejection, he
couldn't help wondering whether Una had been keeping herself for a
white man.

At twenty-five Una had plenty to say about love, and covered sheets
of paper with poems about the pain of love, love and desertion and
unrequited love. In July 1930 she published a pocket-sized volume of
lyrics, sonnets and miscellaneous poems called *Tropic Reveries*, the first
lines of which accurately reflect the book's flavour: 'I cannot tell why I
who once was so gay'; 'I cannot let you hold me in your arms'; ''Tis best
that we should say farewell for aye'; 'I know too well, beloved'. And so
on.

Some of it was intensely emotional, theatrical stuff, representing
slightly different personae: the deserted princess, walking alone in her
rose garden, awaiting the return of her handsome prince:

> In vain I build me stately mansions fair
> And set thee as my king upon the throne,
> And place a lowly stool beside thee there,
> Thus as thy slave to come into my own.

Sometimes the grieving, deserted woman is jealous:

> I know too well beloved
> That thou art not for me
> That other hands and other hearts
> Will minister to thee.
>
> I know those eyes so tender
> On others still will shine
> And that your kiss will linger
> On other lips than mine.

Sometimes the lonely woman longs for deeper physical passion:

> Play bridge! when each fibre of my aching heart
> Yearned just for the touch of your hand.

Una published her collection, at her own expense and priced 2*s* 6*d*, with an introduction which suggests a coy and diffident personality:

> Of their worth it is not for me to speak, except to say that they are the heart throbs of one who from earliest childhood has worshipped at the shrine of the muses and dwelt among the open spaces and the silent hills where the cadences of Nature's voice tempt one to answering song.

The *Jamaica Times* writing about *Tropic Reveries* on 5 July 1930 referred to her 'fine talent' and from the three subsections – Love, Nature and Miscellaneous poems – had selected 'Vows', a sonnet said to be reminiscent of Elizabeth Barrett Browning, and the parody 'To Wed or Not to Wed'.[1]

Such parodies show that, although much of Una's poetry was pure Romantic derivation, she was aware that feminist consciousness could strain sexual relationships and that women had to struggle internally against subservience and passivity. 'Race' and colour were also an issue for her and, while expressing sexual desire, she confronted the fact that men did not find her beautiful. Although she counted many men among her acquaintances, several have commented negatively about her physical appearance: 'In those days the emphasis we placed on beauty and form was so different.'

For Una the consequence of womanly desire, feminist consciousness and male prejudice was inevitable disappointment: 'love and grief' were 'twin souls'. In her short story 'Sojourn', a young, dark-skinned Jamaican woman, Helen, who falls in love with an Englishman, Sidney, is portrayed as needlessly sensitive about her colour:

> 'Why does she object to going out with me? You should have pressed her if she were not willing. Maybe she does not like me,' said Sydney a bit peevishly.

'Nonsense,' said Harry, 'She's alright. She has her own ideas and takes a bit of knowing, but when you get to know her you will find she has a heart of gold. She's awfully sensitive and reserved.'[2]

In time Helen realises that Sidney's affection for her is genuine and discards the self-imposed barrier between them, but the relationship does not develop because he is called away to England and Helen is left wondering whether it might have blossomed. Sexual fulfilment between the 'races' remains at the level of fantasy and desire. Una portrays Helen as needlessly sensitive while Sidney is seen as oblivious to the shade distinctions between them; this is an idealised picture of racial attitudes in Jamaica.

Her second collection of poems, *Heights and Depths*, published a year after *Tropic Reveries*, reveals more succinctly how conscious she had become of the social environment and continues to assert an interest in women's experiences. In the title poem, the 'heights' to which Una refers are a peopled arcadia where she is admired and cherished, 'the depths' the real wilderness to which she is obliged to return:

We have known the heights together
I have known the depths alone
We have joined in merry laughter
But the tears have been mine own.

No one can say for certain whether Una, twenty-six years old when *Heights and Depths* was published, had had a sexual relationship or not. She was probably still a virgin, but, since she was a public figure who was outspoken on the relations between the sexes, her love poetry raised questions about her own sexuality. She knew and observed how men frustrate women's lives, but her own desires, unfed by any sexual experience of her own, remained ardent. If there was a man in her dreams, he was strong, long-suffering and kind, a protector, respectful of feminine virtue. He was also, at the same time, destructive, inadequate, selfish and weak. All her life Una guarded her independence ferociously, perhaps because her father had died in her early teens and she felt like an orphan for whom emotional security carried an exaggerated value. Like so many insecure people, she devoted much of her time to shoring up others – the abandoned, the hopeless and the undistinguished. These she picked up, in recognition: 'The cry of the children is for life and health and joy.'[3]

No man heeded her cry.

It is a shame that Una Marson's first collections, *Tropic Reveries* (1930) and *Heights and Depths* (1931), invite a wild goose chase after male lovers, not only because their identities matter less than the inner world of the woman herself but also because emotional involvement with women was the more vital force in her life. Her bond with Ethel and later friendships with feminist women abroad provided the source from which Una was able to grow and enjoy a positive self-definition. There is, however, no evidence of a lesbian relationship in the accepted sense.

Her early writing, poems and her play *At What a Price*, examined relations between the sexes in a male-dominated society. In her play, a tale of innocent girlhood and the deceptions of man, a young middle-class country woman migrates to Kingston to work as a stenographer. The heroine, Ruth Maitland, is then seduced by her attractive boss, a foreigner, becomes pregnant and, on discovering that she has been betrayed, has to return home as a penitent.

While the ending was nothing but safe and conservative, the play itself presented emancipated women in a world still hostile to their independence in which only the fairy godmother could express the contradictions of the New Woman's existence: 'As much as I long for a home, honest love and motherhood and all that sort of thing, I can hardly conceive of myself getting married.' And the heroine warns her boyfriend: 'Don't you dare to be so absolutely Victorian to tell me that the woman's place is in the home. Those words are only used today as a topic for debating societies.'

The play was written in summer 1931, when Una was twenty-six. A year before she wrote it her mother had died and Una, released from the past, felt free to explore the contradictions of her upbringing, weighting the play in favour of her own values and demonstrating, in a lovely, light-hearted scene, how happy young single women can be in their own company. She had after all, asserted in *The Cosmopolitan* that this was 'the age of woman'.

When the play was staged at Kingston's Ward Theatre on Saturday 11 June 1932 Una had her first taste of being a celebrity. She had devised the play in collaboration with her friend Horace Vaz, but it was chiefly her work and he later praised her as a pioneer who had stressed the importance of Jamaican themes, characters and settings. The critics were mostly impressed. The *Daily Gleaner* (13 June), while recognising that the play was 'weak in spots', called for 'more such productions' and greater public support for local writers.[4] Back in 1911, George Bernard Shaw had visited Jamaica and in pontifical fashion had said:

You want a theatre with all the ordinary travelling companies from England and America sternly kept out of it, for unless you do your own acting and write your own plays, your theatre will be of no use; it will in fact, vulgarise and degrade you.[5]

According to the *Jamaica Times* Una Marson had 'branched out ... successfully in drama'; the review continued, 'it is to her credit and ours and may be the beginning of a Jamaican dramatic literature. ... There are some remarkably good flashes of humour in the play and Miss Marson has steeped herself in local colour and used it with discretion and insight.'[6]

She had drawn out the conflicts between urban and rural dwellers, highlighting the stresses caused by mass migration to the cities, given a voice to the peasant class and probed the question of sexual virtue. When the play closed, after a short run, Una was again thrown back on her own resources. When she looked upon the international renown which Claude McKay, Jamaica's famous poet, had won in the USA, she felt a mixture of national pride and private envy. By any standards the range of her achievements at twenty-seven was considerable. She had now tried her hand at three literary genres – poems, short stories and plays – and won local recognition for her 'talent, executive ability and courage',[7] a combination which, it was confidently predicted in the press, would take her far. But to realise that lucent promise Una had to travel abroad, as Claude McKay had done, in order to broaden her experience, find a wider, perhaps more challenging audience, and, if all went well, win the greater fame she so earnestly craved. Her literary apprenticeship was over; she decided to visit London.

In deciding to travel to England, Una took no advice and confided in no one. She just went ahead and booked her fare – £50 return. America had been suggested to her as a more likely destination, but Una did not care for the United States where she knew thousands of Jamaican women were struggling to make ends meet, working in American factories, in the tobacco industry, in restaurants or as maids and trying to send something home. Una's worst nightmare was to end up working in someone else's kitchen, reigning over greasy pots and pans, storecupboards, brushes and mops. The more she heard about life in the USA, the more resolute she became: she wouldn't go to the States, she 'didn't have the energy for it'. Her attitude was to change later in life.

And so Una had settled on England. England had captured her imagination. It was the birthplace of Keats and Shelley, the land of gracious living. Her naive and youthful mind was enchanted. Her personal strength, her 'zest to taste life all at once', a quality which a forgiving Aimee Webster was later to pinpoint, convinced Una to make the Atlantic leap.[8] When on 9 July 1932 Una arrived in Plymouth, England, on board the SS *Jamaica Settler*, her pockets lined with the slender profits from *At What a Price*, she was, so she later claimed, intending to stay for a three-month holiday.[9] Four years later, by the summer of 1936, she was still living in London, weary and, in her own words, 'heading for a nervous breakdown caused by overwork'.[10]

NOTES

1 'Tropic Reveries: Poems by Miss Una M. Marson', *Jamaica Times*, 5 July 1930, p. 5.
2 'Sojourn', *New Cosmopolitan*, February 1931, p. 8.
3 'Can Education Save the Children', *Public Opinion*, 20 March 1937, p. 10.
4 *Daily Gleaner*, 13 June 1932, p. 6.
5 Quoted by Errol Hill, 'The Emergence of a National Drama in the West Indies', *Caribbean Quarterly*, vol. 18, no. 4, December 1972, pp. 9–40.
6 'Drama Wise Author Writes Local Play', *Jamaica Times*, 18 June 1932, p. 23.
7 Review of *Tropic Reveries*, *Daily Gleaner*, 5 July 1930, p. 19.
8 Aimee Webster Delisser in a letter to the author.
9 West India Committee Circular, 21 July 1932, p. 302.
10 'Racial Feelings', *Public Opinion*, 17 July 1937, p. 3.

6

The arrivant

U NA found lodgings at 164 Queen's Road, Peckham – a spacious, rambling Victorian house – with a Jamaican family, the Moodys. Theirs was a comfortable, four-storey property with a middle-floor entrance leading to a small, often cluttered hall and, beyond that, large dining and drawing rooms. Up a flight on a half-landing was Una's bedroom which looked out on to a grass tennis court and the colourful, rose-filled back garden. By the time Una arrived on his doorstep, Harold Arundel Moody, her landlord and would-be guardian, was a portly gentleman in his mid-fifties with all the avuncular manners his shape might have suggested. Born in Kingston, Jamaica, in 1882, he had travelled to England in 1904 to study medicine at King's College, London. Six years later, 'a distinguished medical graduate', the young Harold Moody came face to face with the institutionalised racism of his chosen profession.[1] He was refused a hospital appointment. Matron said 'no'; even the poor of Camberwell wouldn't have him. So, forced into self-employment, Dr Moody MRCS LRCP MB BS set himself up in practice at 111 King's Road, Peckham, around the corner from his house which he bought in 1913. Moody lived there for the rest of his life with his wife, Olive, a warm, affectionate English nurse, and their children.

Harold Moody had long decided to turn his home into more than a family house; it was open to all the travelling black people who couldn't find a room or a meal elsewhere, and Olive joined in the spirit of things. Never muttering in an ill-tempered way, she used her culinary skills to make people feel at home and 'extra numbers did not worry her, if my father walked in and said so and so is staying for a month, she'd just get on with it', recalled Christine Moody, their eldest daughter.[2]

At the Moodys' house tea was always in the pot, and most evenings Harold attended committee meetings in attempts to fight 'the colour bar', the racial barrier which kept black people out of decent housing, well-paid jobs, hostels, hotels, bars, restaurants, clubs, colleges and nurseries. Harold Moody had a wide acquaintanceship within the religious and philanthropic circles who were trying to counter the colour bar and on 13 March 1931, having enlisted sufficient supporters, he set up his own organisation, the League of Coloured Peoples, Britain's first significant black-led organisation, into whose clutches his lodgers would be drawn.

Una was not the Moodys' only lodger. Down the hall was Sylvia Lowe, a Jamaican student whose father was someone big in the Jamaica Banana Producers. Sylvia didn't think much of her newly arrived countrywoman who was definitely

> looking for something, maybe a job, but she was seeking, seeking something. She didn't know what she was about and couldn't make up her mind what to do. She could have become a teacher or something, but she was always looking around her to see what she could do next.

Sylvia decided that Una was 'odd', not least because 'she frequently remonstrated on the subject of population growth, addressing whoever would listen, then she would explain that a country's true wealth was its people'.[3] When Una had finished, her jaw stiff and strong, Sylvia would leave her bemused. Unaccustomed to such political talk, Sylvia simply dismissed Una as barmy.

Una was in fact responding to the notion of race supremacy which was inherent in the eugenics debate in which calls for class unity, imperial dominance and 'survival of the fittest' masked state control and attempts to subjugate black life. In both England and Germany there had been calls for high fertility and healthy motherhood following the war; in England even the Fabian socialists had argued for social reform to improve the physique of the working class.[4] She was observing some of the developments black activist Angela Davis noted in the USA in the 1980s. Birth control and reproductive rights had carried a 'racist edge' from the nineteenth century, and in the 1930s black men and women had to recognise how racist population control was being presented as an individual right to birth control.[5] Garvey had also spoken about this. Now as a black woman Una was theorising how black female sexuality might be controlled by white, male authorities – not subjects with which her young housemate was at all familiar!

The small, male-dominated black community that gathered around the Moodys' home didn't know what to make of this bohemian gentlewoman. On the rare occasions single black women travelled to England, they came as students. They lived like Stella Thomas, the elegant Nigerian barrister, in decent accommodation in Bloomsbury, finished their studies and returned home.[6] Black middle-class women who were born in Britain like Amy Barbour James, a friend of Una's who lived in Acton, 'were not expected to fully participate in political matters but to be artistic and civilised, ideal wives for professional men'.[7] Una didn't fit anywhere.

Before she came to England Una had dispensed with being conventionalised. She had written about sex-role stereotyping and urged women to be themselves, but she hadn't tackled 'racial identities'. In the midst of this Anglo-black formality, Una responded by accentuating her difference in pointed ways. 'She liked to look African. She put her hair as they did ... natural not plaited, and combed out.' The hair, uncurled, untamed, unpressed, corresponded with Una's politics – this Sylvia did not miss: 'She also had a good African flair and was more interested in them [Africans] than in our own affairs ... she was a bit ahead of most people but we didn't think of that in those days.'[8]

Within months of her arrival in Britain Una stopped straightening her hair and went natural, not through lack of hairdressing facilities but from choice. The lotions and curatives which African-American Madame Walker had popularised in the USA did not touch Una's strong, thick locks. Chastising the 'Miss Jamaica' contest organisers, she must have decided, had been only her first step; 'going Afro' was not only an act of defiance against her standard, it was proof of an alternative assertiveness – nappy hair was best:

> I hate dat ironed hair,
> And dat bleaching skin,
> Hate dat ironed hair
> And dat bleaching skin
> But I'll be all alone
> If I don't fall in.[9]

At the same time some of her African sisters were evolving their own sense of couture and coiffure, as Titilola Folarin, a Nigerian law student, explained in the West African Students Union journal, *Wasu*. They wanted, she wrote, a

> systematic refinement to modernise our present style of Buba to induce

our educated girls and others to have more love and respect for their own native dress culture. ... I remember one particular occasion when I and my other WASU lady colleagues put on our native costumes and went as far as Piccadilly Circus. Many of our English friends who saw us expressed their pleasure and satisfaction at the show; but what struck me most was this, that about a week after, while passing through Regent Street in the West End ... we discovered in some of the shop windows a certain number of ladies' hats, almost exactly in the same style and shape of how we tied up our Gele on the day we passed through that district a week before.[10]

No pictures of Una in African dress have come to light, though she did acquire some West African indigo lappas which later adorned her study in Jamaica. But when she went shopping for clothes in London she picked up splendid, rich colours whenever she could find them: loud, bold stripes, multi-coloured dresses and handsome, vibrant accessories. In 1989 Christine Moody, looking at a picture of Una so attired, commented: 'She was not interested in clothes and hair as you can see.' Fashion, the young women had decided, was not Una's forte.

There wasn't much to do all day. There were so many things one might try to do. Get up and go for a walk, have something to eat, talk to Olive in the kitchen, go and try to find a job, hang out with the students. Trail about, write a poem or two. Or not.

It should be a thrill to be in the great city of London, centre of the world. Peckham is only ten miles away from Hyde Park Corner, but Una might as well have been two thousand miles away in Jamaica, for all the good it was doing her. Today Peckham is a byword for poverty: there are rats on the waste ground, unemployment has gone through the roof and inner city deprivation is no longer newsworthy; the 1930s tenement blocks are coming down, condemned housing, they say. They were just up when Una arrived, but already the new buildings were being blackened by the gas works, the bug cinema down the road seemed dirty and cold. It was always so very cold. The minute she stepped out on to the grey flagstones, she started to chill. Staying indoors was better, but so limiting. Dr Moody always had queues of patients awaiting his attention, Olive helped out, the children were at school and Christine already at college. London was waiting to be explored. The truth was that Una dreaded going out because people stared at her, men were curious but their gaze insulted her, even small children with short dimpled legs called her 'Nigger', put out their tongues at her. This was her first taste of street racism. She was a black foreigner seen only as strange, nasty, unwanted. This was the 'Fact of Blackness' which Fanon was to analyse in *Black Skins White Masks* (1952), that inescapable, heightened level of bodily consciousness which comes from 'being dissected by white eyes'. She had no peace outside 164. No safety.

This was where Moody's League stepped in. At first it had been little more than headed stationery, but, by the time Una needed its comfort, a diet of social events was being planned to help such confused aliens – colonial students, visitors and dignitaries: a genteel, compensatory social calendar. During the cold winter months there were small parties at the house, cultural trips, political conferences and endless meetings. When summer came, regular tennis parties were held on the grass court at Peckham, moonlight rambles and respectable dances with proper dance cards kept the misery at bay. Una started to find her feet, enjoying the leisurely round and sometimes playing hostess. Moody, always beneficent, threw a lavish reception in June 1933 at the Waldorf Hotel for the West Indies cricket team who had come to play their first test against England, at which she wittily introduced the team members in verse. He also threw fortnightly garden parties, to which Una often went. It was at one of these that she met the well-meaning but ineffectual Sir Edward Denham, the Governor of British Guiana and later of Jamaica, whose snobbish wife she also found irritating. Guests of honour were not always so prestigious; on 3 September 1932 they were Mr and Mrs R. S. Nehra. Mr Nehra was a former member of the Kenya Legislative council, but now lived in south London. But the League, even in its infancy, had great style. In June 1933 Moody sent an invitation to St James's Palace requesting the presence of the Prince of Wales at a League dinner or function, but the Colonial Office advised against this. The Prince of Wales did, however, receive a copy of the first issue of *The Keys*, the League's journal, published from summer 1933, which included a picture of Una Marson, already a leading member. The Prince, said the Colonial Office, 'noted in *The Keys* the statement of the objects of the League and wishes the League success in achieving them'.[11]

One of the League's aims was to assist in job hunting. Una looked for secretarial work, which was stereotyped as 'women's work' and thus low paid but for which, with her Pitman qualifications, she was amply qualified. Work was hard to find. Since the slump and the General Strike of 1926 morale was low and women had to be inventive if searching for jobs. Someone advised Una to try different agencies and firms, to put herself about a bit. And she did, but all she found was the most blatant racial discrimination:

> I tried to register for work as a stenographer. One agent told me she didn't register Black women because they would have to work in offices with white women. Another agent tried to find me a position and he told me that though my references were excellent, firms did not want to employ a Black stenographer.

Like so many of the West Indian women migrants of the 1950s, Una found herself blocked at every turn. She complained and cried; she felt lonely and humiliated, but she stayed and kept trying. Sylvia, arriving home late one night, saw how 'very emotional she was with frustration … she was crying and working herself up, and crying and crying, looking like a frightened child, helpless'.[12] England was making her feel inadequate; it dragged her low spirit lower.

Una never told lies about this, but she generalised it: writing on the 'Problems of Coloured People in Britain' she pointed out that women faced 'serious problems' finding work, because 'they are more often than not poorly educated'.[13] Perhaps she saw herself as a notch above the poor, black working-class women from the old communities in Cardiff, Liverpool and London, although English employers didn't regard her in a different light. The pain went deep and Una, who was facing tangible economic difficulties for the first time, didn't know how to armour herself.

In one of her poems she engaged in a fantasy, imagining herself in a powerful position, rejecting the English and giving them a taste of their own medicine; she dreamt of going to a Lyons restaurant and ordering breadfruit, 'some fresh ackee and saltfish too / an dumplin hot'. Her fantasy of an unracialised body was an imaginative strategy designed to resist the corrosive force of her oppressive world.[14] Standing by her bedroom window on a Sunday morning, dressed for church, Una tapped into the feeling of Sundays everywhere. Melancholy, religious, stable and quiet.

> Christ, if thou didst bleed upon the Cross
> To bring the world to God
> Let not Thy glorious travail be in vain.[15]

Here in London, with its endless cold days and drizzle, she dressed with woollen vest close to her skin and warm dress and grey coat buttoned up, to follow the parade of Moodys to the Congregational church at the corner of Wren Road, through the grey streets of Peckham.

It was better than nothing, but it wasn't home. The difference was so great that all hope fell into the shadows and Una's striving for happiness became damp and futile. On Sundays the extent of human injustice seemed worse than ever. One Sunday, at a special service at Whitefields Tabernacle on Tottenham Court Road, the minister Alfred Belden referred to his largely black congregation as 'brethren'. The press mocked. 'He Called Them Brethren!' became the title of one of her race poems. Una was discouraged that this superficial warmth should cause such consternation. The gap between white and black seemed wide and terrifying, even though the spirituals her group performed were going down well and Basil Rogers, a Jamaican soloist, was letting them have 'I'm going to play a harp all over God's Heaven.'[16]

After a difficult first year Una gave up looking for work and in autumn 1933 became the League's unpaid assistant secretary, in charge of organising student activities, receptions, meetings, trips and concerts; maintaining contact with other student bodies, training institutions and colleges; obtaining information on the arrival, activities and progress of coloured visitors, students and residents of Great Britain.[17] Moody kept a close eye on her. He had a very clear idea of how he liked to conduct his business, and his stern Christian fundamentalism coupled with his Victorian attitudes kept any radicalism in check. Coming from outside the contemporary scene of left-wing, anti-establishment activism, Moody was in the line of fire of many younger (male) thinkers. (But not with Una.) Ras Makonnen the Guyanese activist found him infuriating: 'You obstructionist', he wrote, 'you are using this balm of aid and garden parties to seduce these young men.' Other people might criticise Harold Moody – the animated young C. L. R. James, then a confirmed Trotskyist, was another feared detractor, but he acknowledged that Moody's letters in the press and informal chats with MPs 'mattered because there were too few black people around'.

James had published *The Case for West Indian Self-Government* that year with Leonard and Virginia Woolf's Hogarth Press. That statement of WestIndianhood, politely received in England, was thoroughly debated at the League's conference, thus advancing Una's political education.

Now that Una lived and worked at 164 Queen's Road, she could stop going out, but as she opened all the mail and dished out the requests for lectures to other members it was easy to pass on the mundane requests and cream off the best invitations for herself, including lunch in town with John Masefield, the Poet Laureate. This sort of Machiavellian administration was the quickest way to wriggle out of the company of the students; Una gained the reputation of being 'a true loner who didn't exactly seek out company', and some League members countered by refusing to take notice of her.[18] Yet her regular haunts, aside from the Moodys' home, became the Memorial Hall in Farringdon Road where League meetings were held and the West African students' Camden Road hostel where they congregated to rail against colonialism, lack of opportunity, the cold country and the cold people. Dr Robert Wellesley Cole, a Sierra Leonean, remembered Una as 'extremely charming, but not one of us'.

Una was lonely, ill at ease and uncertain, but she was also learning about life in Britain and finding ways of overcoming the pseudo-scientific notions of 'race' which hindered her existence, by making quests for validation and recognition within the cultural terrain, as the snippets which follow indicate. In July 1933 she accompanied Harold Moody to Hull, at the invitation of the city's Lord Mayor, to take part in the William Wilberforce Centenary Celebrations, a week-long event. Una took part in a mock Victorian exhibition of freaks and objects, including slave relics. She placed herself alongside a strange tableau of Wilberforce from Madam Tussaud's and was filmed like a model doing a lifelike reproduction of a West Indian market seller, in the exhausting heat of the long brown Mortimer Galleries, in the vain hope of providing a spectacle which would increase racial understanding.[19]

She provided a second, similarly motivated spectacle when she obligingly mounted a League performance of *At What a Price*, involving every available member, at the YWCA hostel Central Club on Great Russell Street on the evening of 23 November 1933. The play, Moody told them, was evidence of what the colonial students were capable of and proof that the League was going places. Una took pride afterwards in the invited audience's appreciative applause and in the *West Africa* review which called the play a 'delightful Jamaican comedy' and a 'capital rendering of middleclass life'.[20] But the bouquet went to Stella Thomas who, in the role of Ruth's friend Myrtle, seized the imagination of the *Manchester Guardian*'s critic: 'Perhaps the most memorable thing of the evening was the sheer beauty of Miss Thomas' walk across the stage. When she came in on one scene in a magnificent orange dress, moving like a slim queen of night, the whole audience broke into applause.'[21]

After Christmas, the play transferred for a three-night run, beginning on 15 January, at the Scala Theatre in Charlotte Street, central

London. The show attracted good reviews even from the mainstream press and Una received some welcome attention for her directorial debut, but there were some counter-indications of her theatrical judgement. A modern director would choose only actors whose accents were recognisably Jamaican, but Una had little option: the *Daily Herald* reviewer picked up 'the rich language of the African coast, the staccato sing-song of Jamaica, and a genuine Cockney accent' among the supposed Jamaican band. Una took it all in her stride and enjoyed her success which was duly noted in various West Indian papers, proud to report an 'All Coloured Play in London'. Although the play failed to make money, it did make history as the first black colonial production in the West End, which was a considerable achievement.[22] Even during the 1980s, a decade notable for the visible accomplishments of black women artists and writers, only three had the distinction of directing plays in London's West End.

The importance of the League, from Una's point of view, was as a gateway to wider circles. On its own, it was too narrow a world for the twenty-seven-year-old who longed to be involved in London's life and letters, but it gave her a start. She arranged and compèred an evening's entertainment at the Indian Students Hostel, engaging a distinguished line-up including the American singer John Payne, who had worked with the Southern Syncopated Orchestra; Bruce Wendell, a first-class pianist; and Rudolph Dunbar, the Guyanese clarinettist. She became editor of *The Keys*, which in 1934 had a circulation of over two thousand worldwide.[23] It was well-designed, well-illustrated and comprehensive in its coverage of race issues both at home and abroad, from the case of the Scottsboro boys in the USA to the problems of colonial seamen in Cardiff.

This editorial experience provided fruitful ground for Una. She had never had such wide exposure to pan-African political issues or handled such varied copy. She logged every issue and every regional problem discussed and was able to draw on this vast body of data in later articles, speeches and debates. 'It is impossible to live in London, associating with peoples of other Colonies of the British Empire without realising that British peoples the world over are working for self-realisation and development towards the highest and the best', she wrote in September 1937.[24] London, the centre of the empire, was also cradle to the pan-African movement, a sort of boomerang from the horrors of slavery and colonialism, to which Una, like many of her generation, was being steadily drawn.

Una continued like this for many months. Gradually, imperceptibly, something was happening to her. It was as if the despair had gone out of her. She was now the centre of the League, the editor of its journal, its spokeswoman (second only to Harold Moody himself). She had the feeling that she mattered again. Sometimes, even in Peckham, the sun was shining. For a long time she didn't say anything publicly about the transition towards contentment. Perhaps she didn't even think about it, but the next play she wrote was a witty comedy called *London Calling* based on the experiences of colonial students in London; she began to master the feelings of alienation and to empower herself and others in relation to negative imagery by countering the myth of black inferiority:

> I am black
> And so I must be
> More clever than white folk
> More wise than white folk
> More discreet than white folk
> More courageous than white folk.[25]

Her instincts urged her to come to terms with the disappointments of the 'Mother Country' and to branch out to preserve her sense of uniqueness. In summer 1934 she found a viable way out of the League's confines. The answer lay in an alternative strategy – not only encouraging her 'audiences' to debunk racist and sexist ideologies but also re-fashioning herself.

NOTES

1 D. Vaughan, *Negro Victory* (London, Independent Press, 1950, pp. 27–8.
2 Christine Moody interviewed by the author, Kingston, Jamaica, May 1989.
3 All quotations from Sylvia Lowe from a telephone interview with the author in Jamaica, May 1989.
4 S. Rowbotham, *Hidden From History* (London, Pluto Press, 1973), p. 106.
5 Angela Davis, *Women Race and Class* (London, Women's Press, 1981), p. 215.
6 Material on Stella Thomas from her Inn, Middle Temple.
7 J. P. Green, 'Amy Barbour James and the Negro Spiritual', unpublished article, Crawley, December 1987.
8 Sylvia Lowe interviewed by the author.
9 'Kinky Haired Blues', *The Moth and the Star* (Kingston, Jamaica, 1937).
10 T. Folarin, 'Our Native Dress', *Wasu*, vol. 4, no. 4, October 1935, p. 56.
11 Public Record Office, London, PRO CO323/1244/11805.
12 Sylvia Lowe interviewed by the author.
13 'Problems of Coloured People in Britain', no date, Una Marson papers, Box

1944B, National Library of Jamaica. As this piece is undated and Una Marson doesn't state the date of her job search it is impossible to confirm that it coincides with her arrival in Britain. However, this seems to be the most likely period of her unemployment.

14 'Quashie Comes to London', *The Moth and the Star*.

15 'He Called Us Brethren', *The Moth and the Star*, p. 15.

16 'Negro Singers Hold a Congregation Spellbound', *Daily Herald*, 29 May 1933, p. 3.

17 'The League of Coloured Peoples' from PRO CO323/1244/11805.

18 Robert Wellesley Cole interviewed by the author, London, May 1988.

19 'The Englishmen Who Broke the Slave Trade', *West Africa*, 29 July 1933, p. 788. See also *West Africa*, 22 July 1933, and 'The Wilberforce Centenary Celebrations: Hull July 23–29th', in *The Keys*, vol. 1, October 1933, p. 22; A Programme for Hull Celebrations, Local History Library, Hull.

20 'At What a Price', *West Africa*, 20 January 1934, p. 39.

21 Quoted in 'At What a Price', p. 39.

22 Interviews with C. Moody, Sylvia Lowe and notes from *The Keys*, journal of the League of Coloured Peoples, British Library, London.

23 *The Keys* owed its title to the Ghanaian educator Dr Aggrey's analogy of the piano keys, a sign of racial harmony. See also p. 21.

24 'A Call to Downing Street', *Public Opinion*, 11 September 1937, p. 50.

25 'Black Burden', *The Moth and the Star*.

Una in her late teens.
Courtesy of the
National Library of
Jamaica

'Miss Una Marson',
from the *Jamaica
Critic*, March 1928.
Courtesy of the
National Library of
Jamaica

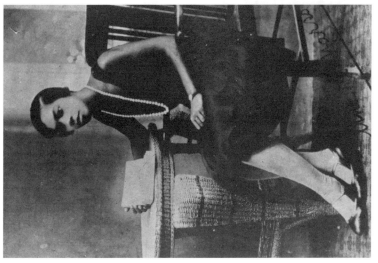

A view of the harbour showing steamers moored at the wharves on the Kingston dockside, with mountains in the distance. Courtesy of Cambridge University Library

A view of the harbour looking along King Street towards the mountains in the distance. The street itself is crowded with promenading Jamaicans, while in the foreground stands the Metcalf Statue with the Victoria Market to the right. Courtesy of Cambridge University Library

Conference Group, Second Annual Conference of the League of Coloured Peoples, High Leigh Hoddesdon, March 1934. Courtesy of the National Library of Jamaica

Conference Group, Second Annual Conference of the League of Coloured Peoples, High Leigh Hoddesdon, March 1934. Courtesy of the National Library of Jamaica

Una Marson, as compère of *Calling the West Indies*, the weekly programme broadcast from London on the BBC Overseas Service. Courtesy of the BBC

facing, above Calling the West Indies Christmas party and third anniversary celebration of the programme, 1943. Una Marson with Gerry Wilmot, the well-known BBC compère and producer. Courtesy of the BBC

facing, below Una Marson with Learie Constantine in 1942. The famous Trinidad cricketer was doing a broadcast for *Calling the West Indies*, about his work as the Ministry of Labour's Welfare Officer for the 200 Jamaican technicians working in factories in England. Courtesy of the BBC

Broadcast of *Voice*, 1942, the monthly radio programme which broadcast modern poetry to English-speaking India, on the Eastern Service of the BBC. From left to right (sitting): Venu Chitale, a member of the BBC Indian Section; M. J. Tambimuttu, a Tamil from Ceylon, editor of *Poetry* (London); T. S. Eliot; Una Marson; Mulk Raj Anand, novelist; Christopher Pemberton, a member of the BBC staff; Narayana Menon, Indian writer. (Standing): George Orwell, who produced the programme; Nancy Parratt, his secretary; William Empson, poet and critic. Courtesy of the BBC

Una Marson with Victor Feather of the Trades Union Congress in 1942. He gives a series of talks on the BBC's Shortwave Service to the West Indies on the birth, growth and development of trade unionism in Britain. Courtesy of the BBC

Una Marson at the BBC during the Second World War. Courtesy of the National Library of Jamaica

Hello West Indies, 1943. Courtesy of the British Film Institute

Una and William Macmillan. Courtesy of Mona Macmillan

At home at 101 Hope Road, Liguinea. Courtesy of Erica Koch

Alexander Bustamente 'wore a lovely colourful shirt just right for photographs, with the mass of grey hair framing a very classic face'. Courtesy of Erica Koch

In the garden at Liguinea, May 1951. Courtesy of Erica Koch

'Women and Development', November 1964. Courtesy of Mount Carmel International Training Centre for Community Leaders, Haifa, Israel

'The brolly points to Jamaica': 1964 Leaders' Seminar at Haifa. Courtesy of Mount Carmel International Training Centre for Community Leaders, Haifa, Israel

7

Identity politics – 1930s style

THE AFRICAN king Sir Nana Ofori Atta Omanhene of Akyem Abuakwa (not far north of Accra in northern Ghana) came to London in July 1934, leading a Gold Coast delegation to the Colonial Office. He was fifty-four, charming and brilliant. He believed fervently in the acquisition of western education as a foundation to building a modern African state and he was promoting this ethos with some vigour amongst his many – fifty-plus at one count – children. Neither wholly traditionalist nor vapidly modern, Ofori Atta was comfortable with the notions of women's advancement, tolerant of religious freedom, astute in business development and a pioneer in race pride. The King liked Foyer Burlington cigarettes, whose boxes were embossed with his name, he favoured large American cars – a Studebaker and a Chrysler – and fine wines, port and champagne. In London he was staying at the Grosvenor. He was such an intriguing personification of modern and ancient Africa that the Colonial Office studied his manoeuvres with keen precision.

In July 1934, when Una officially welcomed Ofori Atta on behalf of the League of Coloured Peoples, she was enthralled. They first met at a well-attended garden party held in his honour at the house in Peckham to which the king turned up attired in 'a suit of gold and purple velvet, leopard skin, sandals with gold clasp and a large golden cloth umbrella'. Short and stout with a gentle demeanour and fetching smile, Ofori Atta promptly won everyone's affection. Christine Moody thought he was lovely: he had a cracked, musical voice and 'whether he sang in a chorus or as a solo, he always provoked great laughter'.[1] Through keeping Ofori Atta's company, Una was to learn much about African politics and culture that proved useful in her work as League secretary.

Una and Ofori shared many tête-à-tête conversations that summer after his tiring excursions around the city, visits to Cadbury's and Colonial Office meetings. For Una it was a new experience to be socialising with this type of man, and she savoured the moments. She escorted him to meetings, prepared his farewell speech for the BBC Talks Department and shared his private thoughts during his long absence from home. She was impressed by his interest in English historical monuments – the statues, houses, books and shrines of England's heroes – and 'could not help feeling that he returned to Africa determined to help his people to pay more honour to those who had served them well'.

In summer 1937, when she was in the process of writing up some of her England experiences, Una wrote obliquely and briefly about her time with Ofori Atta, adding 'I do not propose in this article to generalise on that experience, rich as it was'. One wishes that she had generalised more.

It appears that they became, briefly, lovers. But what exactly happened between them remains a mystery. Certainly Ofori Atta had no need of secretarial services. He had a sizeable delegation and his secretary was his half-brother, the lawyer and doctor J. B. Danquah, whose considerable legal and managerial talents would have made Una professionally redundant. But his wives were home …

There is a letter to him which the English historian Richard Rathbone came across while researching in Akyem Abuakwa in Ghana in 1991. It is a typed letter, with an indecipherable signature from a young woman, breathlessly happy and longing for renewed contact with the great man. It seems likely that it comes from Una – its phrasing, tone and style are consistent – and, as it is the only evidence of an intimate relationship, is quoted here in full:

My Dear Nana
I was terribly disappointed to realise that after I telephoned you this morning that I would not see you until Sunday evening at the earliest. Why are you so cruel? Never mind, there is nothing to be said or done about it. I am ever so jealous. I keep wondering who is talking to you and if they are give [sic] you jokes and if you laugh as heartily as you do when I am with you. I keep wondering where you are, how you are and if you miss me at all. It is silly of me to write to you again especially as I am at work as there is much to be done. But I think you will be pleased to have a letter from me, will you not? And will you write to me to cheer me up since I shall not see you until Sunday evening. Please

do not blame me for this. It is no desire of mine, but I must respect the wishes of a King who is accustomed to be obeyed. I am glad you went out yesterday evening and enjoyed yourself. I wish I could have been with you. You will be out this evening so you will not miss me. I shall go to a meeting on African Drama.[2] I would much rather be with you. My holiday has been cancelled and my friends are very distressed but they are here always; in a few weeks I shall be losing my royal guest. My heart is very sad because I miss seeing you so much but Sunday will soon be here when *I hope* to have the pleasure of your company. In the meantime may I hope to hear from you?

Your loyal little friend.[3]

This is probably Una's voice. She was in touch with the British Drama League over African drama, following her production at the Scala. Multiple official and unofficial sources show that she was the only woman to have been closely associated with Ofori Atta's 1934 visit to London. While the evidence for an affair may be circumstantial, it is persuasive. Una was transformed by her encounter with Ofori Atta as is rarely the case with purely intellectual, platonic encounters. Their long private conversations were cross-fertilisations: 'he was gleaning Western ideas and I was probing the mind of an African Paramount Chief'. Una's next play, *London Calling* (1937), which she began writing shortly after Ofori's departure, centres on an African prince from an imaginary colony, Novokan, whose travels to England and encounters with the British aristocracy are farcical and pertinent. Prince Alosa, the main character, grew from Una's acute observation of Ofori Atta during those glorious sunny days and the colony, Novokan, from her knowledge of Akyem Abuakwa, about which he spoke with such intense feeling. Critics realised that the impressionistic, though heartfelt, portrayal of the African ruler was clearly based on an original model, and they were impressed.

Ofori Atta's delegation had come to London to plead several grievances. They hoped to amend the Gold Coast constitution, to increase the elected number of Africans on the Legislature and to moderate the power of the Governor. Sir Philip Cunliffe-Lister, Secretary of State at the Colonial Office, refused to contemplate any 'alteration in the constitutional system under which the Governor had not the power to pass whatever legislation he thought was right in the public interest'.[4] Complaints about high water rates and the confiscation of supposedly 'seditious' literature also fell on deaf ears. J. B. Danquah, acknowledging that such genteel protests were futile, wrote in *The Keys* that the Gold

Coast people were very much upset, but had learnt a lesson, namely that the old grandfatherly policy of the Colonial Office was dead. The notion of Colonial Office gentility was dead and buried.

This was not lost on Una. The special impetus and the collected insights of Ofori's summer were urging her to give the African continent a new look and to reassess her attitudes towards British colonial policy. She didn't like what she found. During the next year her newly discovered animus towards the British system produced a clash at a Royal Empire Society meeting, in spring 1935, when Una argued with the widow of a former Gold Coast governor, Lady Guggisberg. Feeling 'somewhat diffident' about discussing colonial policy, which she typified as careless and incompetent, Una acknowledged that she couldn't speak frankly without causing offence. When she did speak, offence was caused. Colonial countries were suffering and allowed to muddle along, she explained, because Westminster had no colonial policy, governors came and went, imposed their own idiosyncrasies and ideas of progress, and no governor was obliged to carry out his predecessor's pet scheme. It took a governor two years at least to find his feet, in the third he made up his mind and laid his plans, in the fourth his plans were set in motion, and before he had time to see them in action he was promoted not 'to glory' but to a more lucrative position.

Lady Guggisberg replied that the poor governor was simply 'worn out' after five years and needed a rest. Una retorted that the 'dear lady' had her sympathy, but a tired governor harassed and bewildered by colonial policy was simply 'not good enough'.[5]

Colonialism had been an enigma to Una. And she was now keen to deconstruct its powers as she had never before. Her culture, as far as she had been aware, was English. To her chagrin she recalled how back in 1933 she had been shepherded along to a British Commonwealth League conference by Trinidadian Audrey Jeffers, an older, more liberal activist, and assured her audience that in Jamaica there was no 'native' mother as such since the country's laws, language and culture, in her estimation, were entirely English, unlike in Africa or India.

But Ofori Atta had changed all that. Una was confidently addressing African issues at conferences; she began to read African books, articles and pamphlets; she sustained good relationships with many student activists such as Lapido Solanke, the founder of the West African Students Union, Desmond Buckle, Louis Mbanefo, Sackefyio, Prempeh and Giviira. When Una came across the International Institute of

African Languages and Cultures, a small publishing venture, based in central London, which brought out fiction, descriptions of African life, biography and grammars of African languages, she was thrilled. She read *The Story of an African Chief* by Oxford-trained anthropologist Akikik Nyabongo, and *Africa Answers Back* by an African village school teacher. The sociological work about ordinary lives revealed a shrewdness which Una would have thought characteristic of a well-travelled aesthete, and in a later article she held this text up as a model for Jamaican authors.[6] She focused hard on the African at home and in the diaspora and was able to see the potential of West Indians through 'African' eyes.

In late November 1934 Una attended the Women's International League Conference in London, *Africa: Peace and Freedom*, and made a speech entitled 'Social and Political Equality in Jamaica', in which she said:

> As regards health it is significant that more people die from tuberculosis than from any other disease, due largely to poor economic conditions, bad housing and poor food. The people live chiefly on starchy foods grown in their own soil and the peasants are very rarely able to get milk, eggs or other nutritious foods. Wages are very low, but high if compared with Kenya or Tanganyika ... the cost of living is high, which is partly due to the fact that the people are not allowed to buy cheap Japanese goods now, as they are very loyal in the matter of buying British goods, and anxious to help poor Lancashire.[7]

Britain's many women's organisations called Una up to make speeches. She was always happy to accept invitations and by 1936 had developed a wide range of contacts within the Women's Freedom League, the Women's Peace Crusade, the Women's International Alliance and the British Commonwealth League, of which she became an ordinary member, attending many meetings, speaking at conferences. To one of these she took a new friend, Jomo Kenyatta, the pan-African radical and an anthropology student with Malinowski at the London School of Economics, who was campaigning on behalf of the Kikuyu over land rights and beginning work on *Facing Mount Kenya*.[8]

Like Ofori and Jomo Kenyatta, Una regarded the quality of education as a key to progress. Hers had been entirely European and had equipped her with the skills to be able to address sizeable English gatherings, but she still regarded it as inadequate and inappropriate. The challenge was live and fierce, just as it had been a century before when in a speech on Indian education Lord Macaulay had argued that the

English could not 'attempt to educate the body of the people. We must do our best to form a class who may be interpreters between us and the millions whom we govern; a class Indian in blood and colour, but English in taste, in opinions, in morals and in intellect.' In the West Indies Una would have become one of these interpreters, but she argued, as reported in the newspaper, that all colonies had

> far too much of the old Imperialist propaganda and British training. The child using books which upheld the glory of Empire grew to manhood or womanhood knowing nothing and caring less, for the land of his forefathers, Africa, and the race to which he belonged. Duty to one's own country and people should be taught before duty to an Empire that took little interest in these children. They grew up with an inferiority complex. Out of date books were shipped to the colonies and special subject books such as history books extolling the glories of the British Empire which were not used in England, were sent to colonial schools. The aim of colonial education should be to produce useful citizens of their own countries and not merely flag-waving Britishers.[9]

She was so incensed that such education, a 'technology of colonialist subjectification', should be allowed this false universality, where other social benefits never reached her people. She parodied it and pigeonholed it along with the situation in South Africa, where £25 a year was spent on each white child a year while the government granted a mere £2 3s 7d subsidy to the missionary bodies who were teaching 300,000 black children.

Teach him? – that; –

> And then, I grant, we put a sting in him
> That at his will be may do danger with
> The abuse of learning is when it is given
> To subject races: And, to speak truth of Negroes
> I have known when they have turned to serve us
> Once they are taught.[10]

Una's encounter with Ofori Atta signified a change in direction, a change in political consciousness. She came to the realisation that Africa mattered: that its cultures, people and wisdoms equalled those of Europe and that, without the persistent attention of African people, its history would be lost, neglected and denied. She was not the first to make this re-connection; or indeed the last.

Avoidance would have been easy. Neither family nor friends nor society urged her in this direction. On the contrary, on Una's return to

Kingston, some of her Anglophile associates thought her African obses-
sions 'odd', others wondered whether she was unpatriotic, and only a
few judged that she was visionary.

From this period onwards the pan-African movement provided a
sphere through which Una could envisage a better world. Feminism
was another; through its ideas, organisations and activities Una saw a
way of influencing emancipatory movements both in Europe, particularly England of course, and in the Caribbean islands and to a lesser
extent in Africa. Along with English feminists who were also interested
in developing international networks now that the vote had been won,
Una's contributions, preserved in the historical record mainly through
her various speeches, include debates on the definition of needs, the
scope of rights, equality and 'difference'. These words, along with her
powerful creative writings which explored questions of 'race', gender
and sexuality, revealed that she was fired by her own experience as
much as by that of women as diverse as Mary Wollstonecraft, who
penned the *Vindication of the Rights of Woman*, and former-slave
woman orator Sojourner Truth. Moreover, as a twentieth-century feminist of African descent, Una's perspective was rare. She looked locally
at the politics and experiences of women in her audience and globally
to women of African descent. She took part in the 1930s in a white-
dominated women's movement and put the case of black women in
terms of economic justice, international peace, and personal and political rights. The relation between black feminism and the mainstream
white movement concerned her as deeply as it concerned the second-
wave feminists and womanists of the late twentieth century.

Una was active in the British Commonwealth League, formed in
1925 to encourage the development of women's groups within the
Commonwealth. It was renamed the Commonwealth Countries
League when most of the members became self-governing states.
Among the BCL members during the 1930s was Myra Stedman, daugh-
ter of suffragette Myra Sadd Brown, who recalled:

> The All India Women's congress had been affiliated to them, Mrs Rama
> Rau [*sic*] had addressed several meetings when she was in England also
> Una Marsden [*sic*], Jamaican poetess of the Jamaican Federation of
> Women and others from Commonwealth countries, both coloured and
> white including Sarofini Naidu, a well-known Indian poetess.[11]

According to its constitution, the BCL aimed to raise the 'status of
women of the less forward races'.[12] This little phrase, well-meant but

alarming, points to the double-edged experience Una was to have within it.

Her membership, though it lasted more than six years, was sometimes troublesome. For although she was fond of many of the women personally, politically she was estranged from their way of seeing. At her first conference in 1933 she spoke cautiously about the 'Rights of the Native Mother' in Jamaica in a debate with Audrey Jeffers from Trinidad. But, as she became more confident within the BCL, she became more critical of their approaches to 'native women' and protested at the use of the word 'primitive'. Women of colour had 'exactly the same feelings as other women, [and yet] they were looked upon as individuals apart, as strange creatures. Not only the wives of Governors, but others who went out to the colonies, seemed to think of people there as beings who should remain at a certain fixed low standard of living', she said.[13]

Women who knew her through these organisations retained similar impressions. Lydia Tovey, meeting Una in 1935, thought her eloquent and bright. Others, even casual contacts, were struck by her knowledge, insight and quick-wittedness. Her usual topics were Jamaica, race, politics and the experiences of black women in England and overseas. Her feminist preoccupations gave her a wide platform and even, on occasion, made the news. Yet she found herself in the classic predicament of the black woman activist who, in the absence of groups which are both race-conscious and gender-conscious, must contribute to both black and women's organisations. Una shared a platform with a variety of speakers, some of whom made her see red: 'I gathered from the speech by the white Rhodesian that African women do not exist in Rhodesia, in any case they did not loom large enough on her horizon for even a casual mention there', she later wrote about one gathering.[14]

Una found, time and again, that she was facing audiences of anxious women, anxious because she represented additional stresses within the Empire. The British Empire on which the sun never set had been part of everyone's childhood teaching. As little girls, they had become accustomed to maps with a quarter of the world's surface tinted pink, to history books which told of Britain's mission to civilise backward peoples and to stories of English men's daring in the dark continent. But now their adult consciousness warned that the unobliging sun was slipping towards sunset after all. Indian nationalists had buttonholed successive government officials in elaborate enquiries, reports and negotiations about self-rule. Who could say how rapidly other people would follow? Knowledge of Jamaica may have been scant, but many women who had personal ties with the Empire would have looked upon Una with a mixture of curiosity and suspicion. For among their friends and families were numerous ex-colonial civil servants, their successors, businessmen with colonial interests, Empire-minded naval people, and declassed semi-intellectuals who found themselves more at home abroad.

But there were exceptions. One of the English feminists Una had wanted to meet, and did meet through the BCL in 1934, was the novelist Winifred Holtby. Una had been aware of Winifred Holtby since she arrived in London, but had refrained from making contact out of shyness. Winifred showed an intensity of emotion in her writing and her activism which was exciting and attractive. She had an absorbing interest in the struggles of black South Africans. Following her visit to South Africa in 1926, she had provided funds for Cape Town's Industrial and Commercial Union and had sponsored Scottish trade unionist William Ballinger to act as its technical adviser. Una had heard of Winifred's London-based activities through Moody, who knew her through another group. Then late in 1933 Una had been given a copy of Winifred's passionately anti-colonial novel, the ironic *Mandoa, Mandoa* which Una was to describe as 'a most brilliant satire'. Thus it was that, when Winifred Holtby did appear in real life, Una was delighted. They were both down to speak in the debate 'Bars to Careers' on the opening day of the BCL conference in June 1934.

Una had no difficulty in recognising Winifred, who, nearly six feet tall with pale flaxen hair and blue eyes, was a distinguished-looking woman:

> As I walked into the crowded hall I looked around and my eyes caught those of Winifred Holtby. I knew instinctively who she was and she told me afterwards that she recognised me from what she had heard about me. After the meeting she spoke to me and invited me to lunch with her.[15]

Winifred's own account, written within a month of the conference, is a casual reference in a letter (9 July 1934) to her friend Norman Leys. She is describing another conference and exploring the similarity between black and female experience:

> There was one clergyman who at tea made the kind of jokes about the 'fair-sex' and the 'dominating influence' of women which make me feel

that I know exactly what a Negro feels when called a Nigger. In fact, I know it is so. Because after I told a small audience at the British Commonwealth League Conference just how I did feel, Kenyatta, *a brown girl from Jamaica* and an Indian, all came and told me that what I described as my own feeling really was exactly what they had felt. I sometimes feel it is an advantage to be a woman, I can tolerate opposition; but facetious patronage makes me BOIL.[16]

Una did not separate 'black' and female experience. While Winifred talked about the colour barrier in South Africa, Una quickly pointed out that there were equally insidious barriers in England, and she demonstrated her point with the case of Eva Lowe, Sylvia's sister, who had received numerous rejections though well-qualified.[17] She had finally settled for a place at the London County Council Hospital, St Nicholas in Plumstead,[18] though not before her father had collected more than twenty flimsy excuses including this:

> It is not the colour we personally object to, but it is the very difficult time the girl would have with other nurses. I am afraid the insular prejudice against colour dies hard, and I have a young and enthusiastic class of women, numbers of whom are Army men's daughters and whose prejudices are very strong. I am afraid for the girl because she might be ostracised and then she would be so unhappy.[19]

Una's intervention was reported in the press.[20]

So, when Una and Winifred departed for lunch, the young Jamaican had, as many modern black feminists have done, brought the debate back home. They had much to discuss: politics, feminism and literature. Later they spent an evening together at Winifred's Chelsea home discussing Una's writing, an experience which Una later called 'one of the most beautiful memories of my life'.

And Winifred? Sadly, the nature and depth of her attitude towards Una remain uncertain, since none of the correspondence has survived. Winifred Holtby's literary executor has taken the view that she would have 'had all too little time to see very much of Una Marson' because she had such a 'tremendously full and busy life'.[21] But Una was outspoken and insightful and her politics are likely to have added an unusual dimension to Winifred's social life.

Winifred kept in touch with Una for the rest of her short life. When Una heard of her death in September 1935, she was devastated. She had received a letter from Winifred just a few days before, but was apparently unaware of how serious her illness was. Una treasured her letters from friends and correspondents worldwide, and not until many years after her death were these thrown out. Among these papers lay the private thoughts of these two friends and especially Winifred's side of the story.

In the space of three years Una had become the leading black feminist activist in London, but although she attended more than her fair share of meetings and conferences, giving speeches and passing resolutions, her activism was bound to take the form of writing. The fundamental questions in her emerging works were all about identity and cultural revolution, what it meant to struggle against multiple oppression, how to re-invent oneself. Una's work ranged over many personal concerns: instances of racist and sexist oppression; love and trouble; woman as lover and labourer; Jamaica as home not tropical isle; and Africa as a spiritual source. Above all else, her writing was built upon a contradiction. How could the black woman, sentenced to an eternal invisibility and silence, find her own voice, speak and be heard in a world that had long misjudged, misplaced and misconceived her? As Toni Morrison, the African-American novelist, was to write of another black heroine: 'She had nothing to fall back on: not maleness, not whiteness, nor ladyhood, not anything. And out of the profound desolation of her reality, she may very well have invented herself.'[22]

NOTES

1 Nana Sir Ofori Atta, from *The Akim Abuakwa Handbook* (London, 1928).

2 *Journal of the British Drama League*, vol. 13, no. 9, June 1935. The 16th Annual Report of the British Drama League gives an account of the work of the African Drama Committee's third conference which was held in London on 27 July 1934. Una Marson was involved with the BDL at this time and later formed a Jamaican Drama League, an affiliated group.

3 Letter from Akyem Abuakwa State Council Archives, Kyebi, Ghana, AASA 9/57.

4 Quoted by J. B. Danquah, 'The Gold Coast and Ashanti Delegation: a Gesture and a Lesson', in *The Keys*, vol. 2, no. 2, October–December 1934, p. 21.

5 'A Call to Downing Street', *Public Opinion*, 11 September 1937, p. 5.

6 'Coloured Contributions', *Public Opinion*, 3 July 1937, p. 11.

7 'Social and Political Equality in Jamaica', a speech to the Women's International League for Peace and Freedom conference, *Africa: Peace and Freedom*. See papers of WILPF at the London School of Economics library, London.

8 Jomo Kenyatta, British Commonwealth League conference, 1934. See BCL papers, Fawcett Library, London.

9 Una Marson to the British Commonwealth League conference, May 1935. See BCL papers, Fawcett Library, London.

10 'Education', *The Keys*, January–March 1935, p. 53.

11 From notes of an interview with Myra Sadd Brown by Brian Harrison, 2 March

1977, London, in the possession of the author.

12 The BCL was formed to continue the work formerly done by the British Dominions Women Citizens Union and the British Overseas Committee of the International Woman (*sic*) Suffrage Alliance.

13 Una Marson to the British Commonwealth League conference, 1939. See BCL papers, Fawcett Library, London.

14 'A Call to Downing Street'.

15 'Winifred Holtby as I Knew Her', *Public Opinion*, 5 June 1937.

16 Winifred Holtby in a letter to Norman Leys, 9 July 1934, File 4.4 of the Winifred Holtby Archives, Kingston upon Hull Central Library, Hull.

17 The League continued to challenge discrimination by writing letters and conducting surveys. Eva Lowe's father sent a detailed report on his daughter's experiences to the Secretary of State for the Colonies. The League of Coloured Peoples dispatched a report to the Overseas Nursing Association. And finally, the Overseas Nursing Association carried out a survey of eighteen London and provincial hospitals which confirmed the Lowes' experience: all said they would refuse black probationers. Eva Lowe did well in her training, however; she left England in 1939 and in Jamaica became the supervisor of District Health and Nursing.

18 Una appealed to the BCL to take up the matter. No evidence has come to light to show whether her appeal was acted upon. For details of the debate see BCL minutes of Conference Debate entitled 'Bars to Careers' on 14 June 1934. BCL papers, Fawcett Library, London. The *News Chronicle* of 15 June 1934 is not available, but its coverage was reported in *The Keys*. The story of Eva Lowe comes from the *Annual Report* of the League of Coloured Peoples, 1932, a copy of which is in the Winifred Holtby Archives, Kingston upon Hull Central Library, Hull.

19 Quoted in the *League of Coloured Peoples Annual Report* 1932.

20 *The Keys* also reported that the *News Chronicle* quoted Una Marson saying that in the United States 'they tell you frankly when you are not wanted by means of big signs, and they don't try to hide their feelings. But in England, though the people will never say what they feel about us, you come up against incidents which hurt so much you cannot talk about them.' *The Keys*, vol. 1, no. 3, April–June.

21 Paul Berry in a letter to the author, 5 June 1988.

22 Quoted by Mary Helen Washington (ed.), *Black-eyed Susans: Classic Stories by and about Black Women* (New York, Doubleday, 1975), p. vii.

8

'The Autobiography
of a Brown Girl'

U NA left the Moodys' busy household in spring 1935 and moved a
short distance to a quieter and leafier part of Camberwell,
Brunswick Square, which, despite its name, was a long, winding road
which curled around a park. Her new home was number 29, a spacious
Victorian four-storey house in a short terrace, with a pleasing view of
the park's shrubs and the crocuses just peeping up through the soil.
Inside things were less elegant. The owner and resident landlord,
Arthur Mepsted, capitalising on London's housing shortage, had con-
verted it into five bedsits and apartments for itinerant lodgers, most of
whom, like Una, would stay only a year. But at last she had the space
and solitude her writing required and a place she could call her own.

For years Una had been toying with the idea of writing her autobiography. Indeed, back in 1931 when she was only twenty-five, she
had confided to her *New Cosmopolitan* co-editor Aimee Webster that
she was working on it. Of course Aimee couldn't see how Una's early
life warranted such a permanent record and later described the very
idea as 'amazing'. Una meantime had been scribbling away in Kingston
under the heading 'Autobiography of a Black Girl'.

Now, just four years later and living in London, she had gained a
new perspective on life as a 'black girl' and had decided to pick up the
typescript once more. She added to and amended the material and
changed the title to the racially conscious and commercially astute
'The Autobiography of a Brown Girl'.

> Little brown girl
> Don't you feel very strange
> To be so often alone
> In a crowd of whites?
> Do you remember you are brown

Or do you forget?
Or do the people staring at you
Remind you of your colour?

When you stroll about London
Seeking, seeking, seeking
What are you seeking
To discover in this dismal
City of ours?

Still feeling 'very hurt by some slights caused by the ignorance of the people', Una would chart the journey of the naive colonial visitor to London where 'everyone seems so far off. You see groups of people and no one you know. It is very lonely.'[1]

The very act of writing her autobiography would have enabled Una to explore both internal and external worlds, bestowing a quality of authenticity upon her experience. Writing her own life was an ideal means of transferring herself from the margins – the baby daughter, the mediocre student, the struggling author – to the protagonist's focal position as writer, editor, traveller, feminist. It therefore accorded her, as did all her plays, a measure of authority rarely unchallenged in real life and an opportunity to experience herself as an empowered black woman.

Una's title, 'Autobiography of a Brown Girl', is reminiscent of the American classic by James Weldon Johnson, the simulated auto-biography *The Autobiography of an Ex-coloured Man* (1912), which Una greatly admired. Following the African-American autobiographical tradition in which the concerns of the collective predominate, Una intended to incorporate her own experiences into a wider picture of black British life.

Una had chatted with others at Winifred's house about her work, Brittain wrote:

> one afternoon an incongruous quartette gathered in her study for tea: Eric Walrond, a negro poet from New York; Una Masen [*sic*], a Jamaican dramatist who was writing 'The Autobiography of a Brown Girl' for Victor Gollancz; Winifred's cousin, Daisy Pickering; and the vivacious cosmopolitan writer, Madame Odette Keun.[2]

The interesting conversation which lasted till 9.45 included the 'colour question, miscegenation, birth control and race prejudice inside out' – all topics on which Una could expatiate. She found her discussions with Winifred herself so fruitful that she decided to dedicate the book to her. Winifred had also encouraged her with the suggestion that such a book would alleviate racial antagonism and 'make for better understanding between the races'.

Una's material was timely. Younger intellectuals, poets and novelists were concerned with the social environment and were setting their characters and conflicts in a wide political context of crisis. J. B. Priestley, the popular novelist, had written the documentary *English Journey*, expressing a Yorkshireman's sense of outrage at poverty in the midst of plenty. George Orwell, despairing at the rottenness of middle-class England after his colonial service in Burma, had shown in *Burmese Days* that the black man, not the white man, was burdened. But black British women authors still were an unknown quantity.

Although Una had some critical support and a prominent left-wing publisher in Victor Gollancz, who co-ran the Left Book Club with Harold Laski and John Strachey, she failed to deliver. No trace of the book has survived, though she continued to work on it on her return to Jamaica and had according to a friend, Rupert Meikle, completed it by summer 1937.

Rupert Meikle at twenty-eight was a literary light of considerable talent and insight. He ran a cultural club in Port Maria, Jamaica, and followed the literary trends of the Harlem Renaissance. Flushed with excitement that summer over two recently published autobiographies – Claude McKay's *A Long Way from Home* (1937) which he thought 'lovely and memorable' and *Along This Way* (1933) by James Weldon Johnson which he judged 'fascinating' – Meikle confessed that both books were 'acting on me and giving me a fever to visit America and make contact with my brothers of blood across the little bit of salt water'.[3] To James Weldon Johnson he lamented Claude McKay's permanent absence from the island and wished he would return for a visit, 'and allow us to see and hear and honour him'; but in the meantime he was encouraging the 'very outstanding' Una Marson, whose recently completed autobiography he longed to read.

Assured that she was set for success, Rupert Meikle pressed Una to follow McKay's lead and publish in the United States instead of England. 'After reading Claude's autobiography, she has decided to write to his publishers', he alerted Weldon Johnson. 'I also advised her to try and get in touch with you and ask your help in getting it over amongst the Americans. It is going to be marvellous reading.'[4]

The autobiography never appeared in North America or in England; autobiographical fragments leavened Una Marson's journalism of the late 1930s, but these are merely scattered crumbs on these European years. It goes perhaps without saying that, had she published, the landscape of twentieth-century Caribbean literary history would be different today. But Una did not publish her autobiography, and today novels such as Sam Selvon's *The Lonely Londoners* (1956) and *The Emigrants* (1954) by Barbadian writer George Lamming stand as the first powerful evocations of the rites of passage of Afro-Caribbeans in London. Perhaps Collins, the writer in Lamming's novel, would have empathised with Una Marson with his grim assertion that 'this is the land of the enemy'. But lost are the intimate details of her experiences with Moody, the League, its students, visiting dignitaries and celebrities. Lost too, without doubt, is a rare item, the reflections of an intelligent, articulate and politically active black woman in England of the 1930s.

On Easter Day (17 April) 1936, at home in her 'little den', she turned on the wireless to listen to the BBC's regional programme broadcasting a service of Negro spirituals performed by the Fisk Jubilee Singers from their chapel in Nashville, Tennessee. Then she heard the voice of James Weldon Johnson, the sixty-four-year-old professor of Negro literature at New York University, reading his celebrated poem 'Creation', a black preacher's moving version of the book of Genesis:

> And God stepped out on space
> And he looked around and said,
> 'I'm lonely
> I'll make me a world'

> And as far as the eye of God could see
> Darkness covered everything,
> Blacker than a hundred midnights
> Down in a cypress swamp.

> Then God smiled,
> And the light broke,
> And the darkness rolled up on one side,
> And the light stood shining on the other,
> And God said, 'That's good!'

When the poetry reading ended, Una was still. To hear the poet's own rendition touched her much more deeply than she would have anticipated. She cherished the memory. Weldon Johnson became a 'dear unknown friend' to whom she had wanted to reach out, but she hesitated, afraid of appearing gauche or pushy. Many months elapsed before she wrote to him but in time they became good friends.

Black literature was beginning to work on Una. She thumbed the turn-of-the-century classics: Booker T. Washington's autobiography and James Weldon Johnson's poetry and novels and *The Souls of Black Folk* by William E. B. Du Bois. She was very pleased with *The Souls*, often told people they should get a copy and wrote that it 'should take pride of place in every coloured home'.[5]

The new musical, jazzy poets stirred her and she dreamt of catching, Caribbean-style, something of this innovative black verve. From time to time she heard more of what was going on in Harlem, admired it and wanted to be in contact with the Harlem Renaissance writers. A steady stream of black artists was trickling into Britain. They brought jazz, they brought blues. Una liked to tap her feet to jazz rhythms and heard the blues at London night spots. The brilliant Guyanese clarinettist Rudolph Dunbar was making a name for himself as a bandsman, took up writing for *Melody Maker* and played for the League's 1934 Christmas dance. England, he had said, was the best place for work and for recognition. In the evenings artists, activists, students drank and supped and kept their spirits high at Amy Ashwood Garvey's West End restaurant. There, according to the Trotskyist writer C. L. R James, the only good food in town was served and, if you were lucky, the 78s of Trinidadian calypsonian Sam Manning, Amy's partner, spun late into the night.

Black musics created the right ambience, but Una's real models were literary. While Langston Hughes could stroll past a bar and hear the 'poem' he was going to pen, Una's main instruction in rhythm and blues came from other writers. Eric Walrond, a Guyanese, came to London via Harlem's clubs and soirées where he'd counted among his friends Langston Hughes, Zora Neale Hurston and Countee Cullen, with whom he had travelled to Europe in 1928.[6] Walrond was not only a good, highly acclaimed short-story writer – his collection *Tropic Death* (1926) had done well – but he was also an editor and critic[7] who sometime gave lectures on contemporary themes in African-American literature.[8]

Who better to bring Una up to date with the writings of her peers in New York! She asked him to review two of these African-American books for *The Keys*: Zora Neale Hurston's *Jonah's Gourd Vine*, the tale of a black Southern preacher, and Langston Hughes's collection of stories *The Ways of White Folk*.

Hurston's language, Eric Walrond pointed out, was the chief interest of her novel – 'Ah means tuh beat her til she rope lak okra, and den again Ah'll stomp her til she slack lak lime' was the kind of thing he had in mind. This did not remotely resemble the kind of language Una had been schooled in using and was 'disturbingly eloquent of the break with the English literary tradition that is so characteristic of the work of the young writers of the American Negro renaissance'.[9]

Zora Neale Hurston knew that there were hundreds of black preachers all over America equalling the 'poetic barbarity' of her hero's famous sermon.[10] Una knew that there were plenty in Jamaica too. Black worship was also 'disturbingly eloquent' of the break with English church traditions, as she was to show in 'Gettin de Spirit':

> Lord gie you chile de spirit
> let her shout
> lord gie you chile de power
> an let her pray
> hallelujua – amen
> shout sister – shout –
> God is sen' you His spirit
> shout – sister – shout[11]

But it was to be her 'blues' poetry which led critics to acknowledge the link with North America and especially with the poetic genius Langston Hughes. Una's blues poems, which are about love and trouble and black women's identity, appeared in her third collection, *The Moth and the Star*, which was published in Jamaica in September 1937. But their music belongs to the London days.

NOTES

1 'Racial Prejudice Not Improving', *Daily Gleaner*, 28 September 1936, p. 5.
2 Vera Brittain, *Testament of Friendship* (London, Virago Press, 1980), p. 380.
3 Rupert Meikle to James Weldon Johnson, 19 July 1937. James Weldon Johnson Collection, Beinecke Rare Book and Manuscript Library, Yale University, New Haven, Connecticut.
4 *Ibid.*
5 'Coloured Contributions', *Public Opinion*, 3 July 1937, p. 11.
6 See R. Hemenway, *Zora Neale Hurston: a Literary Biography* (London, Camden Press, 1986), p. 51.
7 He wrote for the leading moderate black magazine, *Opportunity*, and edited the radical *New Masses*. When Una came across Eric Walrond in London, he was writing for Garvey's newspaper *Blackman*.
8 Eric Walrond's papers are held in Tokyo, Japan, by his grand-nephew.
9 Eric Walrond, 'Jonah's Gourd Vine', *The Keys*, spring 1935. Zora Neale Hurston had also contributed 'moving sketches of Negro life in the South' to *Negro*, an

anthology edited by Nancy Cunard and published in London 1934. It is likely that Una had read this.

10 Zora Neale Hurston to James Weldon Johnson, quoted by Hemenway, *Zora Neale Hurston: a Literary Biography*, pp. 193–4.

11 'Gettin de Spirit', *The Moth and the Star* (Kingston, Jamaica, 1937), p. 76.

9

A man who did much for his country
and another who did much for his race

IT WAS 'the most exciting time in my life',[1] Una told Nancy Cunard in 1941 in an interview. She was talking about the spring and summer of 1935 when she left London for a major international feminist conference in Istanbul. Her morale had not been so high for months.

In 1935 the world's attention was focused on the fascist attacks on democracy in Germany and Italy. Unemployment was high and women's status was deteriorating since more were being ousted from their jobs or being paid pitifully low wages. International trade had broken down and economic stability seemed a thing of the past. Outbreaks of fascist violence had aroused women to take an active stand against aggression, and against fascist rule.

In April Una received a letter from the Women's Social Service Club in Jamaica,[2] asking her to represent it at the 12th Annual Congress of the International Alliance of Women for Suffrage and Equal Citizenship which was to meet in Turkey later that month. This organisation, despite its name, had a strong European bias. It had grown over the preceding thirty-three years from a nucleus of five nations – Britain, Norway, Sweden, the Netherlands and the United States – which had first congregated in Washington in 1902. One founder member, the celebrated Chapman Catt, the American suffragette, though still a member, was too frail to undertake the long, exhausting journey, but her message reminded the younger generation of the progress international feminism had made. At this, the twelfth congress, thirty nations were represented, and societies from Persia, Syria, Palestine and India were admitted to membership. Of the 280 delegates who arrived, one flew five days by Graf Zeppelin from Brazil, Australians travelled via Colombo bearing greetings from Ceylonese women, from India came two Muslim representatives, while delegates arrived from

New Zealand, Romania and the United States, and a party of fifteen from Egypt. But as Margery Corbett Ashby, an English feminist and chair of the congress, was to note on her programme, Una Marson was the 'first delegate from Jamaica and the first woman of African race – Negro'.[3]

Una was delighted by Istanbul. She felt, she was reported as saying, that 'everything was perfect ... one certainly realised how small the world is. It was wonderful to see how everyone was eager to learn something of other countries.' She had travelled with the English delegation which included Margaret Ingledew, then twenty-three, who was equally excited to be attending her first big international conference in the company of Mrs Corbett Ashby, already a veteran feminist. They had never had a conference so far east, and with Turkey's very recent political changes – the President Kemal Atatürk had just introduced equal suffrage – they were highly inquisitive about the country and its people.

Una was exuberant about what she saw in Turkey. Women were beginning to take an active role in public life: she went to afternoon tea with the seventeen new women MPs and met some of the new city councillors. Turkish women, long held in airless harems, were suddenly liberated from wearing their veils, and Atatürk was said to have praised his own wife for her verbal wit, her dancing and her ability to consume cocktails. Una, star-truck by Atatürk, thought he had done 'marvellous work for women', modernising their lifestyles, providing free education (even at university level) for those who couldn't afford it and providing clothes, food and pocket money to boot. She traipsed about the city as much as time would allow, trying to find the clues to Turkish progress, and even spoke to some schoolgirls at the American college whose social commitment seemed to offer a key: 'they tell you they are going out to help their country and peasants ... to help their people. Even in England, one does not get that spirit among young people.'[4] And so, like other western delegates, she ignored Turkey's impoverished peasantry and the persistent inequalities.

The conference was being held at the gaudy, bejewelled Palace of Yildiz, which was set in spacious gardens on the outskirts of Istanbul. It was the former home of the late sultan, and seemed a romantic setting for the sensibly dressed western feminists who were clustering its sumptuous halls.

On the second day, 19 April, Una spoke in a lively and well-attended session on 'East and West in Co-operation'. As she stood alone on the long dais, she could see rows of women, sitting in their delegations before her, with dark-eyed Turkish girls at the end of each row acting as pages. She looked smart and self-assured in her small felt hat and pearls and was holding typed postcards of her lecture notes.

She used her now customary technique for setting the context: giving an outline of Jamaican history and social structure, she talked about the poorest women who suffered malnutrition. It was a highly emotive speech which reduced the delegates to tears, as Una described the women of Africa as 'the little sisters' of the women's movement appealing to the 'big sisters' to give a helping hand.[5] Seasoned Una Marson watchers, however, would have known that this 'great and moving plea', as Margaret Ingledew recalled it, was classic but earnest manipulation. Una began:

> Our country is a British colony. We speak English. We are subject to English laws. We were given the right to vote automatically without asking for it. Since the abolition of slavery 100 years ago, women have progressed. We have women doctors and lawyers. But the situation in the rural areas is not so good. However, our organisation is doing its best to overcome this and provide help for progress. Some of our women are unpaid labourers and work for low wages and live under unhygienic conditions.
>
> There was no marriage during slavery. It was argued that marriage tied people to the home and interfered with their work. Even the whites who came to the island believed this. This resulted in the lowering of morality. Unfortunately, even today, these attitudes seem to be prevalent in the rural areas. We have to do something about this. We have to give children born out of wedlock some legal status and thus ensure their well-being.
>
> I talk on behalf of all the Negroes of the world not only Jamaicans. Although I don't know much about Africa, I consider it a part of my being because my forefathers came from there. There is a lot we have to do for Africa. Whatever the colour, human beings have the same heart … It is necessary that the great powers who have taken in their hands the destinies of Africa should think also of assuring the status of women of that vast continent. And they must do this in all spheres, social, religious and educational. …
>
> You know the situation of American Negroes. I am pleased that in recent years articles in the press have appeared defending their rights. Negroes are asking for things common to all humans. They want justice. How can you accuse people who are being lynched of being 'barbarian'? There is no worse barbarism than the act of lynching. In America the National Association for the Advancement of Colored

People demands a law which shall put an end to the barbarous habit of lynching. Our alliance ought to be able to collaborate in this work. ...

Even in London one sometimes sees discrimination against black people, even those who are British subjects. Negroes are suffering under enormous difficulties in most countries in the world. We must count upon all countries where there are Negroes – for women always possess a better developed sense of justice – to obtain for them a life more pleasant and less severe. Apart from this, however sad the Negroes may be, they smile and hope always and when they see the Negro women side by side with the women of the universe that will reinforce their hopes and make them feel that for them too happiness is not far off. ... I get the impression that representatives gathered here are big hearted and will defend and help my race. We are optimistic for a big future for our race.[6]

Tumultuous applause rang through the hall, as Una finished speaking. Here, at the age of thirty, was Una the persuader, tactful, diplomatic, but not shy of pulling an emotional punch where she judged it right. The attention of the international audience to her speech is not hard to understand. This impressive address was by far the best and most unusual of the whole session. The *Manchester Guardian* reported that this 'negro woman of African origin from the former slave world of Jamaica, brought a new note into the assembly and astonished them by the vigour of her intellect and by her feminist optimism'. Here Una had wielded that optimism with a sophistication and sincerity that were highly effective, calling on feminists worldwide to challenge racial discrimination as a prelude to feminist activism.

'East and West in Co-operation' was hotly debated. European women argued that, instead of their making greater advances in equality, their rights were everywhere under threat. The encouraging progress of Turkish women lifted everyone's spirits, and other 'eastern' delegates were heard with keen interest. Hamid Ali, an Indian delegate, 'insisted that polygamy was still a danger and that it was to it that the abasement of women in China, Japan, India, Afghanistan, Africa and Arabia was due'; the Egyptian representative, Mme Lafuente from Algeria and others from Syria, Australia and Palestine also addressed the forum. The Turkish press made of the event a colourful story: *Cumheriyet* carried a substantial extract from Una's speech. *La République* also had a good photograph.[7]

A welcome opportunity to relax and chat came later that evening when the Union of Turkish Women gave a reception at the ornate nineteenth-century Palace of Dolmabatche with its halls of marble, crystal and ormolu and broad terraces looking out on to the Bosporus. There, the next morning, a bright and cool Sunday, the delegates enjoyed a boating excursion which took them past a series of little villages sheltering in their harbours. Up beyond these hamlets were green hills wooded with cypresses, umbrella pines and horse chestnuts. At lunchtime they stopped at Beylerbey Palace, former home of the last sultan, who had died in 1918. But the treasures still remained: priceless works of art and a blue mosaic ballroom with central goldfish pond. In the sunshine they strolled through the terraced gardens which at that time of year were scented with the pink blossoms of Judas trees.

When the conference was over, on 25 April, Una joined a select party of thirty including the IAWSEC board and made the eighteen-hour train journey, by a specially commissioned train, to Ankara in the heart of Anatolia, where beside the ancient town was rising a modern city with fine official buildings. At Ankara they had a two-hour reception with Kemal Atatürk at his palace. He reminded them that all nations had to 'work together to preserve peace in the world'. These were apt words. And in the interview which Una gave after the reception she explained why the meeting had meant so much for her:

> I have been following from afar how this great person transformed the spirit and condition of his nation. I've read many books about him. How I wish that other races would also produce a personality like Atatürk to fight for their freedom! Atatürk's efforts cannot remain just within Turkey's borders. They are an example to other nations.[8]

Speaking to Nancy Cunard years later Una said that the Turkish leader was a 'most vivid personality who had done much for his country'.[9] The Istanbul trip and especially the meeting with Atatürk had prised her out of the shade of anonymity, where it was boring to linger.

Most of the delegates had to hurry home; but Una did not. She took a leisurely trip covering about a thousand miles via Rome to Capri. Friends in London advised her against this trip, fearing for her safety in Italy: 'talk about war with Abyssinia was on … they said I'd be taken for an Abyssinian'. Nevertheless Una enjoyed Capri, finding it a 'wonderful place'. Her host, a fellow delegate at the conference, was an Italian sculptress whose name, sadly, is unknown. This mysterious new friend thought Una would be a marvellous model for her work and invited her to Rome to sit for her. But they went to her villa in the isle of Capri instead and there the work began.

Capri, largely free from noise and stress, was a delight with its highly congenial climate, its familiar blossoms of plumbago, oleander and the gorgeous purple bougainvillaea. Una posed for the artistic photographs, wearing a dark, cascading headscarf which brought out the effect of a gypsy queen. Her face had grown softer and vaguer over the recent months; her mouth slightly pursed and her eyes fading as if in a dream. Una, after six delightful weeks, decided Capri was the only island in the world that could rival Jamaica in beauty. In her letters to Jamaica she said 'it was like a homecoming'.

Returning to London in June, Una passed the remainder of the summer pleasantly, but not uneventfully. One morning a flattering invitation from M. Avenol, the League of Nations Secretary, turned up asking her to spend that September at the League headquarters in Geneva as a temporary 'collaborateur'. News of her triumph at Istanbul was doing the rounds and as a promising young person she was being given the opportunity to see the League at work. Una was thrilled as she told Nancy Cunard: 'I was one of 30 people invited from 28 countries to do collaboration work. A negro had never been there before … '[10]

Una was in great form. All her life she treasured the memory of her triumph in Turkey and the glorious days spent in Capri. August was set to be a quiet month with time to gather her thoughts before leaving for Geneva, but Una, wobbling slightly on the tightrope of the recently distinguished, spiced it up by entering into a bizarre public dispute with Paul Robeson, the African-American singer and actor, who had been writing a series of newspaper articles.

Robeson had made a name for himself as concert singer, popular recording artist, and actor of international standing in films such as *The Emperor Jones*, and *Showboat*, the Hollywood musical. From 1927 to 1939 Robeson lived in London, where he befriended countless spirited African students, seamen, dockers and labouring men who collectively regarded him as 'a genuine hero to the Black community'.[11] Many of these working men were given guinea-a-day walk-on parts in *Sanders of the River*, the film he made in 1934 with the Korda brothers. Of greater significance to Una, however, was Robeson's charismatic hold over the West African students whose patron he had become. They adored him. She, for her part, was determined to prove she did not.

As Robeson's career progressed during the 1930s he tried to steer away from stereotype and derogatory film roles, researching African culture, linguistics and aesthetics in his spare time. He wrote:

It is astonishing and to me, fascinating, to find a flexibility and subtlety in a language like Swahili, sufficient to convey the teachings of Confucius, for example, and it is my ambition to guide the Negro race by means of its own peculiar qualities to a higher degree of perfection along the lines of its natural development.[12]

He was also keen to devise more edifying scripts and to dispel the 'abysmal ignorance' of African culture. Una had first came across Robeson in summer 1934 when she was looking on at the making of *Sanders of the River*: 'I had never heard of Pushkin [until] ... I conversed with Paul Robeson ... He told me that he found it difficult to get suitable coloured plays and mentioned his interest in Pushkin the famous coloured Russian about whom we know so little.'[13]

At about the same time Robeson was writing articles for papers such as the *New Statesman and Nation*, 'championing the real but unknown glories of African culture'.[14] He also wrote proposing to establish a West End theatre for black plays.

Una's response, which appeared in the same paper shortly afterwards, read:

> I was very interested in Mr Paul Robeson's article 'I Want Negro Culture', published in a recent issue of your excellent paper.
>
> A negro myself, I say without the least hesitation that negroes have a long way to go before they can take a place of equality, as a race, among other races of mankind. It was the great Booker T. Washington who said: No race that has anything to contribute to the markets of the world is long in any degree ostracised.
>
> The cry for negro culture is putting the cart before the horse and the first task of the negro who has achieved is to teach his people the value of unity. The negro worries too much about what the white man thinks of him and too little about what he is himself in the eyes of people of his own race.
>
> There is nothing the negro needs more than sound, wise leadership by men and women able and willing to sacrifice for the good of their own people.[15]

Una Marson was accustomed to being at the centre of things. She had run her own magazine, produced her play in Kingston and London, published two collections of poetry and effectively run the social side of the League of Coloured Peoples – and all in her twenties. But in every sphere, wherever she turned, there was Robeson, upstaging her, an impoverished colonial woman! Following the London performance of *At What a Price* Una had discovered the British Drama League, a network of amateur theatre groups, and had lengthy discussions with its secretary who 'begged her to do what she could to induce people to interest themselves in plays of their country'.[16] Similar interventions had been made by Paul Robeson and his wife, Eslanda, who in 1933 had spoken at a BDL conference on native African drama; Una longed for a British-based black theatre group that could 'produce Empire plays by native people'[17] such as herself, but this idea had come to nothing, perhaps because organising African and West Indian students, a 'floating population', was so very arduous.

Now here was a major international artist, a man well beyond her class, proposing to dominate the black theatre world in London, without even a nod in her direction. Una's anguished, vituperative blast betrayed her real pain. She could not bear to be ignored. She hit back immediately. This letter, probably written at great speed, reveals her inconsistency and distress. There is no logical reason why the formation of a black theatre in the West End should lead to disunity among people. Indeed if Robeson's prime concern were to 'make himself secure' and show off what a 'splendid' man he was, easier paths were at his disposal.

Although Una was good at performing in public, she was not adept at concealing her emotions. While some adults know how to contain their annoyance and resentments, Una exposed her feelings in all their rawness. She was not as sophisticated as she liked to believe. In a small colonial society, supported by family and friends, her authority had not been tested. London was a bigger pond and she a relatively small fish.

The dispute with Robeson could also have had its origins in political differences. Una had recently written a passionate plea for racial unity in *The Keys*, but running deeper than this rational concern was her opposition to communism, then in the ascendancy among London's black student population. It seems likely that Una feared that Robeson would lead the mass of the students away from Moody's reformist politics – some left-wingers had already urged students to quit the League – and towards communism. Although Robeson had not yet been labelled a communist, he was associated with radical thinking, with the workers' Unity Theatre and with Russia. Una wrote emphatically: 'Communism won't help us, we don't want to fight, we are pacifists.'

The West African Students Union which had also printed Robeson's essay on 'Negro Culture' replied to Una Marson's letter in their journal, *Wasu*, under the heading 'Race Enemy no 1':

If anyone thinks the WASU is out to condone the faults or weaknesses of our people, he is sadly mistaken. Self-criticism is essential to progress, and the true patriot is he who turns the searchlight first on himself and on his own before pointing the finger of reproach at others. Hence we welcome the criticism of Miss Una M. Marson which appeared in the *News Chronicle* anent the article of Mr Paul Robeson which was produced in the last issue of this journal.

If Miss Marson is insinuating that Paul Robeson belongs to that class of successful Negroes who are 'boosting' the race in order to focus attention on themselves, we may tell her gently, but firmly that she is mistaken. Undoubtedly there are such negroes, but Mr Robeson is not one of them ... Just as a plant cannot grow without its roots, no more could a culture that is worthy of the name, without due regard to its ancestral heritage. ... It is for them [West Indians and African-Americans] to realise that Africa is the rock from whence they were hewn. That they have a lot to teach the African, goes without saying, but that they have as much to learn from the African, should by this time be equally patent to them.[18]

The West African students went on to express both respect for and agreement with some of Una's criticisms of black disunity, though her emotive rhetoric (putting the cart before the horse) left them angry.

Una Marson was not a revolutionary. Her writing carried left-wing implications and, when she talked of change, social reform and liberal humanism were what she had in mind. She liked to champion Booker T. Washington, that celebrated African-American of the post-emancipation period, known for his reformist politics, who had in 1881 founded Tuskegee Institute to train freed blacks in marketable skills, and throughout his life argued for self-help and a share of economic gain, though not adult suffrage. Following him, Una was to put her trust in education, training and black co-operation. She wanted to see professionals and newly qualified graduates returning home to 'take the stigma away from the race', and wrote in *The Keys*:

> What percentage of these students are studying the problems that face the vast continent of Africa, the problems, though less, that are still unsolved in the West Indies? Whites should not oppress us and use us for their enrichment, and Blacks should not be trying to make money for themselves or quarrelling among themselves.

It wasn't only a question of politics, it was also a matter of style. Since her arrival in England Una had been willing to listen to anti-colonial views and even to express them, but her instincts were towards middle-class protest, negotiation and respectability. She found communism distasteful and aggressive and distanced herself from the likes of Robeson. Una was back in Jamaica when Paul Robeson visited in winter 1948 and she wrote to a friend: 'Paul Robeson is with us in person and Jamaica, as the Americans say, has "fallen for him a big way".'[19] And in spring 1952, when Henry Swanzy saw her in Kingston, he noted that Una was 'heatedly making disparaging remarks about Robeson, but her cousin took umbrage that she should criticise him so much'.[20]

Una Marson had had little personal contact with the great artist, yet the last whiff of her anger endured for years. In 1952, Robeson, miles away from the wrath of Una Marson, was being hounded for 'un-American activities' through McCarthy's anti-communist purge.

NOTES

1 'Negroes in Britain', Nancy Cunard, for the Associated Negro Press, Cunard Papers, Chicago Historical Society, Chicago.

2 The Women's Social Service Club was lead by Mrs D. Cordova and based at 4 Rosedale Avenue, Kingston. For further information on the club's work see 'Women's Work and Organisation in Jamaica 1900–1944', Joan French and Honor Ford-Smith, unpublished research study for the Institute of Social Studies, The Hague, Netherlands. There is nothing to show that Una was a member of the WSSC.

3 Papers of Margery Corbett Ashby, MICA, Fawcett Library, London.

4 *Ibid.*

5 From Margaret Mathieson and Adele Schreiber, *Journey towards Freedom: Written for the Golden Jubilee of the International Alliance of Women* (Copenhagen, IAWSEC, 1955), p. 48. Resolutions were passed in support of East–West cooperation and a pledge given to support women whether they struggled for the eradication of special legal, social and economic disabilities and for the recognition of their rights to equal citizenship in their respective national units or whether they were in danger of losing such rights which they had achieved. See the conference report 'Resolution on East and West in Co-operation', papers of the International Alliance of Women, Fawcett Library, London, p. 18.

6 Large sections of Una Marson's speech were reported verbatim in *Cumheriyet* by the Turkish press (reproduced here with thanks to the Millikephane Newspaper Library in Ankara for selecting the microfilm and to Mehmet Dikerdem for his translation). Six weeks after the conference, the *Daily Gleaner* reported verbatim some sections of Una's speech; these have been spliced into the *Cumheriyet* text. It is clear from oral testimony sources that Una made additional comments on the experiences of black people in Britain. It seems reasonable to conclude that some parts of her speech have not yet come to light in spite of careful searches.

7   Corbett Ashby papers, MICA, Fawcett Library, ref. 484 c18, and conference report.

8   *Cumheriyet* newspaper, 24 April 1935.

9   'Negroes in Britain'.

10 *Ibid.*

11 Susan Robeson, *The Whole World in His Hands* (Secaucus, New Jersey, Citadel Press, 1981), p. 71.

12 Paul Robeson, *Here I Stand* (London, Beacon Books, 1958), p. 34.

13 'Coloured Contributions', *Public Opinion*, 3 July 1937, p. 20.

14 Paul Robeson, *Here I Stand*, p. 35. See also Martin Duberman, *Paul Robeson* (London, Bodley Head, 1989), pp. 159–84; and 'Africa and World Destiny' in *West Africa*, 13 June 1931. This is a report on Robeson's lecture on race and culture at a league meeting.

15 *News Chronicle*, 6 August 1935.

16 'Racial Prejudice in London Not Improving Says Miss Marson', *Daily Gleaner*, 28 September 1936, p. 5.

17 *Ibid.*

18 'Race Enemy no 1', *Wasu*, vol. 4, no. 2, August 1935.

19 Letter of November 1948 to Grenfall Williams in Una Marson file, BBC written archives, Caversham.

20 Henry Swanzy interviewed by the author.

10

Fascism and anti-fascism

A T THE END of August 1935 Una left London to take up her post at the League of Nations headquarters in Geneva. She was thrilled to be at the hub of diplomatic negotiations and was posted for the three weeks within the information section, but wherever she wandered only one topic was ever on her mind.[1] Just as she arrived there the Abyssinian crisis came to a head. It was the moment in world politics which would alter the course of her own life, a shattering moment for Britain and for its empire. This conflict had been brewing since 1934, when Benito Mussolini, the Italian dictator, declared that he would re-establish the Roman Empire in Africa, by conquering the free state of Abyssinia.

This was not the first threat of fascist dictatorship that Europe had witnessed that decade. In Britain Oswald Mosley's British Union of Fascists had attracted a terrifying number of thugs and romantically minded white-collar workers, as well as rich backers from the establishment. In Germany Hitler had done the same. These movements sprang from the hopelessness caused by mass unemployment, the insecurity of the lower middle classes and widespread, paralysing economic depression. In Italy Mussolini offered an old solution to his aggrieved and frightened masses, a chance to see themselves as a great imperial nation once more. He brought unity to the previously warring classes; he gave them purpose; he gave them hope. The military wanted revenge on the Abyssinians. They recalled their humiliating defeat at the Battle of Adowa, Abyssinia, in 1896, and in November 1934 found an excuse to attack when a group of Anglo-Abyssinian land commissioners camped one night on their side of a disputed boundary at Walwal. In the ten months since Walwal two questions agitated opinion in Europe. Would Mussolini attack Abyssinia, and how would the League of Nations, which was formed after the First World War to assure peace among its members, respond to such a crisis?

When Una arrived at Geneva, she was just in time to hear the Britain's honourable call for sanctions against Italy. The government, with a general election pending, wanted to be seen to be taking a tough line. It had been shaken by the recent Peace Ballot organised by the League of Nations union and publicised by the likes of the flamboyant former suffragette Sylvia Pankhurst, who later became a devotee of Haile Selassie through her newspaper *New Times and Ethiopia News*.

At the League all Una could do was to sit and listen. But as her posting came to an end she longed to do something constructive and made contact with the head of the Abyssinian delegation, a fine young general whom she genuinely admired, Tekle Hawariat. She offered to go out to Abyssinia and help, but he suggested a safer post, that of English-speaking secretary to the Abyssinian minister in London, Dr C. W. Martin. At the end of September Una packed her belongings, including the detailed notes of the League's sessions which would have been included in her autobiography, and headed back to London.

Una went over to Kensington, to the Abyssinian Legation, a large, three-storey, white building with grand, high-ceilinged rooms, to meet Charles Martin, an elderly doctor, suffering from chronic asthma, with 'very few staff' to assist him and 'a colossal amount of work' to do. There was no regular typist to handle their correspondence and the legation was staffed by unqualified students.[2] Martin offered Una a job, apologising for the modest wage, and Una, pitying him, agreed to do the work. She had been charming, not only calling at the Legation the day she arrived back, 2 October, armed with notes, but even returning two days later with 'some fine roses', as Martin noted in his diary.[3]

Within twenty-four hours of Una's reporting for duty, hostilities began between Abyssinia and Italy: a hundred thousand Italian troops crossed the Eritrean frontier into Abyssinia at dawn on 3 October. Within days the cities of Adowa, Enticcio and Adigrat had been occupied, without battle and almost without incident. Although Haile Selassie, the Abyssinian Emperor, had strengthened his army since coming to power and had formed a small cadet training school with the help of Belgian military, the Abyssinians were no match for the imperial force. There were some well-trained soldiers, but they had few tanks, the odd Junker monoplane from Germany, and ill-equipped volunteers, some of whom carried ancient bayonets or even sticks – no match for Mussolini's powerful modern army and poison gas.

Meanwhile back in London Una began studying Abyssinian geography, politics, customs and society so that she was better qualified to brief others and to lecture on the situation. Ironically she was called upon to discuss 'slavery' in Abyssinia, which she did with good grace. The Abyssinians, she said:

> produced practically all they required on the premises and the slaves were merely a part of the establishment under a very mild form of serfdom. Many slaves now become free under certain conditions and all children born to slaves are also free. It would be a doubtful mercy to liberate all slaves 'at the stroke of the pen', but the Emperor if free of interference would have liberated all within 20 years. Then if the Abyssinians had been allowed to develop along their own lines, in their own time, not immediately opening up the resources of the country for the benefit of outsiders, their ultimate attainments would have been an advance on Western Civilization.[4]

Abyssinia took over Una's life. She worked alongside a young Abyssinian student, Emmanuel Abraham, who later became a Cabinet minister in Haile Selassie's government in exile, and she and Abraham became passable friends. She struck him as mature, intelligent, tenacious and strongly feminist.[5] There were endless meetings to attend, lectures, discussions and resolutions to attend to in the evenings; during the day she was tied to the office.[6] She dealt with the entire correspondence of the Legation: the Minister made red pencil notes on the letters and sent them to her. She dealt with thousands and thousands of letters, drafting and typing correspondence, answering reporters' calls for up-to-date information and fielding questions on Abyssinia's politics. The diplomatic situation intensified when, finally, the League imposed limited sanctions, but without oil sanctions the war was not halted.

By the end of the year 1935 the British government was supporting the notorious Hoare–Laval pact, a deal which offered Italy everything it wanted in Abyssinia. It was a major step towards colluding with fascism; worse was to follow. Una, like many others, renounced any hope of Britain coming to the rescue of Abyssinia. Black activists who had been encouraged to believe in English justice were forced to recognise the war as a black/white issue, as C. L. R. James told them:

> Africans and people of African descent, especially those who have been poisoned by British Imperialist education, needed a lesson. They have got it. Every succeeding day shows the real motives which move

Imperialism in its contact with Africa, shows the incredible savagery and duplicity of European Imperialism in its quest for markets and raw materials. Let the lesson sink in deep.[7]

It did. April 1936 brought renewed victories for the Italians and almost unrelieved despair to the Abyssinians. Totally defeated in the north, they could count on two remaining assets alone: the Emperor himself and the army of the south. Haile Selassie withdraw from the limelight for days, retreating to the hills to pray and reflect. When he re-emerged it was to announce his decision to surrender and subsequently to leave for England.

In London the news was greeted with both sadness and joy. Selassie was due to arrive at Waterloo Station on 3 June. Una went to greet him and found the station packed with well-wishers and friends of the beleaguered statesman. London had never seen anything like it. The spring was decisive; a clear blue sky and warm sun shone above Waterloo Station. Crowded into the special enclosure on the platform were the dignitaries, the Dean of Winchester, lords and ladies and intimate associates. The crowd, mustering outside, eager and forgetful of its tired feet, clung together in excitement. The legend of English reticence was dead. Old-age pensioners were in the crowd, impatient teenagers, mothers and small children; all the black organisations were there – the Pan-African Federation, the International Friends of Abyssinia, the Gold Coast Aborigines Protection Society, the Negro Welfare Association, the British Guiana Association, the Gold Coast Students Association, the League of Coloured Peoples and the Kikuyu Association of Kenya – many in their African costumes. Above their heads wide scarlet banners were flying. Una was moved to tears by the sight of the flags and armlets, home-made hat bands, badges, buttonholes, in green, yellow and black, the Abyssinian colours.

In Jamaica the followers of Haile Selassie recognised him as their long-awaited black God, the king who would lead them from Babylon – place without redemption – to Africa. He, the Son of JAH, Haile Selassie, Emperor of Abyssinia. Una, whose social background would normally have told her to steer clear of the Ras Tafari Brethren in those days of police harassment and public contempt, was to become one of the first to grant them respect and to fight for social facilities in their communities.

At last the train steamed into the station; O. C. Harvey, private secretary of the Foreign Secretary, Anthony Eden, entered the train to greet the Emperor; flowers were pressed into the hands of his daughter, Princess Tsehai, and eventually Haile Selassie emerged, a diminutive figure, resplendent in his distinctive black cloak, standing proudly before his well-wishers. Defeated in war but not in spirit, he started, 'I am deeply touched by the welcome you have given me today. At this most anxious time to me and members of my family we must express our profound gratitude to you and to the British Government, which has shown us its sympathy and been of great comfort to us.'[8] Una at last had glimpsed the man for whose cause she had been working. What struck her most was his indomitable will, his determination to fight to the last: 'He is intensely religious and has great faith in the British people, the League, and his God.'[9] But she did not meet him then. It was weeks later, at a Hampstead garden party that they came face to face. Since his arrival in London her workload had increased with thousands of letters pouring into Princes Gate: letters of sympathy, offers of assistance, newspaper cuttings and donations from the British public and many foreign countries. There was little sign that officialdom was taking the Emperor's visit seriously.

Haile Selassie was visited privately by the Duke of Gloucester and by Anthony Eden at Princes Gate, but no invitation came from Buckingham Palace, and when the Emperor lunched at the House of Commons the Prime Minister, Stanley Baldwin, hid behind a table to avoid meeting him![10] The intense diplomatic activity of officials in London and Rome seemed endless and futile. Where power really lay, Selassie had no real friends. Nothing exposed this more than when on 10 June the Chancellor of the Exchequer, Neville Chamberlain, made a speech outside the House in which he called the continuation of sanctions 'the very midsummer of madness' since the Emperor could not be restored without military action. Selassie, determined to make his last plea to the League of Nations, decided to go to Geneva. Una decided to go too as a personal secretary.

On 30 June, the day on which Haile Selassie made his last plea to the League of Nations, Una sat in the Diplomatic Gallery when some rash Italian journalists started jeering and heckling. 'They seemed to have had whistles under their tongues and the noise they made was terrible. They would not allow the Emperor to speak and detectives arrested them. It was very upsetting.'[11] 'A les portes ces sauvages' cried Titulescu, the Romanian delegate, as people stared in horror and embarrassment. Selassie, a small, picturesque figure, with famous cape and beard, stood undeterred by the noise; majestically, he spoke in Amharic, asking whether force should be allowed to triumph over the Covenant and so threaten the collective security of small states. Throughout his speech Haile Selassie seemed calm; it was only towards the end, when he asked, 'What reply shall I have to take back to my people?',[12] that his voice cracked and the strain of war showed on his face.

The answer was none. Later that evening, at the Carleton Park Hotel in Geneva where Haile Selassie was staying with his entourage of fourteen, Una received news that the international press was very sorry about the incident with the Italian journalists.[13] The celebrated heiress Nancy Cunard, who was reporting the war for the American Associated Negro Press, called with a companion, William Jones, to see the minister and caught a sight which summed up the day's sorrow:

> The defeated Emperor passed outside the window walking slowly and alone, meditating in his long black cloak, a single and tragic figure in that garden of June roses. And then Una Marson came in in a golden dress, a figure of what is termed 'oriental splendour'. It was fine to see her like this; it made you feel somehow that all of the pleasures of life, despite everything, had not been extinguished for the last country in Africa that is not ruled over by white men and that sometime the wheel would turn again, for Abyssinia to be liberated from the Fascist invader. Inside that golden dress was a capable well-informed secretary.[14]

What Nancy Cunard failed to register was Una's despair and sense of hopelessness at the tragedy. Everything she had been working for at the legation and outside had come to nothing. The English politicians had failed to defend the victim of fascist aggression.

When she returned to London Una began to feel sick and weak in the mornings. Invitations to speak at conferences that she had once welcomed with a keen enthusiasm looked, much to her own surprise, onerous and bothersome. The Abyssinian Association, which was supporting the patriots in exile, lobbying against the lifting of sanctions against Italy and publicising the Emperor's forced exile, wanted her services, but she was too exhausted. (She helped as much as she could, even cautioning the Abyssinians about suitable London dress and telling them to comb their hair before going out into the streets!) She empathised with their sorrows; the worst thing for these exiles, who had left homes and families behind, was the knowledge that their wives and children were not allowed to leave and their properties were being confiscated. 'If they return they will have to be "Italians" and do not know their future. It is very heart-breaking', Una told friends. The Abyssinians' desperation was also reminding her that she too was separated from her loved ones, and quite alone.

She rallied her energies enough to take a short seaside holiday, but the English coast town could not make amends. On her return she consulted her doctor and was told that she was 'heading for a nervous breakdown caused by overwork'. It was time to go home. Una booked a passage on an Elders and Fyffes liner, SS *Cavina*, due to sail from Avonmouth, Bristol, on 10 September for Kingston.

At last, once on board, time was her own for loafing about. Una settled into her cabin for the two-week voyage home, via Turks Island. Entirely at ease as the liner neared home, Una was at last able to relax; she ate in style on her last night – Osetrova caviar, paté de fois gras, snacks of clear green turtle soup and roast partridge, a much richer menu than she is likely to have savoured for a long time.

On Thursday 24 September, after more than four years away, Una arrived in Kingston, Jamaica. It was shortly before eight in the morning when the SS *Cavina* was moored in Kingston harbour. Down on the pier was the customary large crowd, eager to welcome passengers home or simply make contact with the outside world. Among them stood Etty and Edith, quietly waiting for the local heroine. She appeared, looking remarkably fresh, in a smart check jacket with a buttonhole. Happy and relieved to be home at last, she posed for the photographers and had this to say about the war:

> There has never been a man with such faith as Selassie. He certainly has faith in the League and in spite of the fact that he has been let down, his faith is more than ever. We have only to wait now to see how his faith is regarded.
>
> … I regret to say that I am not hopeful about this fight, for the Italians are just waiting for the rains to be over and when they are, nothing will prevent them from going to the Western portion of Abyssinia and taking it over. Abyssinians cannot fight poison gas and they have not got ammunition. I do not know what will happen, nobody knows.[15]

Una's early belief system had taken a bashing. She had undergone an enormous transformation: now she distrusted 'Europe' and looked to 'Africa', and to a greater degree she looked to herself. It was not simply a question of externals. Britain's role within the League of Nations had sustained a vital emotional currency for Una, and the reality of its failure to save Abyssinia carried an inflated value for her. Although she had been intellectually prepared for life in England, nothing had prepared her emotionally and socially for the complex web of political manoeuvrings she had witnessed, or for the harshness of racism or the feelings of isolation. Her personal age of innocence about the 'Mother Country' was over.

Some of Una's anger over the Italian–Abyssinian war was expressed in articles, and one of her poems, prompted by news in February 1937 of Charles Martin's two sons, Joseph and Benjamin, who were fighting under Ras Imru in Wollega, appeared that autumn. Una learnt that Ras Imru had fought four successful battles against the Italians, but in the fifth his ammunition was exhausted and, when he was captured, Joseph and Benjamin were also taken. Benjamin was burned on the face with gas and taken to Addis Ababa for treatment.[16] The following month both sons were executed by the Italians. 'To Joe and Ben', a tribute to the brothers, amounts to a memorial for all the Abyssinian soldiers:

> God I know
> That these thine own
> And thousands more
> Cut down in youth
> And beauty
> Are not dead.

NOTES

1 Una's file, now lodged at the United Nations Library in Geneva, shows that her three-week posting began on 5 September. She was paid 850 Swiss francs.

2 'Racial Feelings', *Public Opinion*, 17 July 1937, p. 3.

3 C. W. Martin diary, in the possession of Gabriel Tedros, Springfield, USA.

4 On 30 March 1936 Una Marson spoke at the West Ealing Congregational church on behalf of the League of Nations Union. This was reported in *Middlesex County Times*, 4 April 1936.

5 Emmanuel Abraham in a letter to the author, November 1989.

6 It is not clear whether Una commenced work for the Legation immediately, and her own testimony does not coincide with the recollections of her colleague Emmanuel Abraham who served as secretary to the Legation. In 'Racial Feelings' Una states that she started work at the Abyssinian Legation at the beginning of the Italian Abyssinian war and remained until early autumn 1936 when she returned to Kingston. In a letter to the author Emmanuel Abraham says she worked there for about six months in the spring and summer of 1936. Common sense suggests that Una's record is accurate.

7 C. L. R. James, 'Abyssinia and the Imperialists', *The Keys*, vol. 3, no. 3, January–March 1936, p. 32.

8 'A Right Royal British Welcome', *New Times and Ethopia News*, 13 June 1936, p. 4.

9 *Daily Gleaner*, 25 September 1936, p. 17.

10 A. Mockler, *Haile Selassie's War* (London, Grafton Books, 1984), p. 151.
11 *Daily Gleaner*, 28 September 1936, p. 5.
12 *Ibid.*
13 'Jamaican Girl who was Personal Secretary to Haile Selassie', *Daily Gleaner*, 25 September 1936, p. 17.
14 Nancy Cunard, *Barbados*, for the Associated Negro Press, 26 April 1941, Cunard Papers, Chicago Historical Society, Chicago.
15 'Racial Prejudice in London Not Improving Says Miss Marson', *Daily Gleaner*, 28 September 1936, p. 5.
16 'Dr. Martin's Sons Captured', *New Times and Ethiopia News*, 27 February 1937.

II

A place in politics

Administration is bad, but a lot of it is 'jobbed' by their own wealthier people, the planters using the 'haves' among the blacks to keep things smooth and easy for their considerable property; peasant holdings are many, and available; but it is bad government ... there are masses incredibly poor and unambitious, touts and beggars and bad country housing, typhoid, no water supplies though plenty of water, and in Kingston filthy slums well out of sight, and plenty of people drifting in to fill them.[1]

THESE WERE the words of the political analyst and historian William Macmillan to his wife, Mona, about social conditions in Jamaica. The letter was written in January 1935, some twenty months before Una returned to the island, but nothing much had changed about Jamaica in that time.

The trouble had been building up for some time, indeed since the end of slavery. During the 1930s conditions in Jamaica grew from bad to worse, and now they were critical. The worldwide depression had battered the island's economy: export prices had collapsed, domestic production was down, unemployment rose steadily and fast. In 1935 Panama and Cuba had put an end to Jamaican migration: this, once the colony's safety valve against employment, was now firmly shut.[2] So Jamaica's problems stayed home and festered.[3]

The colony had a new governor, in the form of Sir Edward Denham, who had arrived in 1934 and shown some commendable interest in slum clearance; but even Macmillan, who had met Denham before, found him 'aloof and official' and resented having to go and play golf alone rather than talk economics. Macmillan had worked in South Africa and had extensive experience of the African continent, but found Jamaica shockingly old-fashioned, dominated by local vested interests and ruled by a locally based civil service with no incentives to innovation.[4] When Una came home, after four years away from the colony, she found it equally disappointing: with its decorative upper crust and its impoverished masses, it was revoltingly hopeless. 'Kingston is repulsive and its people beyond redemption.' Even her friends seemed more gloomy and people were 'on the whole much poorer than they were when I left in '32'.[5]

Una, in self-protection, left Kingston for a restorative visit to the countryside, probably home to St Elizabeth and to the tiny village of Brown's Town, St Ann, to visit her beloved Cousin Angie. Returning to rural Jamaica, to the scenes of her childhood, brought Una in touch again with herself as an individual with freedom, identity and responsibilities of her own. It was here, in the vitality and immediacy of country life, that she could re-assess the original versions of her childhood and the firm conclusions she had drawn from it. At thirty-one, after four years alone, Una felt the need to regain the self-authenticating knowledge of her earliest years and re-direct her life.

At the year's end Una returned to the city, with a new focus. The nationalist movement which started in the mid-1930s released her from the isolation and frustrations of her recent past. So now, at the end of 1936, she was embarking on a happier, more sociable period.

Again she shared with Etty a rented two-storey house, 'Rosebank', 17 Half-way Tree Road in St Andrews, Kingston. It was a pleasant and elegant residential area, within easy reach of downtown Kingston, and was an appreciable improvement on the modest Camberwell streets she had left behind. Una crammed her top-floor flat with books, journals and papers, and, poor as she was, purchased gorgeous cushions and curtains. She had no conscious idea of interior design, however, and, as her friend Isobel Seaton recalled, 'if she saw a lamp with a shape that appealed to her, she didn't worry about incongruity, she'd just buy it ... and yes, flowers ... she'd buy them and people gave them to her'.[6] Una's flat was 'always very homely'.

Once she emerged from this domestic comfiness and from the welcome home parties thrown for her by Suzanne Foster, a friend in the fashion business, and by the Poetry League, Una looked about for new projects. She thought about starting a women's organisation, but dropped the idea because Lady Denham, the Governor's wife, had already established a women's league and was ruling this growth sector, in tandem with the gentle and accommodating black middle-class woman Amy Bailey, Una's later colleague. Una was, however, in great demand, giving talks 'at every conceivable kind of meeting, even at a protest meeting against a proposal to establish house to house metering of water'.[7]

But she couldn't afford much leisure time. Like many a West Indian woman, she was doing a little trading, selling copies of Macmillan's *Warning from the West Indies*, a cogent and timely little book which documented the region's retarded economic and social conditions. Una was wildly enthusiastic about it and was bullying all her influential acquaintances into purchasing copies and sometimes, with a misplaced sense of commerce, handing out free ones: 'I have given copies to other people who should read them but are too mean to buy and as I am not at all out of pocket so that is very good.'[8]

But the main issue on her mind was the banana. Since 1835 the 'Gros Michel' banana had been grown in Jamaica. But it wasn't until 1866, when an enterprising captain, George Bushe, put in at the small northerly port of Oracabessa in search of bananas for the American market, that trade got under way. The local peasants sold him five hundred stems and advised him to try Port Antonio for more. George Bushe journeyed across Portland urging peasants to grow more bananas until, three years later, he was able to set up office in Port Antonio as agent for a number of American fruit companies.

Banana plantations began to flourish: abandoned sugar plantations, neglected canefields and peasant small-holdings were turned over to the crop all over Portland. The Americans held on as the marketeers, leaving the Jamaicans to grow and tend the plantations, but they paid higher prices for the crop, while cutting the selling price so that would-be Jamaican or British competitors were squeezed out. A banana war broke out, from which emerged the plump United Fruit Company, while smaller interests – the British who were trying to enter the market and the West Indian planters – were pulped. This took place at the end of the nineteenth century, but even now in 1936, among those being puréed by the United Fruit Company was the small Jamaican peasant farmer who battled with banana disease and severe hurricanes. It was with him that Una's sympathies lay. 'I don't know – things seem quite mad here', she told Macmillan. 'The co-operative venture – the Banana Producers – has been dissolved and a company formed instead.'[9]

The Jamaica Banana Producers Association, a large-scale peasant-based co-operative, had been formed to market the crop for export.

Peasant families depended upon it for their livelihood. But severe hurricanes during the 1930s, a banana disease in Portland and the subsequent rise in rejections absorbed much of the peasant farmers' often-tried confidence.

Sam Zumurray of the United Fruit Company came to Jamaica to advise the Producers Association to renounce their co-operative venture and, through negotiations with the island's leading lawyer, Oxford-trained Norman Manley, won this concession in exchange for a token charge on each stem exported. This money was to be used for a social welfare fund for the island's rural population. It became known as Jamaica Welfare Ltd.

Manley, as president of the Jamaica Banana Producers Association, insisted that local groups should manage themselves under a co-ordinating leadership which could 'engender a national spirit'.[10] His advisers included the island's chief medical officer, William McCullough, a friend of Macmillan and of Una herself. Manley was 'keenly interested in the formation of these Village Clubs', she wrote to Macmillan. She added:

> Medical work will be included as you suggest. Manley has asked me to work out a scheme for him and I have done so, based largely on the Women's Institute and I have given all the available literature on this matter to him. I also had literature from the Save the Children Fund as I think it is important that very keen interest should be taken in the children. The middle aged people can be helped a bit, but never changed, it's work for turning out a finer next generation. Manley has me in mind about this work which he thinks will not be started for another six months or a year, but just what that means I really do not know. Anyway one can wait and see and in the meantime I keep busy.[11]

While Una was humbly waiting and keeping busy during the first half of 1937, Manley was already recruiting staff and board members for Jamaica Welfare. Thom Girvan, Reggie Fletcher, Eddie Burke, Margery Stewart and Leila James Tomlinson were among those who, following the Women's Institute model which Una had provided, established cottage industries, co-operative societies and 'better village' programmes. According to Manley's biographer, Philip Sherlock, later president of Jamaica Welfare, the Jamaica Welfare eventually won outstanding international recognition, its members serving as consultants and advisers to international agencies and governments. Una, unfairly, was never given such a prominent or secure position. Norman Manley revealed the same imperfections in dealing with Una

Marson as most males reveal in dealing with clever, under-confident women. The frustration and resentment that Una must have felt that spring, at her implicit exclusion while others were taking up Jamaica Welfare's management, can only be imagined. Una has not described it, though she described how later she was placed in an equally invidious position by Lady Denham, the Governor's wife, who had sent one of her aides, a Mrs Moody, 'to ask me if I would serve as secretary of her Research Committee of the Jamaica Women's League and she wanted to discuss what ideas I had etc. Well', Una continued:

> if she really wants to discuss things with me she knows me, we had a long chat in London, she knows where I am. I told Mrs Moody that I could not undertake any work that would take up too much of my time without remuneration as I had no private income. Besides, there does not seem any intention to organise the thing well and run a proper central Office in Kingston and I hate half measures. All these ladies know so much better than I do so I do not think I will inflict myself upon them. When the gods see fit to send some money my way I know just what I shall do with it.[12]

Una, who counted two kings amongst her intimates, was being summoned like a parlour-maid because she was expected to be pleased to rub shoulders with the elites. Lady Denham, the most burnt edge of the upper crust, epitomised what was wrong with social welfare in Jamaica. The same frustration Una had felt towards the first lady turned into bitter resentment when later in the year Lady Denham hit the headlines for setting up an embroidery centre where twenty-five young Jamaican women, earning around £1 a week, were making pretty doilies to be sold abroad:

> All this is to the good and we are grateful – but when our 'one and only' [the *Daily Gleaner*] comes out with a bold headline averring that the unemployment problem for women in Jamaica is finding a solution in embroidery then we begin to think that Jamaica's greatest need next to a Secretary of Labour is a sense of proportion.[13]

Officially there was no colour prejudice in Jamaica, but there was considerable class prejudice, Una had told feminists back in London in summer 1934. Home again, she was getting a taste of it. Her place, she found, was among the agitating middle classes, the equivalents of the English grammar-school set, bright, ambitious and realistic, but without the collateral or connections to revolutionise society in their favour. The Jamaica Progressive League, a New-York-based nationalist group formed in 1936, was calling for self-government, citing unfair taxation, unequal educational opportunities and inequality within local government and the civil service as its main grievances. At home and abroad Jamaicans were waking up to the constitutional disadvantages of their system. Among this set a platform was being prepared for Una.

As she told Macmillan: 'Two young men, friends of mine, are running it and I help as much as I can. Of course, we have no money as usual.'[14] It was the weekly 'news-magazine' *Public Opinion*, which first appeared on 20 February 1937. Una had a column. The two friends were managing editor Osmond Theodore Fairclough and journalist and political commentator Frank Hill.

Fairclough, like Una, had lived abroad for years. In Haiti he had been a senior banking official at the National Bank. But on his return to Jamaica he found that none of the banks would have him. One manager told him, somewhat apologetically, that he could offer him only a porter's job. It was all down to colour. Management posts in the entire commercial sector were closed to dark-skinned people. Just as he had decided to challenge this, Fairclough came across another angry young man, Frank Hill, a journalist on the *Daily Mail*. Hill, who was to become Una's closest male friend, had grown up a devout Roman Catholic, but, now in his mid-thirties, this sensitive intellectual was disillusioned by his Church and particularly by its local Jesuit priests who had unconditionally supported the fascist Spanish leader, Franco. Frank deserted Catholicism for Marxism, Fairclough deserted banking for journalism and together they set up *Public Opinion*. To make a stable triumvirate they enlisted Hedley P. Jacobs, an Englishman who had been teaching at Mandeville College since 1925, to join them.

The paper's offices at Temple Lane became a centre for lively discussion. Every Friday night contributors and well-wishers gathered to help fold the pages and assemble and dispatch the paper as it came off the press. There were occasions when the work, and the discussions, went on right through the night, some of the writers going to work the next morning without any sleep. *Public Opinion* became 'the leading forum for the expression of advanced ideas – advanced, that is, by comparison with the prevailing imperialist and racist concepts which had so successfully permeated the whole of Jamaican society', wrote the Marxist lawyer Richard Hart, one of Una's younger colleagues.[15]

As both catalyst for change and recorder of it, *Public Opinion* would over the next twenty years remain at the centre of Jamaican political life, taking up radical and left-wing positions on domestic and overseas issues. Una, at first its only female writer, filled *Public Opinion* with her feminist opinions. This newspaper was to publish the most trenchant articles she ever wrote. Not only had she the desire to communicate, always strong in her, but she had struck a vein, unique to herself at that time, of material to communicate – her vision for women of Jamaica.

'Should our women enter politics?' she asked in her debut piece, and answered 'A thousand times yes!' and 'A start should be made at once. We must stop saying our City Council, our Legislative Council are no good – anyone can criticise. I believe our women ... could outdo our men in politics – I throw out the challenge – who will be our first woman politician?'[16]

The first response to this article, though not directly to the challenge, was from a founder member of Lady Denham's Women's Liberal Club. Writing in the next issue of *Public Opinion*, Amy Bailey, whom Una had met twelve years earlier through the Jamaica Poetry League, argued that women needed formal, paper qualifications to fit them for political office; degrees in political economy and sociology were, she said, more relevant and valuable than the social work experience Una Marson had advocated. Jamaican male politicians were 'miserable failures' because their minds were 'so untrained that they are left befuddled when big questions come before them'. But the final solution for Jamaica was to be party politics. 'Unlike Miss Marson', Amy Bailey continued, 'I believe that Party Politics would do this country a world of good. Then men and women would think of, and vote for the principles of their party and not confine themselves to personalities as they now do.'[17]

This debate, which many regarded as a sign of healthy discussion among the island's leading women, seems to have marked the beginning of a deeply felt, but rarely acknowledged, rivalry between Amy and Una. Amy Bailey, while she shared many of Una's interests and enthusiasms, did not care for her methods, or her personality. Una, she later explained, was flighty and unreliable, given to embarking on projects she later abandoned, and extreme in her behaviour. When Una's decisive articles, in which she revealed the quality and extent of her feminist associations in London, started to appear in spring 1937, Amy, who had spent all her life in Jamaica and was devoted to Jamaican organisations, might have felt peeved.

Amy was forty-two, ten years older than Una, and a teacher at the Kingston Technical School. In 1894 her parents had founded the Jamaican Union of Teachers in Walderston, her birthplace. Amy and her siblings had learnt to work hard at home 'picking coffee, rat-cut coffee … off the ground'.[18] These well-disciplined Baileys were instructed by their parents not 'to be content to be down at the bottom of the ladder' and as adults all entered various professions. Amy, Ina and three others followed their parents into teaching, Elsie became a nurse and Susie a pharmacist.

Amy, resilient and sensible, was to found the Housecraft Training Centre in 1945 to train unemployed teenage girls in domestic skills. She was an able journalist and activist, though she never joined any of Una's more radical literary circles. Politically she was at home with the nationalists and had been a keen Garveyite in her twenties. Culturally, however, Amy was a child of English liberalism, grateful to the 'white people of culture', ministers and school inspectors who had been associated with her family. This outspoken champion of black working-class women was, nevertheless, tinged with some of the imperialist instincts and beliefs that helped to keep those same black women at the bottom of the social ladder.

Over the next twenty years Una's and Amy's paths continued to cross. Una, after her death, received attention for feminist theory, Amy for her practical work. But Amy Bailey was to have the last word on Una Marson. In a drama-documentary produced in 1990, *Miss Amy and Miss May*, on the lives of Amy Bailey and fellow Jamaican feminist, May Farquarson, the two women are seen in a reconstruction, at a social function. Sipping wine and trading witty and pointed comments on their peers and their times, they observe Una Marson, off-screen, entering the hall. Miss May observes: 'Una Marson is doing good work: look at those articles in *The Standard*.' Miss Amy replies: 'Those articles dignify women's work, but Una Marson goes a bit too far. You know the other day, I bumped into her down Kings Street, carrying a basket on her head!'[19]

Una's proposals for Jamaican feminist activism as propounded in *Public Opinion* consisted largely of a reworking of initiatives she had witnessed and admired in England. She started her second article, 'Some Things Women Politicians Can Do', with the no-nonsense comment: 'I take it that we are all fully agreed that our women should enter politics. And now, what next?'[20] What Una saw as the peculiar challenges and opportunities facing women politicians was informed by the English text *Our Freedom and its Realities* (1935) by five British women, four of whom she knew personally: the Labour MP Eleanor Rathbone; Alison Neilans, an executive member of the International Alliance of Women; Erna Reiss, author of *The Rights and Duties of Englishwomen*; and Mary Agnes Hamilton, Labour MP for Blackburn from 1929 to 1931 and a novelist. Una wrote:

> Our women have initiative and administrative ability. Here and there we see it – it must be encouraged and developed. Our schools must encourage scholars to think for themselves. Our offices must give women the same chance as men and the same pay for the same work. … Let us have women on our City Council and in our Legislative Council, making their voices heard. Women who serve because they must – women above prejudice and intolerance – women on whom the progress and happiness of our people depend.[21]

Una was an independent activist, at arm's length from groups. She made numerous speeches and took part in public debates, but she was to find, to her distress, that, though feminist ideas and activities received a lot of attention, some reactions were hostile. Richard Hart, the Marxist lawyer and activist, remembered that 'she was the one who was always pushing the woman question', but who

> never had any constructive ideas other than the assertion that women must speak up … I used to think her speeches a bit empty of content, I don't think she was very much in tune with the positive ideas that were coming up, the idea that we should rule our own country and that sort of thing, the idea of promotion of culture.[22]

Even though as a young man Richard Hart saw the alternative routes for men, and the inconsistencies of the rules that were presented to his set of male associates, he did not see the alternatives for women of his generation. Not until 1944, when Mary Morris-Knibb was elected to the city council, did women enter mainstream politics, but long before that time many were politically active. History has ignored most of them, but they were there. Una Marson was not born to be a politician in the traditional sense. She was a solo voice. She needed room to manoeuvre and found it in journalism, creativity, conversations with sisters and friends and self-analysis. Her *Public Opinion* column did not have a single arena: it galloped over many topics – employment, unions, community development, the police, tourism, the need for local publishing houses, literary groups and cultural politics. She was bursting with good ideas.

NOTES

1 Mona Macmillan, *Champion of Africa* (Long Wittenham, published by the author 1985), p. 68.
2 Wayne Brown, *Edna Manley, the Private Years: 1900–1938* (London, André Deutsch, 1975), p. 191.
3 Major Orde Brown, *Labour Conditions in the West Indies* (London, Colonial Office, February 1939).
4 *Champion of Africa*, p. 65.
5 Una Marson to William Macmillan, 1 December 1936, in the possession of Mona Macmillan.
6 Isobel Seaton interviewed by the author, Kingston, Jamaica, May 1989.
7 Una Marson to William Macmillan, 1 December 1936.
8 Una Marson to William Macmillan, 17 May 1937.
9 *Ibid.*
10 See Philip Sherlock, *Norman Manley* (London, Macmillan, 1980).
11 Una Marson to William Macmillan, 17 May 1937.
12 *Ibid.*
13 'Wanted – A Secretary of Labour', *Public Opinion*, 25 September 1937, p. 6.
14 Una Marson to William Macmillan, 17 May 1937.
15 *Ibid.*
16 'Some Things Women Politicians Can Do', *Public Opinion*, 20 February 1937, p. 10.
17 Amy Bailey, 'Women's Politics', *Public Opinion*, 3 March 1937, p. 10.
18 Erna Brodber, 'The Pioneering Miss Bailey', *Jamaica Journal*, vol. 19, no. 2, May–July 1986, p. 11.
19 The 1990 drama-documentary was filmed by Honor Ford-Smith, the artistic director of Sistren Theatre Company, a women's organisation in Jamaica.
20 'Some Things Women Politicians Can Do', p. 10.
21 *Ibid.*
22 Richard Hart interviewed by the author, London, 1 February 1991. See also Ken Post, *Arise ye Starvelings* (The Hague, Institute of Social Studies, 1978), which ignores feminist activism in the 1937–38 uprisings in Jamaica.

12

The Moth and the Star

For many decades European writers have been revealing the mind of the Negro to Europeans. Now the Negro is becoming articulate. It is important that he should become more so – that he should have a clear idea of what he thinks and what he wants. These ideas must be expressed so that they can be widely read.[1]

ONE OF the positives of Una's long stay in Europe had been her exposure to a vast literature: journals, magazines, Gollancz's Left Book Club and debates about cultural, social and political subjects had sharpened her mind. It was a world away from McFarlane's pallid Poetry League, and with this newly acquired experience she decided to co-ordinate a progressive literary group to encourage would-be writers by exchanging ideas, offering criticism and sharing new publications. But Una Marson did not feel it would be everybody's cup of tea. She belonged to that educated elite who charge themselves with preserving and developing 'culture' and wrote of 'a board of best brains whose duty it would be to criticise and encourage local literary talents'. Una argued that women and men, such as her group, had the power to determine culture and to make it in their image. Consequently, they would transform existing Jamaican culture, not merely have access to what already existed. In the end Jamaica, she said, would be judged 'not so much by its "sugar and rum," as by the products of its great minds. Gandhi, Pandit Nehru and Rabindranath Tagore are better known than the financial magnates and the gold-laden maharajahs of India.'[2]

Indian cultural nationalism, traceable in the writings of nineteenth-century poet Rabindranath Tagore, had become for Una an ideal for Jamaicans. She anticipated an end to imitative art. Her cultural philosophy, which can be gleaned from several *Public Opinion* contributions, echoes James Weldon Johnson's assertion in the *Book of American Negro Poetry* (1923) that a people's greatness is recognised by one measure, above all others: 'the amount and standard of literature and art they have produced'.[3] Without such obvious and uncontentious cultural manifestations, a people's quality and stature would remain hidden; while, on the other hand, no 'people that has produced great literature and art has ever been looked upon by the world as distinctly inferior'.[4]

It was a distinctly superior set who came to Una's literary group, the Readers and Writers Club, in early August 1937. They were young, bright, professional people, some of whom were writing for *Public Opinion* and most of whom, like Una, had strong nationalist leanings. One of the few women members Una lured back to her side was her one-time colleague at the *New Cosmopolitan*, Aimee Webster. She found the club, the first inter-racial one in Jamaica, 'a very refreshing place to meet people with whom you were intellectually at home'. It was also good to see Una again, after so many years.[5] Una's 'travels had sharpened her perceptions and gave her perspectives that were considered extreme' but she 'demonstrated a great yearning for literature and yet she didn't conceive of herself as a literary figure, had no thoughts of selfishness or of money making'.[6]

The club was at 4 Central Avenue in Kingston Gardens, the building with a modest library it was to share with the Kingston Drama Club and the Poetry League of Jamaica, its cultural siblings. Every Tuesday evening at 8 p.m. the literati gathered, often until the small hours, to discuss books, criticise manuscripts, listen to lectures or, on occasion, have a party. For this club, Una had acquired the patronage of Herbert G. de Lisser as club president. He was a self-made man of creole stock, nearly sixty, editor of the *Daily Gleaner*, publisher of the magazine *Planters Punch*, a novelist, indeed a man of such social and literary clout that he couldn't be ignored. But as 'a figure of the past, of the imperial relationship',[7] de Lisser was humiliated and rebuffed when he came to address the young nationalists and went off in a huff, with Una acutely embarrassed! Una hated this sort of open conflict.[8]

Una was in her early thirties, at an age when many women are preoccupied with husbands and small children, but the club was the centre of her life and its members the demanding brood she could mother. Isobel Seaton, a secretary who had been away from the island for some time, was taken along to the club by a friend. She had read about some of its members and was longing to meet them, especially Una:

You couldn't meet Una without realising that she was individual: alive, interested in everyone and a happy person. You felt you knew her a very long time. I went to the club three or four times and could see that Una was the prime mover in it. She felt intensely about everything and had a very good sense of humour.[9]

Frank Hill, five years older, was like a brother; he and Una talked politics, theatre and writing over lunch at the Esquire Restaurant and stayed late at *Public Opinion* meetings. It was 'total cohesion'.[10] Una was drawn to Frank's sensitivity and practical intelligence: he had a capacity to analyse problems and find creative solutions. He read the first drafts of her plays, giving her constructive criticism – he told her frankly that *London Calling* was rough around the edges – and he sharpened her political awareness. Frank's gentleness may have drawn to the surface Una's more fragile side. On occasion she seemed ingenuous: 'She was never crafty', remembered Stephen Hill, 'but always open-minded and genuine, though slightly puritanical in her outlook and very easily embarrassed by broad humour.' But Frank, preferring to shield Una from offence, refrained from challenging what he saw as her naivety and 'would merely laugh, saying: "Una, you're a very silly, silly little girl", because she liked to believe the best of everyone'.[11] Frank also helped when Una was depressed or inclined to withdraw into herself. Sometimes she tried to do too much and the pressure of work built up to an intolerable degree. Although she was energetic Una was often overstretched. She was invited to give numerous lectures at schools, colleges and community associations because she was a 'brilliant, off-the-cuff speaker [who] could turn her material to suit any occasion'.[12] But once Una became so overwrought in a debate on colonialism that she couldn't answer her opponent, Esther Chapman, a vociferous champion of imperialism, who was often pitched against her, and had to be helped out by Frank and friends.

There is nothing to suggest that Una's relationships were anything but platonic. Much rumour and speculation have been expended on Una's relationships with men, who made up the majority of her companions, colleagues and friends. One of her lifelong friends, the lawyer Clifton Neita, recalled that 'You could always tell the kind of person she'd be pals with. She preferred people of intellect and did not care for the show of things. ... She was always amongst men. And men liked her.' What men seem to have liked was her wit, her intellect and her organising abilities. At the same time male prejudice against brilliant women was rife: clever women like Una, Ethel and Amy Bailey did not marry or, in some cases, ended up divorced.[13]

In spite of the inevitable stress of running the club, there was in Una a joy and a capacity for exuberance which was both very moving and very rare. Clifton Neita, who was meeting Una for the first time, admired the way she 'threw herself into whatever she was doing. Other people didn't always understand this. She had to put her heart and soul into whatever she was doing and spoke with a passion when she wanted to put something across, but she wasn't over demonstrative.'[14] He often ran into her at art galleries, book launches and parties and, years later, when he came to know her better, used to visit Una at her house. They had several mutual friends, among them writers and journalists such as the Englishman A. E. T. Henry, a BBC wartime reporter, and Neita's best friend, Roger Mais, author of *The Hills Were Joyful Together* which Cape published in 1953 and which was hailed as 'a literary phenomenon', for it was 'the first native work of major quality to come out of Jamaica since that island was discovered by Columbus on his way to America'.[15]

Una was also forming literary alliances abroad. Her few, but lengthy and copious, letters to James Weldon Johnson lodged in the Beinecke Library at Yale span two years. He replied to her correspondence and, though they never met, it is clear that Una depended upon Johnson's letters, fussing about whether hers were tiresome and intrusive, worrying about letters lost or not yet answered. The concern was mutual; he wrote to her (11 April 1938):

> some months ago I wrote a letter of some length to you in answer to your letter which was dated October fourth, 1937. In the letter I expressed my high opinion and appreciation of your work. At the same time I sent you a photograph of myself inscribed to you. It is difficult for me to understand how this letter should go astray. I am sure it had the right postage.

In open-hearted letters Una told him about her literary aspirations and accomplishments. He in turn commented on her writing and literary groups, and gave her news of the African-American literary scene. He was a mentor whose good opinion she cherished and, when her third collection of poems, *The Moth and the Star*, was published in September 1937, her longing for his good opinion was as deep as it was sincere. She waited weeks for a response and finally it came. *The Moth and the Star*, he said, was a 'beautiful book'; he had 'liked [it] very much'.

In the weeks before her collection appeared Una's life was extremely hectic. She had to select the items herself, supervise the book's production, direct the marketing and help plan the launch. This was hosted on 27 September 1937 by the Poetry League at the Institute of Jamaica to mark the opening of its autumn programme. Una's friends from Kingston and further afield came for the evening's readings and musical entertainment and to buy copies of this plump volume of over a hundred pages priced at 4s. Rupert Meikle, who had recommended Una's autobiography to James Weldon Johnson, was in the audience and purchased a copy. He sent it to the American professor without delay, hoping that 'the Negro literati will like Una Marson and her work' for she was 'very strongly racial'.[16]

The Moth and the Star, a title which Una took from Shelley's 'To the Moth and the Star' (1821), which was quoted as an epigraph to her work, was indeed 'very strongly racial'.[17] Una had chosen several poems concerned with racial issues and reflected observations which, although fresh and surprising to Meikle and other readers, grew out of a body of thought and experience that had matured over several years. She had spent many hours pecking at her typewriter, drafting and re-drafting poems. Sometimes Una was unable to concentrate on her work at home, so she transported her typescripts to friends' houses and revised the work there. Unfortunately no early drafts of *The Moth and the Star* poems have survived, but it is clear from comparing some poems in her first collections with their earlier magazine versions that she was in the habit of editing her own work. This time, she also paid attention to selection, excluding poems which had appeared in *The Keys* in London and aiming to represent a range of styles and subjects.

Philip Sherlock, co-editor of the *New Age Poetry Books and Caribbean Readers*, observed in his perceptive and favourable introduction to the collection:

> It has been remarked that the Blues of American Negro Literature have in them a 'primitive kinship with the old ballads' and Miss Marson has made good use of the opportunities for effective repetition and for simple quick description. She has written blues which seem spontaneous rather than artificial, and that in itself is an achievement. The Blues as well as other dialect pieces are 'divinations and reports' of what passes in the minds of our people.
>
> A number of poems deal … with the facts of race and colour. We often adopt a false attitude, and pretend that no such difference exists

... they do exist ... and we sometimes quite wrongly suffer injustices and insults on account of them.[18]

One of the poems of race and colour, 'Black Fancy', ends:

> My John told me I was sweet
> I did not believe him
> Thought he would go mooning around
> Some whitewash girl
> But maybe he means it
> For I am not so dull
> Yes, I am sure he loves me
> His black ivory girl,
> And I love him
> For he is young and strong and black.

Writing against the cult of 'ideal womanhood', Una portrayed black women as strong, attractive beings, challenging social conventions and taking pleasure in their sexuality. Whiteness had become for Una a devaluing force for the black woman, associated with lack of confidence in her beauty, confused sexuality, fear of invisibility and fear of isolation. In 'Cinema Eyes' a mother, who as a young woman used to adore the 'beautiful white faces' of the screen, tells her daughter:

> Come, I will let you go
> When black beauties
> Are chosen for the screen;
> That you may know
> Your own sweet beauty
> And not the white loveliness
> Of others for envy.

And she admonishes:

> I know that love
> Laughs at barriers
> Of race and creed and colour
> But I know that black folk
> Fed on movie lore
> Lose pride of race
> I would not have you so.

The Moth and the Star was an admirable book. It was the result of years of experimentation and hard work. Una, following the examples of Langston Hughes, Zora Neale Hurston and James Weldon Johnson, was infusing her poetry with black musical notes: the blues and jazz-style song. These were among her most vital and perceptive poems: in the sad dry notes of the blues poems and in the inventive use of irony in her 'social' poems Una revealed her particular strengths. Her style was often clipped and conversational; it was more feeling than intellect. She had cut and curtailed her Romantic inclinations, although she included over forty poems on 'Nature' and 'Love'. The other two sections, 'Poems written in England' and 'Poems on Life', are the finest, centring for the most part on the female world, though 'At the Prison Gates', written in 1937, pleaded on behalf of 'the poor men of Jamaica who went to the jails, knocked at the gates and spoke to the director of the prison'.

Una was presenting to Jamaica a new poetic style. In terms of her response to British society she had more in common with the West Indian poets who were to publish in the postwar period than with her peers. Like these later poets, she showed her incorporation into the society and her isolation within it; she reflected her settled condition, her insecurity and, also, an underlying explosiveness.[19] And just as later West Indian writers, such as George Lamming in *The Emigrants* (1954), were to reflect upon the mixed relationship, so too did Una.[20] In 'The Stranger' she projects on to an inquisitive English gentleman:

> You like talking to people like me
> Friend with the wistful smile
> To foreign girls who are brown of skin
> And have black kinky hair
> And strange black eyes.

She had observed the Englishmen around her but she had felt obliged to keep her thoughts to herself and later to poeticise them. Some men must have fancied her, chatted her up and even taken her out, but such men were only distant beings. Her smile was as wistful as the stranger's.

Passion is reserved for the 'blues'. These all hark back to intimate, self-reflective moments where she had put aside all thoughts of political correctness, international relations or social conditions. They are woman-centred and stir up images of women talking, laughing, dancing, even howling together over food and drink and tales of love and trouble, with no need to make believe or dissimulate. Bessie Smith, the extraordinary singer of blues, was Una's darling. There is something double-edged and strong, something ironic and piquant in Bessie

Smith's voice which Una had in mind. The satire on black women's self-hatred 'Brown Baby Blues', is for singing:

> I got a brown baby
> Sweet as she can be
> I got a brown baby
> Sweet as she can be
> But she ain't got no papa
> Cause he's gone to sea
>
> I love me baby
> But she don't got no name
> I love me baby
> She don't got no name
> Well wha' fe do
> Dat is not her shame.[21]

In literary terms the blues poems were clearly indebted to the younger Langston Hughes, who from the early 1920s had been experimenting with these rhythms. In an article on the blues Carl Van Vechten, the jazz-lover whose novel *Nigger Heaven* was a bestseller in 1926, had quoted the twenty-four-year-old Hughes, saying: 'The Blues always impressed me as being very sad, sadder even than the Spirituals, because their sadness is not softened with tears, but hardened with laughter, the absurd, incongruous laughter without even a god to appeal to.'[22] Una's blues seem more decorative, less wild than Langston Hughes'. He was always delighted by the raw American voices he heard in bars, cafés and even churches and wrote out of that experience. Una had also found musical forms in other Harlem Renaissance literature such as Helene Johnson's 'Poem' (1923) which appeared in Countee Cullen's anthology *Caroling Dusk* which she had read. This employs the Harlem street life vernacular:

> Little brown boy,
> Slim, dark big-eyed
> Crooning love songs to your banjo
> Down at Lafayette –
> Gee boy, I love the way you hold your head
> High sort and a bit to one side
> Like a prince, a jazz prince.[23]

Una's 'Banjo Boy' was an imitative poem which mixed a Harlem beat with standard English:

Black boy,
How you play that banjo
Gee – it goes right to my toes
I could dance all night
And through the day again
How your face beams
Do you love it
I'll say you do

The publication of *The Moth and the Star* should have been a turning point for Una in the West Indian literary world; it justified her extensive thoughtful work. It was accepted by de Lisser as 'genuinely good work'.[24] But Una's experimentation in free verse and dialect elicited a haughty response from him:

> The peril with so much free verse is that it tends to be more prose than poetry; and though one may mention Walt Whitman in contradiction of this view, one must remember that Whitman was a giant. … While some of Miss Marson's verses in dialect are excellent we do not profess to think that she achieves her best in dialect any more than Claude McKay has done. As a matter of fact, as an educated woman, she does not think in dialect; her normal medium of expression is cultured English and some of her best poems are therefore in a language that is so perfectly and inevitably natural to her.[25]

Una fared no better with Clare McFarlane. In an eight-page review he griped about her modern 'sociological bias' and dismissed her quest for a specific language to record the lives of Jamaican women:

> Beauty in the artistic sense is rarely possible in a broken language; this is because the words, the materials with which the artist is building, are blurred in outline and unshapely. The materials themselves are indifferently mixed from dissimilar elements which do not always blend harmoniously. There is in the language itself something ludicrous which, while it heightens humour, often lends a farcical appearance to tragedy and makes burlesque of pathos. This is why an audience will laugh at 'Stonebreakers' when it ought to feel compassion.[26]

There is no doubt that Una's detractors were unjustified. They didn't understand or like the collection which challenged the maidenly, elegant, socially discreet tone that they expected from young women. Una had become a worldly woman, light years away from other Jamaican poets who still adhered to the great Victorians. But she was no literary orphan. Una joined a class of poetry which was highly conscious of its place in history, of modern psychology and social class.

But because she was a black woman poet (not following in the foot-steps of the left-wing Auden set) she was embracing another viable tra-dition – the African-American tradition. The spirit of *The Moth and the Star* might, as indeed it did later, have won admirers for her among more radical black and feminist critics. By the early 1980s Una Mar-son's name had emerged as *the* pioneering African-Caribbean woman poet, the foremother of contemporary black women writers in Britain. Only the canon and the curse of literary history that has concealed women writers of one generation from the next had separated Una from her African-Caribbean daughters. But in 1937 in Jamaica those who had a 'voice' gave her poetry a deflated value and trampled upon her emerging confidence. Wisely Una mentally put de Lisser and McFarlane in the doghouse and looked elsewhere for advice and com-fort. For a year after the book's appearance James Weldon Johnson, at Fisk, was a splendid ally.

Early in 1938 Una had solved her problem of how to outshine the Jamaican critics. She wanted an American publication and had even toyed with the idea of going to the United States. No longer an uncrit-ical writer, she was able to select the better poems for a collection and to laugh at her juvenile efforts: '*Tropic Reveries* is so "young" that I blush to read it – still one or two might be used.'[27] She had been receiv-ing favourable reports from other American friends, too. Adelbert Hamilton, a professor of classical philology at Elmira College, New York, who had frequently summered in Jamaica, liked the book. He had sent also her a copy of Edna St Vincent Millay's *Conversation at Midnight* and she was 'thrilled with it'.

About the same time as Hamilton's gift came, an encouraging letter arrived at the *Gleaner*'s offices from Van Riemsdyck Book Service, New York, asking for particulars of Una's publications. Una was not sure how to deal with the firm for, though she was keen to have either *The Moth and the Star* or a selection of her work available in New York or London, her publishing experience was local and self-managed. To keep the price down she had brought out *The Moth and the Star* with a soft cover, but now she was afraid it looked second-rate: 'I am won-dering if I should send this book as it is to these people. They want prises [*sic*] trade discounts? I am particularly anxious to have 'The Moth and the Star' on the market there but would like to go about it in the right way. Can you please advise?', she appealed to James Wel-don Johnson in January 1938.[28]

Prudently mindful of the need to be free of constraints she was glad not to have come across Millay, an extremely popular American poet, before completing her own book: 'it is perhaps just as well that I had not come under her spell before publishing my book'.[29] A friend had pointed out some similarities between the two poets, which pleased Una very much.

Edna St Vincent Millay's most arresting qualities were bluntness and a tart freedom. *Conversation at Midnight*, a daring long poem, was an attempt to understand the male world. With its many voices – a painter, a poet, a Roman Catholic priest – it aimed to defend disparate values, juxtaposing for example the businessman Merton and the poet-communist Carl. Una probably liked its discursive tone and wit and the varied display of masculinity. Men scarcely figured in her poetry, except as unidentified or ungenerous objects of love, but in Una's plays men appear more fully – as pompous, unkind, insensitive, cruel, tyrannous, foolish and generally disappointing.

Una's portrayals of men amount to a consistent attempt to free herself from their contempt and from the feelings of anger, fear and insecurity which they inspired within her. As a woman writer she was haunted, just as Virginia Woolf was, by the Angel in the House and still had 'many ghosts to fight, many prejudices to overcome': 'I like the *Moth and the Star* better than *Heights and Depths*', she told James Weldon Johnson:

> that may just be conceit in feeling a later work should be better! I should love to have your opinion. It is nice to know you enjoyed *Heights and Depths*. Sometimes I am not sure that I am a true poet in feeling and execution, feeling, well yes – but I have not written a line since I published *The Moth and the Star*.[30]

NOTES

1   'Readers and Writers Club', *Public Opinion*, 31 July 1937, p.10.
2   *Ibid.*
3   James Weldon Johnson, *Book of American Negro Poetry* (New York, Harcourt Brace, 1923).
4   *Ibid.*
5   Aimee Webster Delisser interviewed by the author, Kingston, Jamaica, May 1989.
6   *Ibid.*
7   Richard Hart interviewed by the author, February 1991, London.
8   Archie Lindo interviewed by the author, May 1989, Kingston, Jamaica.
9   Isobel Seaton interviewed by the author, Kingston Jamaica, May 1989.
10 Stephen Hill interviewed by the author, May 1989.

11 *Ibid.*
12 Wycliffe Bennett interviewed by the author.
13 Rhonda Cobham-Sander, 'The Writer in Jamaican Society 1900–1950', Ph.D. thesis, University of St Andrews, 1982.
14 *Ibid.*
15 Andrew Dakars in *John O'London's Weekly*, 1 May 1953, quoted by Daphne Morris in the introduction to R. Mais, *The Hills Were Joyful Together* (London, Heinemann, 1981), p. 3.
16 Rupert Meikle to James Weldon Johnson, 19 July 1937, James Weldon Johnson papers, Beinecke Rare Book and Manuscript Library, Yale University, New Haven, Connecticut.
17 Marson uses other Romantic allusions. 'A Dream' in *Heights and Depths* opens with a modification of Shelley's 'Indian Serenade', 'I arise from dreams of thee', and, when considering her fading youth in *The Moth and the Star*, Marson makes reference to Byron.
18 Introduction, *The Moth and the Star* (Kingston, Jamaica, 1937), p. 3.
19 James Berry, *Bluefoot Traveller* (London, Limestone Publications, 1976).
20 In Lamming's *The Emigrants* (London, Allison and Busby, 1982) Caribbean women discuss this shortly after their arrival in England: "'And you'll never get an Englishman to ask out one of us." "Not that we particularly want them to, but that is the sad part of the story. You'll get our boys who come up here to study treating the English girls to everything, and you'll never find an Englishman to even look in our direction." "And if they do, you can look out, they're some queer type, thinking it would be an experience to sleep with somebody who looks different"' (pp. 148–9).
21 'Brown Baby Blues', *The Moth and the Star*, p. 97.
22 Hughes quoted by Carl Van Vechten in 'The Black Blues', *Vanity Fair*, August 1925.
23 'Poem', from *Caroling Dusk: an Anthology of Verse by Negro Poets* (New York, Harper & Row, 1927).
24 Herbert G. de Lisser, 'Miss Marsons Poems', *Daily Gleaner*, 27 September 1937.
25 *Ibid.*
26 Clare McFarlane, 'Review of the Moth and the Star', no date, Una Marson papers, Box 1949B, National Library of Jamaica.
27 Una Marson to James Weldon Johnson, January 1938.
28 Una Marson to James Weldon Johnson, 4 October 1937, James Weldon Johnson papers, Beinecke Rare Book and Manuscript Library, Yale University, New Haven, Connecticut.
29 Una Marson to James Weldon Johnson, January 1938, Beinecke Rare Book and Manuscript Library, Yale University, New Haven, Connecticut.
30 Una Marson to James Weldon Johnson, January 1938, James Weldon Johnson papers, Beinecke Rare Book and Manuscript Library, Yale University, New Haven, Connecticut.

13

A woman's little madness

THE WARD Theatre, the largest in the Caribbean, with 950 seats, a pale-blue edifice with white-iced trims, was in a whirl of excitement. Here they were again, the best and the brightest of Kingston's intelligentsia, preparing to present the first performance of the Kingston Drama Club. The scene was contemporary Jamaica and the huge cast a curious combination of men and women; the posh set dressed in blazers and summer frocks, or gowns made by Suzanne Foster's professional outfit, the others wearing the long, white robes of the pocomania cult members, some stitched by Una herself. There were musicians and dancers, singers from the East Street Baptist Fraternal, and hangers-on, including the sixteen-year-old Winston White who, hearing the weird and wonderful pocomania songs emitting from the Ward one night, had slipped in and joined the fun. Una, a quietly firm producer, had just signalled with a look and nod that silence was required backstage. The children, Sheila and Toinette Ableton and their stage cousins Fitzroy and Carl, were already on to the set. Una, looking glorious in 'a white Paris evening gown with double train and sequins dotted over', was later presented to the Governor, Sir Edward Denham.[1]

Pocomania opened at the Ward Theatre in Kingston on 8 January 1938 and was scheduled to run for two nights only, but its première was so successful that the company heeded calls for more performances.[2] *Pocomania*, everyone agreed, was Una Marson's best play. It was to be Una's last major creative work, to become the single one that consolidated her reputation and the one that most Jamaicans still associate with her name. In the six months since *London Calling*'s more modest success Una had found a way of crafting a truly Jamaican play. Topical and controversial, *Pocomania* was flawed neither by farce nor by parochialism. It was, wrote the *Jamaican Times*, 'a landmark in what we hope to refer to in the future as Jamaican theatre'.[3]

The subject matter was compelling. At its centre was the story of a young women's desperate search for herself; through this religious conflict and family strife come to the fore. The island's ecumenical history reveals how through centuries of European rule and influence Christianity had come to prevail and flourish. And yet by the 1930s, even within the bounds of the Christian church itself, increasing numbers of Jamaicans were looking to their African home for spiritual inspiration. African spirits and European saints had been sharing the province for centuries. A mere six years after Columbus left the Caribbean for the final time, the Spaniards went about wiping out every other religion and massacring its adherents in the name of God. Although the Arawaks, like any other careful farming folk, had guardedly scattered their piety among various *zemes* (spirits), after Absolution the New World Christians massacred most of them anyway. When Africans were brought as slaves to the Caribbean, they brought their Islamic and animistic religions with them. These 'soul' religions encompassed the belief that life comes from spiritual source not matter, and is everywhere.

In early Jamaica one manifestation of animism was *kumina*, a myal cult incorporating ceremonial music and dance with *kimbanda* and *kyas* drums beating out the rhythms.

> A kumina queen sprinkles the drums with white rum, then fills her mouth with the liquid, spitting sheets of alcohol over the participants. … The queen calls and sings in quavering shrills mixed with Ancial African words. Then a goat is hugged and petted before an executioner severs its head in sacrifice. Blood gushes out of the goat's trembling body. It is mixed with rum and fed to the participants.[4]

According to Edward Seaga, an authority on revival cults in Jamaica, pocomania emerged as a cultural resistance to missionary Christianity during the 1860 revival which swept the island after emancipation. Outsiders viewed it as 'a little madness' corrupting its true African name *pukkumina* (little *kumina*), a syncretism of *kumina* and Christianity.

Pocomania the play, like the cult on which it was based, flustered the status quo. It is set not in Kingston but in the lush, quiet countryside Una Marson knew in her childhood. The prologue, a nursery scene, shows Stella, six years old, aroused by the beauty of the African drums playing in the distance. It is as though the drums, like a disembodied voice, speak to the soul of the restless child, calling her to rise and find her psychic place of origin. She gets up, dancing to the timeless rhythms, falls in a trance and, since she is too young to know better, collapses. Her elder sister, Dawn (the stable, daylight child who becomes the 'Angel in the House') is displeased with this nocturnal spirit, and calls the nurse, Sarah, who arrives with bay rum to resuscitate Stella and promises to take her young charge to 'witness' a cult meeting one night.

Years later, in the yard of revivalist leader, Sister Kate, the Brothers and Sisters, robed in white and wearing turbans, are practising hymns when Stella's father, Deacon Manners, arrives with Parson Craig. They accuse Sister Kate of enticing members away from Elizer Baptist church into her cult, of corrupting them and allowing evil practices at her meetings: 'we have agreed', ends the Parson, 'that we must ask you to leave our Church.' Furious, Sister Kate denies their charges and asserts her right to belong to both the established Christian church and the pocomania band. Finally, exasperated, she plays her trump card, informing on the Deacon's children: 'Dem stan' in a bush oneside but de spirit tol' me dem was dere. It was many years ago but I not forget.'

In the drawing room of the Deacon's rural home Stella talks to her sister, Dawn. Stella, again sensitive to the homing signal, expresses boredom with predictable country life. She has become uninspired and restless in her narrow world of voluntary work, family matters and church attendance. It is clear she is on the brink of 'something'. Dawn, tragically failing to sympathise with this instinctual longing, is critical and cold. Contentedly mending the Communion cloth, she chastises Stella for being 'rather on the fast side', adding that Parson Craig, her fiancé, also disdains her 'ultra modern ideas'. News of the death of John, Stella's close friend in England, pushes her over the edge. When next she hears the pocomania drums, she is mesmerised, drawn from her physical abode to her spiritual home.

Two weeks pass. Stella, still grief-stricken, visits Sister Kate and, in a long conversation, discloses her fascination with pocomania. Discerning the young woman's naivety, the revivalist leader explains the significance of the drums: 'Troo de drum de spirit speak – de Lawd Himself speak to de soul of him people.' But only after Stella has left does Sister Kate expound her philosophy in full, explaining that social class bars the likes of Stella from the cult: 'Tek dem upper classes if dem come to de meeting and shout and sing dem will be sick but eben dough some ob we people is tear wid de debil dey get up nex day so go long about dem business.'

In the months that follow, Stella, unable to curb her fascination with the cult, secretly attends 'meetings', disguised in a turban. She has rejected the advances of David, a doctor, who suspects her obsession with the cult and tries to deflect her from it. In the final scene, Stella attends the Nine Nights wake for the now deceased Sister Kate. Hiding in the bushes, she watches as the evening degenerates into a brawl, gusty drinking and debauchery. Frightened, she turns to rush away, and is 'saved' by David. She agrees that there will be 'No more pocomania' and that love will now satisfy her need for 'a little madness'.

It is convention that directs this denouement. Throughout, Una Marson's sympathies seem to lie with Stella, who is powerless to escape the Baptist church's suffocating and binding teaching that denies her the right to define for herself an independent or distinct culture. However, in the end Una Marson undercut her own critique by settling for a conventional literary and social ending: rescue by the gallant hero, security for the heroine in love and marriage. What first appears to be a challenging exploration of structural opposition between African, progressive, and feminist values as against Christian, conservative and non-feminist values does not lead to a firm endorsement of the former. Instead, Una Marson used the recuperative dramatic moments to condone the value systems she had implicitly satirised; and punishes the very values her play implicitly affirmed. Failing to explore to the end the new avenue she had so vigorously taken, she delivered an abrupt and contradictory denouement, thereby repeating in this serious drama, the choice made in her first play, the comedy *At What a Price* (1932).

The story of Stella Manners, a creative, expressive soul, is also a tale about the ambitious but trapped New Woman. This was a trap in which Una herself had felt caught. C. G. Jung wrote: 'It is not possible to live too long ... in the bosom of the family, without endangering one's psychic health. Life calls us forth to independence.'[5] This might have been written for and about Stella Manners or Una Marson, women whose wild natures called them out into the world. *Pocomania* admonishes women against trying to sneak freedom while suppressing large parts of themselves. Had young Stella rebelled, run away and joined the cult, she might have been 'saved', but she stayed and stayed. In so doing she allowed the patriarch to tame her, to teach her compliance, peacemaking and servitude. In adulthood Stella finds it increasingly difficult to be assertive and to follow her instincts. Conventional the ending might be, but it is also a saddening reflection of the errors of timid women.

Pocomania is, however, an incisive critique of the early twentieth-century middle-class Jamaican society in which young women who crossed the class barriers and defied sexual conventions were regarded as deviant and treated as insane. Stella Manners complains that her family are 'never completely moved or stirred, never give full vent and let go', so much so that she wants to scream. Una's screams were vented in early combative articles, protest poems, plays and the life script she had chosen for herself. In that very year, 1938, with female unemployment figures rising, she was campaigning hard for women's rights and was appalled when the *Daily Gleaner* applauded the needle-work scheme which Lady Denham, the Governor's wife, instituted for twenty-five women as *the* solution to female unemployment.

And yet, *Pocomania* is not overtly feminist, although its point of view is emphatically female. The sisters represent diverse perspectives on middle-class womanhood, and it is the relationship between Sister Kate and Stella which gives shape and meaning to the action. The dramatic structure privileging the middle section, the moment of dramatic change and action, belongs to them, with the dialogue weighted in favour of Sister Kate's values and attitudes. As in the former communities of slaves which Barbadian historian Kamau Brathwaite has described, Sister Kate is a sacred–secular, multi-dimensional character operating as mother, sister and counsellor and prevailing at the centre of a small but complete world, while Stella, the Europeanised educated woman, moves psychically and physically from one environment to the other.[6] Stella is an alienated soul, attempting to negotiate an identity; she is both rejected and rejecting. Her predicament, reminiscent of Lamming's succinct summation of the statelessness of exile – 'I have lost my place or my place has deserted me' – acts as a metaphor for the fledgeling groups, both nationalist and feminist, in which Una was active.[7]

Much like her white creole contemporary, Jean Rhys, Una was exploring the psychology of women as they make progressive journeys. In both *Pocomania* and Rhys's *Voyage in the Dark* (1934), both autobiographically inspired works, dreams and the fragmentary, circular movement of events contribute to the sense of how women try to define themselves and react against their silencing. Eighteen-year-old Anna Morgan, like Stella, is a motherless, naive young woman, desperate to bond with a mother-substitute and heal her pain. Both heroines find only transient support from others; Anna is merely accommodated by her aunt and successive landladies; Stella finds Dawn cold comfort and even Sister Kate is only a short-term ally. These frail and sensitive Caribbean women whose identities are so flimsy seek redemption in memory. An exile in London of 1919, Anna, a fifth-generation Dominican on her mother's side, needs her bitter–sweet recollections of her island home. Stella, a black Jamaican, who 'owns' nothing so immediate, digs into the collective memory pool to reconnect with her own lost ancestor, her spiritual mother country, Africa.

Shaped through contrasts of history and present, light and dark, masculine and feminine differences, Apollonian and Dionysian religious practices, *Pocomania* nudges the audience to make choices. Sister Kate's life-affirming spirituality is open to the needs of its adherents; she welcomes exchange and participation and she listens attentively to Stella. A strong female character, her attractiveness arises from her refusal to restrict human behaviour even among those who would easily descend into brawling. The respected woman is contrasted with the respectable Deacon Manners, whose ever-diminishing power is lodged in the Church's rules, procedures and form and who forbids emotive truths.

The failings of the traditional Church are emblazoned here; elsewhere Una was more moderate in her analysis of religion and only mildly critical of her father's legacy.[8] In her article 'Women and Religion' (1937) she argues that religion fortifies women in personal, familial and community roles not least because they are so often alone and because men turn to them for their own spiritual support and guidance.[9] She urged women to hold on to their religion, even though it was no longer fashionable; women, she concluded, had nothing else of a spiritual nature to give them courage.

In *Pocomania*, without limiting herself to facile opposition, African/European, or Baptist/revivalist, Una Marson had shown a world where several positions co-exist and where synthesis within individuals is desirable. In the words of Sister Kate, accused of subverting Elizer Baptist church members: 'The debils, I is tell dem to go to Church and worship de Lawd dere too. You can't worship de Lawd too much Minister.' Strategies for cultural resistance should not be reduced, she suggests, to simple contest. Instead, *Pocomania* advances an attitude towards cultural resistance which was readily accepted from the black arts movement of late 1960s – the use and preservation of an assertive 'nation language', the validation of black (folk) religions, drumming and African music, the inclusion of the knowing ancestor or symbols of that ancestral presence. In 1938 none of these signs of a black literary theory was being employed, and the alternative social world depicted in Una's *Pocomania* represented a radical shift from the normal Anglicised bourgeois setting:

> Sister Kate: Yes, but I don't kip wid respectable ladies like she fe come to de meetings. Dem can't understand it. It is not possible to be respectable and common at de same time.
> Sister Mart: But we not common, we is destant.
> Brother Kendal: We is quite destant.
> Sister Kate: Yes, destant in de eyes of de Lawd but not in de eyes of de worl'. I don't care what de people wid larnin say, dere will alwys be de common people and de better class people. I know I like to stay in the common set, for den I can spress meself widouten noting happen.[10]

Here, in the black culture of 'the common set', their freedom of expression is not subjugated or dominated by a white 'other'; in fact here class and race are dismissed in favour of 'being'.[11] History informs the right to 'being' and is relevant to understanding the cult. The most radical aspect of the cult's representation is the assertion that Sister Kate is conserving an alternative history based on common memory and folk experience, demonstrating that the revivalists do not belong just to themselves and to the present but are essential to a redemptive historical scheme that is playing itself out: drumming is the motif for this:

> Stella: Do you know the drummer?
> Sister Kate: Know Josiah, mam? Josiah who is beating drum fe de meeting dem from he is a little boy. Him used fe beat de drum fe me when I was on me foot. Lawd, he can beat it sweet man.
> Stella: Who taught him to beat it like that?
> Sister Kate: No him puppa mam.
> Stella: And who taught his father?
> Sister Kate: Him puppa, dat is Josiah gran fader come ere a little boy pon slave ship from Africa.

The authorities and the missionaries had tried unsuccessfully to eradicate the drumming by the likes of 'Josiah gran fader' by legislation and persuasion because they recognised that it retained and transmitted distinctive elements among the slaves.[12] Marson's demonstration of that retention is an early literary attempt to reconnect Africa with the Caribbean. This, above all else, has prompted contemporary critics to review *Pocomania*.

Una herself was satisfied with the result, and wrote to James Weldon Johnson that 'Pocomania had been staged with the greatest success' of all her plays. The press was less enthusiastic and gave it mixed reviews. The *Jamaica Times* pointed out that the script was 'uneven' and in places 'superficial'; and was correct to comment that it required some editing.[13] In *Public Opinion* Clare McFarlane wrote that it was a 'decidedly moderate and somewhat idealised' version of the cult, and the *Gleaner* also rapped her knuckles for trivialising the cult:

> Beneath the throbbing of the drums, the howling of the hymns, and the prancing and posturing and foaming at the mouth, runs a strong undercurrent of negro mysticism that cannot but command a certain respect. Pocomania to the pocomaniacs is a real and even terrible thing – but Miss Marson represents it as a happy, boisterous and comparatively innocent evening's amusement with an occasional interval for refreshments. To the pocomaniacs, there is only one god and the 'shepherd' is his prophet, and to both individuals they accord a respect of no mean order, whereas in Miss Marson's play Brother Kendal is simply Master of Ceremonies at a rather enjoyable semi-religious 'bram'.[14]

Other spectators liked it rather better. They thought it was serious, reflective and innovative. Its political undertones were not lost on Una's clique. Philip Sherlock regarded it as a product of the new insight, 'a spirit of national consciousness'. Clifton Neita thought *Pocomania*

> excellent; Una was the first person who tried to examine in a helpful way these religious sects which we have in Jamaica and to find some reasons why people, especially the lower classes, believe in them. Roger Mais, my best friend, came afterwards and did much the same things in his books. No doubt Una influenced him.[15]

Una herself saw the pocomania cult as a branch of other African folk religions, and told James Weldon Johnson, 'Our pocomaniacs must be something like the "Shakers" used to be in your Southern states or perhaps like the "Holy Rollers" in Nassau.'[16] She also told West African journalist Victor Delumo in an interview seven years later, 'pocomania is the nearest thing to Africa that we have in the West Indies', adding, 'our African ancestry is still with us'.[17] By that time, the mid-1940s, *Pocomania* had even been performed before a sympathetic Lagos audience in May 1940,[18] and Una was dramatising African short stories for use on the continent, the only surviving typescript being 'The Courage of Bokindi', a sentimental sketch set in a Central African village. It is much less interesting than *Poncomania* and does little to exalt her reputation as a dramatist.

Pocomania touched on social conditions in a manner which alert viewers noted, but the labour rebellion which was about to overtake the island's leaders – so blinkered to truth – shocked the Governor, Downing Street and Jamaica's ruling elites. The trouble had been brewing for some months. Towards the end of March 1938 Tate and Lyle, the sugar magnate, announced in the press that it was about to employ vast numbers at its Frome plant and then reneged. At Frome in Westmoreland a thousand labourers who were building the Frome factory went on strike, demanding one dollar a day as minimum pay. The strike proved to be the beginning of a new era in Jamaica's history. It became so violent that the Governor, Sir Edward Denham, declared a state of emergency and the labour unrest was later investigated by the British government.

On 1 May the strikers walked swiftly through the streets of Frome, breaking into a march as they reached the sugar offices. As they stood with sticks three to five feet long, stones and lead pipes, they were joined by crowds of working people, gathering behind, all voices raised in the chant 'A dollar a day'. The local police stood round in considerable numbers, then attacked; many were on foot but a mounted division of forty Kingston police were later drafted into the area. For hours the entire space was blocked with people. Bit by bit, with repeated charges the police hurled themselves against the swelling crowd. People tried to run away, others dodged the blows of heavy truncheons falling on their heads and backs. Then, fighting back, they hurled stones and old iron axles through the air, some of these straight at the windows of the Frome offices; the glass and timber of the buildings smashed and splintered. Shooting then started. The police with rifles were firing straight at the crowds, amid shrieks and cries for help; some fell to the ground, others staggered away, or crawled on hands and knees to safety. The ground was strewn with weapons and red with blood. The dead and wounded lay motionless on the ground. They were only strikers, some not even strikers, but unemployed labourers, desperate for work. Four people were killed, hundreds injured during that clash with the police. When darkness fell they retaliated, burning the canefields for miles around.

Una was at the scene of this strike. In February she had started writing for the new daily, the *Jamaica Standard*. Over the next few days she reported on the strikers and police action and on the responses of Alexander Bustamante, the trade union leader. Of partic-

ular concern to Una was the part played by women in the labour uprising. At the Savannah-La-Mar Hospital she interviewed several women
caught in police fire.[19] The injured told tragic stories of the riots:

> One Elsie Brown had been going from Georges Plain to Frome to see
> her daughter when she was attracted by the large crowd. Almost
> immediately shots were fired, she ran with the rest, but was shot in the
> leg and tumbled in the dust. In the neighbouring bed was Beatrice Pow-
> ell, a domestic who lives in Burnt Savanna. She was on her way to the
> shops to buy soap. She was caught by the rush of the crowd and shot in
> the leg.

For weeks what had turned into a major labour rebellion rolled on,
involving, during May and June, a series of strikes by wharf workers,
street cleaners, labourers, factory workers, clerks and shop workers,
men and women. It was mid-June before normality returned to
Jamaica. Alexander Bustamente devoted his energies to restoring
order and unionising workers under his Bustamente Trade Unions. In
London Arthur Creech Jones of the Fabian Colonial Bureau asked
questions in the House, letters and reports of the rebellion appeared in
The Times, Harold Moody tried to push the government, which
responded by appointing a Royal Commission under Lord Moyne to
investigate social and economic conditions throughout the Caribbean.
Strikes had occurred across the region in St Kitts, Trinidad, St Lucia,
Barbados and St Vincent.

The Englishman William Makin, Una's editor at the *Jamaica Standard*, was very impressed by the continuous flow of Una's excellent
reports and wrote in his autobiography that she was one of Jamaica's
finest. She was a keen reporter; up at dawn, she travelled miles in
search of a story and was often ahead of the *Gleaner*'s more rigid clan,
bringing a woman's angle to the general strike, but also braving the
violent scenes which erupted here and there. Those, like Una, who
were watching the national mood judged what was needed. Action,
she wrote in 'A Call to Downing Street', was urgently required to avert
mass strike action:

> It is no use to say that Britain is too busy with bigger affairs ... . Are we
> going to wait for a strike to take place before we act? I fully believe that
> the Colonial Office would welcome a deputation of people who had
> facts to lay before it. I think those of us who feel a passion for our coun-
> try, who realise what the possibilities are, should consider this matter
> seriously.[20]

Realising that the Colonial Office, local employers and the wealthy had no interest in ordinary Jamaicans, Una planned to launch an organisation for children and working mothers based on the English Save the Children Fund, of whose Child Protection Committee she was still a member, and called for community support. It was hard work. In the afternoons she would don a hat and plod up and down central Kingston begging for money.[21] Makin, her boss, took note and encouraged her. When finally £230 had been raised, the Jamaica Save the Children Association, commonly known as Jamsave, was launched on 11 June at the Readers and Writers Club premises, with Una as secretary. On the executive committee was Dr Oswald Anderson (who had resigned as Mayor of Kingston because his calls for social action had been ignored), Hedley Jacobs from *Public Opinion,* and the social worker Amy Bailey.

At the *Standard* Una continued to file reports on Jamsave's progress and sift through the heavy postbag of letters, donations and requests for help from parents and children. Businesses rallied to the cause, donating food, clothing and cash; the committee visited schools asking for additional places and made contact with needy families. They aimed to open daytime play centres for children of working mothers, feed them, clothe them and, if necessary, give them a basic education.

A few days after the launching of Jamsave, Makin suggested that Una should return to London to report on the Moyne Commission, which was to investigate the causes of the disturbances. She was pleased to pack. The members of Jamsave, a nucleus of pioneering social workers, saw the advantages of having Una in England as a fundraiser. Later there was bitterness from Dr Verma that Una received more praise and pay than was her due, but the surface relationships seemed smooth and professional. When the problems of allowing their secretary out of sight began to surface, Una was already back in London. She had left behind her in Kingston nearly all her possessions – her notebooks, books, letters and papers – and her dear sister, Etty, and friends. Work had torn her away from home again; it would be several years before she returned.

NOTES

1 'Social and Personal', *Jamaica Times,* 29 January 1938, p. 4.
2 A typed script of the play is held by the National Library of Jamaica, Marson Collection. Secondary copies which show minor variations, e.g. age of children, are also held by the Library.

3   'Pocomania', *Jamaica Times*, 15 January 1938, p. 42.
4   Paul Zach (ed.), *Jamaica: Insight Guides* (Kingston, APA Publications, 1993), p. 98.
5   Carl Jung, *Collected Works* (London and New York, Routledge, 1978).
6   Edward Kamau Brathwaite, *The Folk Culture of Slaves* (London, New Beacon, 1981), briefly discusses the role of the African religious leader who, because 'there is no real distinction between secular and sacred', fulfils several functions within his or her community.
7   George Lamming, *Pleasures of Exile* (London, Allison and Busby, 1984), p. 50.
8   Consider her poems 'Getting de Spirit', which echoes the black Church's exuberance, and by contrast 'He Called Us Brethren', which challenges the world to see us as one in Christ.
9   'Women and Religion', *Public Opinion*, 17 April 1937, p. 10.
10 *Pocomania*, Act 2 Scene 1, p. 18.
11 In time the notion of the free expression of the peasantry became almost a prescription for modern Jamaican theatre. Frank Hill in *Upheaval* (1939) and Archie Lindo's *White Witch of Rosehall* (1945) came to the Ward with their own middle-class distillations of the peasantry.
12 Prologue, *Pocomania*. See also Act 1 Scene 1: 'Sister Kate: I tells you I don't wants drums here in me yard. Next thing the parson hear de noise and come down' (p. 5).
13 'Pocomania', *Jamaica Times*, 15 January 1938, p. 42.
14 'Pocomania Given Great Reception', *Daily Gleaner*, 10 January 1938, p. 10.
15 Based on second-hand experience of the Afro-Christian religious cult, *Pocomania* depicts Una's version of a social reality which, when compared with sociological and historical documentation, differs from the actual religious practice in some important ways. Other contemporary 'outsiders'' documentation reveals similar lacunae in understanding and knowledge.
        Writing of her travels in Jamaica during the mid-1930s, African-American anthropologist, novelist and folklorist Zora Neale Hurston described pocomania as 'a craze' among the peasants. She met two of the pocomania leaders, Mother Saul, 'the most regal woman since Sheba', and Brother Levi, 'a scrotonous-looking man' who informed her that it started as a joke and become something important (*Tell My Horse: Voodoo and Life in Haiti and Jamaica* (New York, Harper Row, 1990), p. 3).
16 Una Marson to James Weldon Johnson, January 1938, Beinecke Rare Book and Manuscript Library, Yale University, New Haven, Connecticut.
17 Interview by V. Delumo, BBC African transmission. Recorded 2 March 1945.
18 See Una Marson to John Fletcher, 20 May 1940, Una Marson papers, Box 1944B, National Library of Jamaica.
19 'Shot Woman Tell', *Jamaica Standard*, 4 May 1938, p. 1.
20 'A Call to Downing Street', *Public Opinion*, 11 September 1937, p. 5.
21 Child Protection Committee Annual Report of SCF 1936/1937, p. 26, Save the Children Fund, London. See also '"Children of Jamaica": A Save the Children Fund?', *World's Children*, September 1937, p. 180.

14

To the BBC

MUCH OF Una's mental energy during 1938 went into publicising Jamaica's economic and social hardships through talks and articles. On 30 September she gave evidence to the Moyne Commission. A detailed report, which captured the light-hearted atmosphere of the session, appeared in *The Times* the following morning. Una Marson had proposed a special tax on Jamaican bachelors and had suggested the money raised in this way should be spent to give 'children with no support from fathers the simple amenities of life'. Una Marson argued that co-habiting couples who had children should be treated the same as married couples after ten years. In particular their children 'should not be stigmatised as illegitimate'.

> Lord Moyne asked if it would be practical to tax bachelors who were not earning much money.
>
> Miss Marson replied that the problem should be tackled. It was the women who always suffered. Men did not seem to care much and in many cases did not know whether their children were being supported or not.
>
> Dame Rachel Crowdy inquired whether it would help to get some system of registration of fathers.
>
> Una Marson replied that that would help but it wouldn't solve the problem. 'They didn't seem to get on so well after they were married,' she added amid laughter.
>
> Dame Rachel Crowdy asked 'Who is afraid of marriage, the men or the women?'
>
> Una Marson: 'I think it is about equal. The men don't want to be tied and the women feel that the men very often take advantage of them and do not want to work so hard after they are married.'[1]

On the same day Una went to the League of Coloured Peoples'

special meeting on the West Indian situation at the Memorial Hall in Farringdon and, sharing the platform with Lord Olivier, famous as a colonial administrator and ex-Governor of Jamaica, and Bishop Hardie, the Bishop of Jamaica, described her experiences and perceptions: 'The Jamaican labourer, or any other Jamaican worker, for that matter is not a lazy person', she said, and attributed the unrest to 'the inconceivable poverty of the people'.[2] Una continued her work by pleading in the 4 November issue of the Quaker journal, *The Friend*, for donations and lecturing opportunities, and in the *World's Children*, the Save the Children Fund magazine, she described how Jamsave had 'started with £150, most of which we were forced to spend on children who really could not go to school because they just did not have clothes to wear'.[3]

Una's responsibilities for Jamsave were no more trying than her private worries over money. Back in Jamaica, imagining that the streets of England were paved with gold, individual Jamsave members were becoming increasingly suspicious of Una's protracted stay. It was decided to send a scolding letter, to which Una, clearly on the defensive, replied:

> Other work has delayed my stay longer than I anticipated … I have not yet sent in my resignation as organising secretary as while I am here some possibility for getting a good sum for the fund might turn up … appoint a secretary. …. I shall do my best here for present and it is well to remember that criticism does not make charitable work easier.[4]

Una's personal financial situation towards the end of 1938 was dire. Fundraising was difficult and not really to her taste. The first flush of excitement, aroused by starting the organisation, had collapsed. In early March 1939 she turned as a last resort to the Save the Children Fund in London, requesting a £15 personal advance. Gently but firmly they turned her down. It was not within their powers, they explained, to release money to her as 'funds here are held in trust for the work in Jamaica'.[5] She could not honourably follow their advice to supply written authorisation from her honorary treasurer in Jamaica since only £217 had been raised in London, of which only £67 resulted from the fundraisers' individual efforts. Another problem dogged her work: the lack of harmony between herself and Amy Bailey, who was also in London.

Amy Bailey had been instructed by Oswald Anderson, the president of Jamsave, to travel to England to assist Una's fundraising efforts.

Arriving in Liverpool in July 1938, aboard the prestigious *Rio del Pacifico*,[6] Amy had travelled to London where Una, who had arrived two weeks earlier, was already at work. Amy felt that Una, resentful and suspicious, was shunning her. Amy, even in extreme old age, had not forgotten the hurt:

> I hardly saw anything of Una, it was Peter Blackman, the Barbadian, who introduced me to lots of people, communists – Paul Robeson and Sir Stafford Cripps who later spoke at the Ward Theatre to launch the PNP [Peoples National Party]. Blackman told Moody about me and suggested I talk to the Royal Commission, so Moody organised a meeting.[7]

Inevitably others realised that all was not well between Una and Amy. At one of Harold Moody's tea parties Amy casually remarked on Una's absence and was told by Peter Blackman, 'Una Marson has not been invited because she has excluded you from anything worthwhile.' Una, as deeply affectionate as she could be annoying, was in different humour one cold December morning when she went to say goodbye to Amy, who was returning to Jamaica, at Liverpool Street Station. Una, nervous, shivery and uncertain, came to wish her farewell. On this, her second visit to England, she had started to view her homeland in a negative light, and what she saw as Jamaica's ingratitude for her tireless efforts left her feeling belittled and disregarded. Amy realised that Una's judgement had been coloured by her long residence in Britain and that she was torn between a desire to 'do the right thing', which meant returning home to build Jamsave, and a compulsion to fulfil her potential as an artist, which seemed to imply staying in England. Without cynicism, Amy told Una what she wanted to hear: she might well be happier remaining in England and could still serve her country that way, but England would never be her home.[8]

Summer 1939 was enlivened for Una by the arrival of two Caribbean visitors, her sister Etty and the recently crowned 'Miss Jamaica', Winnie Casserley. This was Etty's first visit to England, where she was to follow a one-year course in librarianship. But first the sisters paid a visit to France, only weeks before the start of the Second World War, with two friends. Una loved Paris, especially its elegant fashion houses and street cafés. There was optimism in the air, and talking to French people she had the feeling, she was later to recollect, that 'those who had suffered so much in the Great War still hoped for the best, but were prepared to meet the worst. But none of us visualised this "worst" which has come upon France.'[9]

Una's meeting with Winnie Casserley, another blonde, blue-eyed Miss Jamaica, brought in its wake only good news and fun. Visiting London as part of her prize, Winnie Casserley had been invited to the Annual Radio Exhibition, RadiOlympia, which was almost exclusively about television that year. Una, covering 'Miss Jamaica' for the *Jamaica Standard*, went along too. She and Winnie had a wonderful afternoon; they walked about the exhibition together and saw scenes coming up on the television sets. There was tremendous interest because people were seeing television for the first time. Miss Jamaica was televised, then the producer interviewed her and asked Una to take part in the programme, plying her with questions.[10] A few days later an invitation to the BBC's headquarters at Alexandra Palace arrived at Una's flat – she was now living in Mill Lane, West Hampstead – from Cecil Madden, the energetic producer of the popular magazine programme *Picture Page*.

Una's first impression of Cecil Madden was of a 'kind and gentle' person who was 'tall, wiry, sharp-nosed and eagle-eyed'.[11] He offered her freelance work on *Picture Page*, which involved contacting suitable interviewees, especially colonial visitors to London, drafting three-minute interview scripts and ensuring the safe and prompt arrival of her guests for rehearsals and interviews, which were conducted by Leslie Mitchell. To give her a feel for the work, Una was interviewed in 'a very hot studio'. Then Etty, who had accompanied her there, talked about her work as librarian at the Department of Agriculture at Hope, in Kingston, and described some of the island's tropical plants and flowers.[12]

Alexandra Palace, the BBC Television headquarters, was a site of unpredictable chaos inside with cables all over the floor, some of them as big as water hoses and others very narrow. To reach the camera, artists had to climb over this morass of wire, since cameras were not moved and the cameraman, with a black hood over his head, stood rigidly behind. That first summer at Alexandra Palace Una was tutored by Madden, who, she said, 'consistently produced programmes to a very high standard',[13] and his assistant, Joan Gilbert. It was a nerve-racking but amusing experience, since cameras broke down suddenly: 'cut, the camera's gone', someone would shout. A few weeks before the outbreak of war Una, representing West Indian interests, chose cricket for her last broadcast. The West Indies test match team, on tour in England, featured Learie Constantine, George Headley, Ben Sealy, Bertie Clarke and Alfred Valentine, who together made 'a really great programme'.[14] On the afternoon of the broadcast Una met the team to shepherd them across town in complete blackout. They stumbled around in the dark, and Una and Ralph Grant, their captain, anxious about them dropping a team member, kept stopping them to count that all were present.

Britain's declaration of war on Germany in September 1939 had a dramatic effect on Una's social and professional life. With some colonial students heading out of town as their universities evacuated to the north, and others retreating home overseas, 'the Negro colony in London had diminished'.[15] Being on the margins of this shrinking corpus – a few law students, medics and nurses – Una wanted a good job to latch on to, now that television jobs had been discontinued at the beginning of war. She pinned her hopes for employment and security on Aggrey House, the students' hostel. 'It ought to be a valuable centre for Africans and West Indians', she reasoned, 'the secretary assures me that it has not been greatly affected by the war.'[16]

Aware that new students might not brave the dangers of the sea to take up university posts, the Aggrey House trustees were considering proposals for reorganisation. Hearing this, Una wrote John Fletcher, their chairman, on 20 May 1940 suggesting that she be appointed as a social secretary, adding that, since all the trustees were acquainted with her achievements, a detailed résumé or programme was unnecessary. About her general intentions, however, she was specific: 'I do not propose to live on the premises and would work from 2.30 p.m. to 10.30 p.m. My work would be to organise meetings, study groups, parties, dinners etc. I would particularly like a Negro dramatic club.'[17]

While her proposal to Fletcher came to nothing, Una, one of few black women around still, felt she ought to do something to help and volunteered to be an air raid shelter marshal. 'It may sound very grand but I chose the job with the most time off for my writing and domestic duties', she said, 'I shall only have to see people into my shelter when there is an air raid and then keep them there till the all-clear goes.'[18] She gave occasional lectures at the Imperial Institute (which became the Commonwealth Institute in 1962) and did some freelance journalism and, later, talks and some scriptwriting work for BBC radio. In May 1940 she earned two guineas by devising a short, patriotic Jamaican scene which was incorporated into a Scottish production called *Brothers in Arms*. A more important early broadcast was her talk, 'Simple Facts: Jamaica', which was deemed worthy of publication in the 27 July 1939 edition of the BBC's respected journal, *The Listener*. In an equally valuable, more autobiographical programme, 'Talking it Over', Una was to describe her introduction to poetry and her early literary preferences.[19] Like many good broadcasters, Una had a knack for blending general social commentary with personal illustrations and humour. This gave even her early broadcasts a quality that makes the scripts lively reading today.

Keen to make her mark, Una Marson kept in frequent contact with Cecil Madden, occasionally suggesting programme alterations for West Indian broadcasts; 'Negro spirituals are to be preferred to dance music on Sundays',[20] she asserted. Grateful and impressed, Madden took up a number of her suggestions, forwarding them to his colleagues. Whenever possible he aimed to increase and improve the West Indian service, he told them in December 1940, 'with Una Marson's help as she is very intelligent'.[21] Since the BBC would shortly require a specialist to oversee West Indian programmes, this compliment amounted to a fine testimonial for an underemployed journalist.

BBC broadcasts to the Caribbean region were abysmally few. A detailed BBC memorandum written in 1929 had exposed the lack of facilities in the West Indies and colonial Africa and the discrepancy between this and the service to other parts of the empire. No attempt was made to serve the West Indies except on special occasions such as test matches, and therefore no in-house expertise existed. With the outbreak of war therefore, the quandary troubling senior staff at the Empire Division responsible for West Indian programming was twofold. One issue was the delicate handling of British policy towards colonies where nationalist activism had been in the ascendancy during the late 1930s – a political challenge also for the Ministry of Information under whose general influence the BBC now operated. The second, lesser consideration was the staffing of this section, bearing in mind financial and other managerial constraints, such as supervision.

At the Ministry of Information the West Indian press officer, Rudolph Dunbar, a well-known classical clarinettist, was, with the blessing of his superiors, doing his utmost to push for a weekly feature for West Indian troops to send personalised messages home. Meanwhile Una Marson, in a meeting with the Secretary of State for the Colonies, Lord Lloyd, appealed for a West Indian club for the five hundred servicemen now stationed in England. Through more frequent contacts with Cecil Madden, Una continually reminded the powers that be of the political imperative to boost the morale of West Indians at home and abroad. The pressure jointly exerted by Una and Rudolph

Dunbar had its effect. She was invited to broadcast morale-boosting talks on West Indians and the war effort:[22] 'The Empire at War and the Colonies' went out on 1 April 1940 and 'West Indians' Part in War' later that month. She ended one broadcast: 'I am trying to keep the flag flying for dear old Jamaica in my own way here and I am always in a rush as I used to be over there. Special love for you, my sisters.'[23]

For such overseas programmes the corporation required a broadcaster, acceptable to both sides, who was able to convey sincerity through the medium of a talk. This Una did very well. She was given more varied freelance work, particularly music shows, and tracked down some excellent West Indian bandsmen at West End clubs, checked over their details and supplied Madden with colourful, though not impeccably typed, guidance notes. Yorke de Sousa, 'pianist of rhythm and classics', the St Vincentian pianist William Wilson, a long-standing acquaintance she had first come across twelve years earlier at the YMCA in Kingston, and Cyril Blake's band, which played calypsos, paseos and swing-style music, made it to the studios. Her first interview, however, was with the celebrated bandsman Ken 'Snakehips' Johnson, whose West Indian Dance Orchestra had cut several records and was playing the fashionable Café de Paris.

By Christmas 1940 the first 'West Indian party' was scheduled to be broadcast on Boxing Day from the Criterion Theatre. This consisted of music and messages home sent by servicemen. By 10 January Madden, 'so taken by the enthusiasm of the West Indian Xmas party Miss Marson did for us', was sure they could do more 'quite easily and with guaranteed success'.[24]

In 1940 Una Marson, like most other people in Britain, was adjusting to the changing circumstances. She loved her West Indian service pals and many a night when they came to her flat after midnight she got out of bed to give them food – but instead of eating they just went on drinking beer. Una became a reasonable cook, turning out edible dishes from her rations and the food parcels her guests brought. She was living at 14 The Mansions, Mill Lane, in West Hampstead, a very large three-bedroomed flat with a long, drawn-out corridor. In the lounge, which was always full of servicemen's laughter, was a piano, on either end of which stood two bronze lions. Una was fond of hosting rowdy parties, dinner parties and song-singing sessions with the West Indian servicemen. They were her 'chicks', she took pity on them because in their hostels the menu was 'spuds on Monday, spuds on Tuesday, etc.'. She was keeping the Kingston spirit alive in London and even taught the Larsens, a Jewish refugee couple, 'Linstead Market', the popular calypso. From time to time the neighbours complained about the noise.

Una made some enduring friends among West Indian servicemen, Kenny Ablack, a fellow broadcaster, and Ulric Cross, a pilot officer. Thomas Wright, another of these, remembered how[25]

> Una spent enormous amounts of time and a good deal of her own slender resources in helping West Indians, and especially Jamaicans, when they got into some sort of a jam, which was often. She gave a rather delightful impression of absent-mindedness mixed with a great kindliness. But if anyone took this benevolent vagueness as a chance to put one over on her during her hours of work, they were certain to receive a rude shock. She had a good brain and was an able administrator, and all of us had a deep affection for her.[26]

Una's friendliness was not superficial. She invited the Larsens to dinner to meet her West Indian companions, but they, with no experience of black people save a solitary bar man in Prague, 'made cheap remarks to ourselves that she would have us for dinner'. That night there was a black-out too and 'around the fireplace there were six pairs of big eyes, but we didn't turn tail … and the whole thing fell into a beautiful evening'.[27]

The Larsens remained friends always. Egon and Ursula Larsen found her warm, enthusiastic and open, a complete contrast to her flatmate Linda Edwards, a fellow Jamaican and a student at London University. Linda appeared 'very harsh in her contemplation of the white world … was not at all interested in white men and wanted to "go back to Africa"'. Later she did, by marrying Robert Gardiner, the Ghanaian air commissioner.

The Larsens had a chance to know Una better when in summer 1940 they stayed at Mill Lane for a week when they were temporarily homeless. Ursula Larsen noticed the unkemptness of Una's home: 'The kitchen was always full of unwashed dishes, the place was very untidy and very uncomfortable for everyone who came there but no matter who came there they were always very welcome.' They had thought the bronze lions very poor taste and said so; the lions disappeared.[28]

The Larsens also reported how, with considerable relief, they believed they had successfully scotched Una's romantic liaison. Una was seeing an Austrian, from Vienna, called Rosenstein. He was a baker's son of twenty, fifteen years younger than Una and, the Larsens pointed out, not of her social class. But this was apparently a serious affair which lasted more than three years and during which Una contemplated marriage. Only the Larsens have been able to report on this relationship and their view is that it was flawed. Egon explained:

> One look at this young man and we could tell what kind he was; he wasn't even especially good looking or anything ... I had the feeling that there was a third language in which these two would have had to converse because his English was just beginner's and Una was very good, of course.

Ursula agreed:

> Not being familiar with each other's language sometimes when you meet foreigners, you will see them in a beautiful light before you recognise their foibles and shortcomings, and we said 'for heaven's sake Una, don't marry that man. The first row you'll have, he'll turn round and call you the Austrian equivalent of a "dirty nigger".'

These exchanges took place in 1940, shortly after the Larsens had become friendly with Una. But she was having some fun with Rosenstein, who also lived on Mill Lane. Una reported to the Larsens that she was already learning a few Austrian words; she knew the basics and had mastered what sounded like 'deeperter tottle', Austrian for 'silly fool'. If Una had continued with Rosenstein, she would have been able to return his abuse very competently.

On 3 March 1941, her BBC trial period over, Una was appointed full-time programme assistant on the Empire Service, compering and co-ordinating broadcasts under the title, *Calling the West Indies*. Cecil Madden was nursing her consistently through all her broadcasting work and there were some 'growing pains'.[29] The memos and letters exchanged by Una's bosses that May show that there were still some ambiguities concerning her role. With no one to 'assist' and without the formal authorisation to initiate projects Una was attempting to alter or, rather, expand the existing meagre schedule. To curb her informality, the Director of Empire Services, R. A. Randall, wrote to Madden: 'Miss Marson's function as West Indian Programme Assistant is to recommend to Mr Grenfall Williams a plan for these programmes and ways and means of executing them.' With the approval of Williams, the African Service Director, various sections would then be expected to produce programmes in accordance with the proposals and in co-operation with Una Marson. The bosses were temporarily satisfied. Madden sensibly shrugged it off, saying he was 'only too glad to think that other sections will be asked to share in carrying out the new plan' which contained 'no programme that she has not asked for at different times, though her views change from day to day, which has been a little disconcerting'.[30]

Accustomed to creative independence and autonomy, Una, now thirty-six, was finding the pressures and rigidity of bureaucratic life more constricting than the casual homespun cultures she was familiar with. Over the next five years, however, she made a success of it.

The BBC's Broadcasting House at Portland Place, with its plaque reading 'Nation Shall Speak Peace Unto Nation', was only eight years old, but Una did not work there. She had a little, cramped office in the old Bedford College in Regents Park which was the 'temporary home of the Empire Talks Department until an oil bomb got it',[31] and there her West Indian broadcasters and a young woman, Mary Treadgold, a recent graduate of the college, would pop in for regular chats. Mary, who shared an office with writer Eric Blair (George Orwell), was pleased to see that Una Marson stood out from the other BBC women. They were all obliged to dress formally, no plunge necklines, but Una stood apart not only because she was black, had a strong, lyrical Jamaican accent and was always talking about the West Indies, but also because she appeared much less stuffy than the others. She was an outgoing woman with a 'most vivid personality', and a relaxed attitude towards artists: 'I remember her being horrified with me when I said that as well as being good artists and good players, I would like them to be good in themselves as well', Mary recounted. 'Una said "You wouldn't just want them to be just good, would you?"'[32]

Una was as warm and reassuring as she was bewildering and the friendship which radiated so quickly was challenged by a strange episode which left Mary puzzled and offended. 'Una had left the office for about five minutes, I think a summons from the head of her section. About 10 minutes after her return she suddenly said very slowly and softly, in a voice quite different from her normal one, "Mary, why have you looked through my handbag while I was out of the room?" I simply stared open-mouthed, it seemed so out of character.'[33]

Una did not perhaps intend her question to take on the sinister tone it did. Paranoia played some part in her relegation of Mary to the enemies' corner. It was the first intimation of her deep-seated unhappiness. The BBC was a sizeable, busy organisation; her work was a social and invigorating experience; but beneath the sparkle and effervescence of her broadcasting profile, the old doubts and insecurities were still present. Mary Treadgold glimpsed the underlying sad anxiety. The reasons why Una was both anxious and sad were not immediately clear, but they were noted and awoke a loving concern.

Una experienced several difficulties at the BBC. In autumn 1941 she was in a state about what she experienced as the patronising meddling of the West India Committee, a London-based organisation representing planter and business interests. Her particular grievance was against Lady Davson and her War Services Committee which Una charged with embarrassing volunteer broadcasters by requesting that they 'boost' the West Indian Committee in their fifty-word messages sent to their families back home. 'I do not think', Una wrote to Grenfall Williams, 'that we can continue the policy of advertising this committee constantly in our programmes as we have been doing for months. There will definitely be a feeling in the West Indies that we are trying to popularise this organisation. In several scripts which I have had censored, the very mention of a make of bicycle or a Lyons cricket club has been struck out.'[34]

Una saw Lady Davson as an interfering harpy. Her imperious behaviour remined Una of Jamaica's spoilt upper-class ladies. 'I am anxious', she continued after making recommendations, 'that West Indians here should feel proud of the fact that they have a place in Overseas broadcasting and do not send a message through the charity of the West India Committee.' She continued:

> I would like to add that when I was forming the Save the Children Organisation in Jamaica, white people suggested that I was usurping their special privilege of doing charitable work for the coloured people. And the fact that the West India Committee feels that it has the privilege of controlling anything to do with the West Indies is in the old tradition.
>
> I think it is possible for you, and all progressive peoples, to get them to realise that with the help of God the backward coloured peoples are now gradually able to take a hand in looking after themselves.[35]

That, of course, was not the end of it. Lady Davson continued to criticise Una. By March 1942 she had discussed the West Indian service with Harold Nicolson, a BBC governor, who forwarded her notes to J. B. Clark, controller of Overseas Services. Clark, while admitting to dissatisfaction with the 'general standard of the West Indian items', was quietly supportive of Una Marson. She had, he wrote, 'a most modest nature, although her achievement in the white western world is of real significance'.[36] A fellow member of the West India Committee, Clark was nevertheless aware of its 'emphasis on the interests of the white merchants rather than the coloured races'.[37] But Una was not home and dry.

Outsiders also sometimes blamed Una Marson for the shortcomings of the West Indian service: Dr Morgan, a Labour MP, criticised her for telephoning him to take part in a broadcast rather than making a more formal approach; the Trinidad Information Officer in Port of Spain complained about the focus on Jamaica, adding that the programme was 'not really liked in Trinidad';[38] and in London Robert Adams, a West Indian actor and former BBC broadcaster whose contract had been terminated because neither 'the quality [nor] the accuracy of his material'[39] was thought to be satisfactory, was constantly stirring up trouble.

Taking her side in all these disputes, Una's bosses were aware that 'as the only West Indian employed' in that section her position was 'a very difficult one'.[40] But for all this sympathetic backing, Una Marson was still in the time-honoured position of the institutional gate-keeper, caught between a self-protective bureaucracy and a divided and suspicious community on the outside. Two factors, however, ensured her survival: the continuous approval of the Colonial Office staff who 'thought that she had done well',[41] and the conviction of John Grenfall Williams, the African Service Director. In March 1942, Williams, feeling that he had traced the source of the troubles to Aggrey House, the students' hostel, was swift to alert his colleagues of his findings. In a four-page memo to Randall, the Assistant Controller of Overseas Services, he expatiated upon the evidence which had been culled from a variety of sources including:

> Sabine, Edmett and Wilson of the Colonial Office, Miss M. Cox, a white West Indian who is a real enthusiast about the West Indies, in a small way, [Ernest] Eytle[42] who has been doing the West Indian Newsletter recently and has to spend a good deal of time in Aggrey House and, more recently, and rather surprisingly, by Robert Adams, the coloured West Indian actor, who was at one time a violent anti-Marson partisan but has now become reconciled to her.[43]

Williams's report, which was marked 'very urgent', continued:

> Aggrey House, it seems, seethes with gossip and backbiting ... It seems clear that Miss Marson's appointment to the BBC, far from creating universal feelings of pleasure at the success of a fellow West Indian, had a most unpleasant effect in some West Indian quarters, and the resultant

envy, constantly chewed over, developed a hard core of people who not only criticised Miss Marson, but were prepared to go to the length of doing something about it. Any choice of speakers in West Indian programmes, any rejection of a speaker, any reported remark of Miss Marson's, in fact almost any step Miss Marson took was and still is concern of everyone in this particular group.[44]

It was alleged that one faction at Aggrey House claimed to be 'out to get Miss Marson and anyone who protected her out of the BBC at all costs' and had 'collected for ammunition' accusations of the 'foulest' kind which they unwittingly confided to Miss S. Cox. This anti-Marson faction had apparently begun with a slanderous statement to the Colonial Office about Una's activities in and out of broadcasting and, when this ruse failed, had used first Dr Morgan, the Labour MP, and then the already prejudiced Lady Davson for their purposes.

Certain that Una was 'the only coloured West Indian in this country capable of handling these programmes' Grenfall Williams asked Una to write a report on the programmes which, it appears, won the approval of her seniors. So the matter was settled. 'In fairness to her, I must say that with the limited material at her disposal and the extremely hard work involved she has done a very good job', wrote John Grenfall Williams in March 1942.[45] The following month, Una's 'extremely hard work' was rewarded by a promotion to West Indies producer.

Faced with such consistent attack, Una began to feel the strain. Never adept at looking after herself, she now tended to look drawn. As producer, Una made it her business to find West Indians 'everywhere' for her four-night-a-week talks. Periodically, Una travelled to Scotland to arrange programmes for West Indians there. As the *Glasgow Evening News* reported: 'Among the senders were servicemen, doctors practising in Glasgow, children and students. It was odd to hear one West Indian student begin his message in cultured voice, "'Dear Mammy, Pappy"'.[46] The message parties were 'an idea of her own which brings young airmen and war workers to the mike to talk to their families at home'.[47]

Broadcasting also gave Una access to influential people in all walks of life and among her interviewees were Sir Harry Lindsay of the Imperial Institute, Dr Matthews, the Dean of St Pauls, and the actor Clive Brook. In an interview on *Close Up*, Una's interview programme, Malcolm Sargent, the conductor, observed that Samuel Coleridge Taylor, the black British composer, was both 'very remarkable and very individual'.[48] Vic Feather, of the Trades Union Congress, though not yet General Secretary, gave a series of talks promoting trade union development in the West Indies.

Una was in regular contact with the West Indies cricketer Learie Constantine, who was Welfare Officer in the Ministry of Labour, responsible for the 200 Jamaican technicians working in English factories, and, as always, she was in touch with Moody. Moody, who had successfully campaigned to remove the colour bar in the armed forces, introduced newly arrived West Indian servicemen to Una so that she could arrange broadcasts. In January 1943, Moody's younger brother Ronald, the sculptor, who had escaped from Paris in June 1940 two days before the Germans overran the city, appeared on *Close Up* and told of his arduous and terrifying escape from occupied France, before turning to his creative work.

Later that year, Una took part in John Page's short propaganda film, *Calling the West Indies*, acting as hostess and nudging the speakers – service men and women – towards the microphone. The high point of 1943 was Una's highly praised and politically motivated series on the Women's Institute movement in Britain. It was, she told Nancy Cunard, one of those 'programmes on useful social work liable to produce results'.[49] It shaped the later Jamaican Federation of Women, formed in 1944 by the new Governor's wife, Molly Huggins, with the conservative motto, 'For Our Homes and Our Country'.

Una did not commit herself to a particular form of women's organisation, she simply announced:

> I am convinced that the future progress of the West Indies is largely in the hands of women; though women can contribute a good deal to their country's welfare individually, it is through solid organisation that they can be most useful. I know that you are working in your own way and it must be in your own way, but I am sure you will be interested to hear something of what the British women are doing.[50]

But she would certainly have hated the mass weddings which Molly Huggins later organised to force stable monogamy on Jamaica's black unmarried mothers.

The record of Una's BBC years seems like an account of internal battles, troubled moments punctuated by happier ones, *ad hoc* interviews and the tiring routine of bringing service men and women to the microphone to greet distant relatives. Una experienced these years in fragmentary fashion: she lived without the emotional backing of family or close friends and she worked long hours, quite often alone.

Several of her colleagues cared about her, but they had their own war-time stresses. Besides, Una hated to be dependent in an obvious way. There were genuine contradictions in her role – broadcasting to the West Indies in a cheery manner suggestive of unspoilt imperial unity, just two years after the West Indies had thrown sticks and stones at London's policies. But also, on a practical level, broadcasting, even the BBC chiefs admitted, was a national affair and Una was in every sense a long way from home. For the first time she was earning good money in a secure job. The insecurity arose, at the same time, from the anxiety of travelling alone during air-raids, lying in her bed listening to doodle bombs fall and not knowing how her sisters were faring at home.

NOTES

1 'Tax on Bachelors', *The Times*, 1 October 1938.
2 'BWI Affairs, Topic of Talks at League Meeting in England', *Daily Gleaner*, 1 October 1938, p. 10.
3 'And Now Jamaica – New Outpost of the Save the Children Fund', *World's Children*, January 1939, p. 57.
4 Una Marson to the Jamsave Committee in Una Marson papers, Box 1944B, National Library of Jamaica.
5 Save the Children Fund to Una Marson in Una Marson papers, Box 1944B, National Library of Jamaica.
6 Jamaica Save the Children Fund 50th Anniversary booklet, *The Early Years*, p. 9.
7 Amy Bailey interviewed by the author, May 1989, Kingston, Jamaica.
8 *Ibid.*
9 'West Indians in the War', 25/26 June 1940, BBC written archives, Caversham.
10 'Television Remembered', no date, Una Marson papers, National Library of Jamaica.
11 *Ibid.*
12 *Ibid.*
13 *Ibid.*
14 *Ibid.*
15 'Wartime in Britain', no date, Una Marson papers, Box 1944, National Library of Jamaica.
16 Una Marson to Fletcher, Una Marson papers, Box 1944B, National Library of Jamaica.
17 *Ibid.*
18 Una Marson papers, untitled piece about black people and war.
19 'Talking it Over', broadcast 11 July 1940, Home Service, Una Marson, BBC written archives, Caversham.
20 Cecil Madden in a memo to G. H. Payton, 3 November 1940, Foreign General: West Indies (1939–1950), file E2/584, BBC written archives, Caversham.

21 Madden, memo to OPP (name unknown), *ibid.*

22 For Una's programmes see BBC written archives, Caversham, for 1 April 1940, 'West Indians in the War', 26 April 1940, and 'West Indies at War', 31 July 1940.

23 *Calling the West Indies*, 6 September 1940.

24 Cecil Madden in a memo to OPP, 28 December 1940, file E2/584, BBC written archives, Caversham.

25 Cross interviewed by the author, London, 1992.

26 *Daily Gleaner*, 11 May 1965, p. 12.

27 Egon and Ursula Larsen interviewed by the author, London, 1988.

28 *Ibid.*

29 Cecil Madden in a memo to Director of Empire Services, R. A. Randall, 15 May 1941, file E2/584, BBC written archives, Caversham.

30 *Ibid.*

31 Mary Treadgold in an interview, 18 October 1989.

32 *Ibid.*

33 *Ibid.*

34 Una Marson in a memo to John Grenfall Williams, 15 October 1941, file E2/584, BBC written archives, Caversham.

35 *Ibid.*

36 J. B. Clark to Mr Nicolson, 7 March 1942. Clark's concerns were shared by his colleagues, one of whom had earlier written: 'The speakers and the material available, the impossibility of having a large West Indian staff and the amateurishness that inevitably results from the introduction of a new programme run by an untrained official leaves scope for improvement.'

37 *Ibid.*

38 Mr Minsall, Information Officer, Port of Spain, Trinidad, in a letter to Cecil Madden, 25 October 1941, file E2/584, BBC written archives, Caversham.

39 R. A. Randall in a memo to Controller Overseas Services, 7 January 1942.

40 John Grenfall Williams, 'Service to the West Indies: Lady Davson's Criticisms', internal memo, 11 March 1942, E2/584, BBC written archives, Caversham.

41 *Ibid.*

42 Ernest Eytle of British Guiana was one of Una's broadcasters and was featured as 'Man About Town'.

43 Williams, 'Service to the West Indies'.

44 *Ibid.*

45 *Ibid.*

46 'Midnight Broadcast', *Glasgow Evening News*, 16 September 1942.

47 Cunard, 'Three British Personalities of Color', for the Associated Negro Press, Nancy Cunard papers, Chicago Historical Society, Chicago.

48 Malcolm Sergent in an interview with Una Marson, December 1942.

49 Cunard, 'Three British Personalities'.

50 *The Women's Institute*, broadcast West Indian Service, 6 May 1943, p. 5.

15

A Caribbean voice

IN NOVEMBER 1942 Una Marson contributed to *Voice*, a broadcast which had important consequences for her and for Caribbean writing. *Voice*, a six-part poetry magazine edited by Eric Blair (George Orwell) of the Indian Section, aimed to expose younger poets who 'have been handicapped by the paper shortage and whose work isn't as well known as it ought to be'. In several instances the poets themselves read extracts from their work, an innovation which broke with the old-fashioned format of literary broadcasts but also meant that problems sometimes arose in getting everyone around the microphone.

Una took part in the fourth programme. T. S. Eliot, who was to have appeared, was absent. This broadcast, devoted to American poetry, opened with William Empson reading 'The Burying Ground by the Ties' by Archibald McLeish, chosen to represent contemporary pioneering work. Expatriate America was then represented by a reading of Eliot's 'The Love Song of J. Alfred Prufrock'. The script, which has survived, then proceeded:

> Orwell: Again, we ought to have a bit of prose to balance that. But we
> haven't time. Before we go on to nineteenth century writers we must
> have something to represent the Negro writers.
> Marson: Well, there are James Weldon Johnson, Countee Cullen, Paul
> Laurence Dunbar …
> Orwell: But we'd like you to read something of your own. We are lucky
> in having a Negro writer with us in the studio today, Una Marson is
> her name. What do you think you could read us?
> Marson: Well, I've one here called 'Banjo Boy.' That might do. It's only
> short though.
> Orwell: All right, go ahead. Here it is. 'Banjo Boy.' This is Una Marson,

the West Indian writer, reading it.

Una Marson reads.[1]

For those with more than a cursory knowledge of African-American poetry, this scripted exchange was a pathetic window on that field and the impact of Una's reading 'Banjo Boy' might have been to suggest that minstrelsy and coyness characterised Black poetry:

Black boy,
How you play that banjo
Gee – it goes right to my toes

That was not, however, Una's sole experience on *Voice*. For the December programme she was featured alongside a cosmopolitan set of writers including M. J. Tambimuttu, a Tamil from Ceylon and Editor of *Poetry* in London, Mulk Raj Anand, Narayana Menon, William Empson and T. S. Eliot. Though a much reproduced photograph of this gathering survived, the script has not. The series was a great success and a further one was planned for spring 1943. Meanwhile Una set to work, devising a similiar programme which she called *Caribbean Voices*: it proved to be her most enduring and her most constructive creative invention.

Caribbean Voices, twenty-five minutes long, was first broadcast on BBC's West Indian service on 11 March 1943, with June Grimble as announcer and Cameron Tudor reading a short story by R. L. C. Aarons, 'Mrs Arroway's Joe'. The following week the late-night broadcast displayed a wider range of Caribbean authors, including Neville Guiseppe of Trinidad, John Wickham, Barbadian short-story writer and later editor of the influential literary magazine *Bim*, and Ruth Horner, a Jamaican poet. The Jamaican literary journals, Edna Manley's *Focus* and the Poetry League of Jamaica's yearbook for 1940 were used as sources. Constance Hollar, the Jamaican poet and an acquaintance of Una's, who had died earlier that year, was the subject of the third programme.

Wartime Britain was home to few West Indian writers; only published works could be used. In later years *Caribbean Voices*, particularly under the direction of Henry Swanzy, altered and improved its remit: unpublished work was sifted regionally. In Jamaica Cedric Gale Lindo worked through local contributions and sent the best to the BBC in London for critical appraisal. Una, with fewer contributors to hand, struggled to make it work, but the idea caught on and *Caribbean Voices* ran for fifteen years until 1958. In its heyday all the nascent talents of the region appeared, either reading or as short-term editors: George

Lamming, Sam Selvon, Edgar Mittelholzer, Andrew Salkey, Vidia Naipaul, Shake Keane and Edward Kamau Brathwaite. Many were sorry to see it end. Michael Anthony, the Trinidadian novelist who had been persuaded in 1954 by Vidia Naipaul to try to write short stories, and had his first, 'The Girl and the River', accepted early in 1955, surmised that 'naturally, English magazines were not so interested in West Indian stories'. For Edward Kamau Brathwaite, an authority on the oral tradition, *Caribbean Voices* was 'the single most important literary catalyst for Caribbean creative and critical writing in English', a 'tremendous archive' which 'alas, the BBC has [had to] scrub'.[2] The scripts survive, monument not only to its creator's belief but to the writers who, for the first time, were endowed with respectability, recognition and financial reward.

By the time *Caribbean Voices* came off the air, Una's creative work, like that of many Caribbean authors, had been noted in America and England, but at the start Anglo-American indifference had yet to be overcome. Her later assessment was that the programme was based on her own appreciation of

> our poets and short story writers ... during the war years, I introduced the programme called Caribbean Voices and invited all West Indian writers to contribute. BBC standards are high, but through the years the programme has been maintained and has provided an inspiring outlet for our writings.[3]

However great were the stresses of her BBC life, Una continued to write and promote her own poetry. In 1941 she wrote to Cecil Madden of an idea for 'something different in West Indian things ... a programme with poetry and music'. This, her own memo testifies, was an attempt to help others as much as herself:

> There's a boy medical student who is writing a good deal of poetry and has had some published. He could do a couple of short poems and I have had three books of poetry published and have written some war ones. ... I have done a recording for the London Transcription Scheme and could bring the record for you. Only perhaps on short wave it's not so good for poetry.[4]

Few of Una's poems were broadcast, including 'At the Prison Gates', a portrayal of Jamaican destitution, in September 1942 by Noel Sabine at the Colonial Office. Reassurance from the producer had been sent: 'it was clear that it was the period of depression'. Only her least contentious poems were heard on the air, many on the service *Calling West Africa*.

The racial isolation, pride and wartime zeal which characterise Una's war poems would not have been the qualities the BBC was seeking. 'Convoy', which appeared only in the League of Coloured Peoples' journal, *Newsnotes*,[5] is a narrative poem describing a walk during which she sees a truck convoy, lets it pass and observes that every man on board waves to her. Marson wrote:

> For they were my own blood brothers,
> Brown like me …
> And there souls were glad to greet me
> In the great white busy mart.
>
> Our gay hearts grown sad and wiser
> Stirred to life a second then
> A thousand words unsaid, were spoken –
> And we each took heart again
>
> Oh my brothers, in the conflict
> Of our own bewildered life
> How much strength we bring each other
> What fine courage for the strife.[6]

The mass of the BBC's written archives on Una Marson's literary programmes document her work with British authors whose contributions seemed to have been sought to educate Caribbean listeners to what were deemed to be appropriate standards. Under Una's aegis L. A. G. Strong, a novelist, short-story writer and experienced broadcaster, presented many programmes, including a series of talks, *Poetry in Times of War*, in spring 1942, and another on short-story writing. Una developed a productive relationship with Strong and he, understanding her requirements for West Indian broadcasts, tailored his material accordingly: 'Don't be put off by the antique spellings of the poems!', he reassured her, 'I'll make them intelligible and we can add any further explanation that may be needed or repeat a poem.'[7] They also discussed her proposal for fifteen-minute historical and dramatic sketches of West Indian subjects, an idea which appealed to Strong. Una had tried to get Louis MacNeice to do this, but without success.[8]

Not belonging to any literary club or clique, Una found her BBC work useful. When in spring 1944 she decided to put out another collection of her poems, Strong was approached to write a preface. There he revealed both the length and the nature of their acquaintanceship:

Some years ago I received a letter from the West Indies containing a few poems. The personality revealed in the letter made an immediate appeal to me and it was manifest in the poems. More letters followed and more poems. Then the correspondence ceased and I heard no more of Una Marson, till, to my great surprise, she wrote from the BBC and invited me to broadcast for her to the West Indies.[9]

Strong was not Una's first choice. In June 1944 Una had approached T. S. Eliot, but he declined. Fortunately for Una, at a time when she was probably feeling bereft of literary support, she made friends with Stella Mead, an English poet and short-story writer who had a special interest in Third World peoples and had travelled extensively. Among the titles of her many books were *Round the World Poetry* and *Tales from Many Lands* (1956). Stella helped Una select poems for the collection, and in June 1945 *Towards the Stars* was published by the University of London Press, which had also brought out several of Stella's books.

Slightly more than half the poems were culled from the earlier volumes. The collection was in three parts: 'Nature', 'Love' and 'Life'; but, unlike Una's earlier works, the ubiquitous lonely woman persona was hardly present. Instead, as the critic Erika Smilowitz has remarked, 'the new poems represent a triumph over a constricted, self-centred view of life'.[10] Marson expressed her anger over racial discrimination and her disillusionment at war. A personal and spiritual voice emerges in the penultimate poem, 'For There Will Come a Time', in which Una looks forward to racial equality and prophesies:

For there will come
A time when all the races of the earth,
Grown weary of the inner urge for gain,
Grown sick of all the fatness of themselves
And their boasted prejudice and pride,
Will see this vision[11]

A more acerbic note is sounded in 'Politeness':

They tell us
That our skin is black
But our hearts are white
We tell them
That their skin is white
But their hearts are black[12]

In spite of such occasional flashes of insight, the collection had a tired heaviness about it, which would seem to explain why Una's work did not find a larger audience. The *Times Literary Supplement* briefly noted the collection and it was mentioned in the *World's Children*, the Save the Children Fund journal. Haydn Perry in the *Teachers' World and Schoolmistress* called it 'splendid stuff', some poems being 'as primitive as the island of Jamaica on which the authoress was born; others are pure Song of Solomon or W. H. Davis in outlook'.[13] Una, by this time, was too depressed to ruminate over whether her work appeared 'primitive' or whether she and Davis shared a poetic vision.

Towards the Stars had been compiled at a time when Una was feeling lonely, insecure and unloved. Romance had not completely eluded her. In 1941 Una had met and fallen in love with a Jamaican RAF man, Flight-Lieutenant Dudley Thompson, who was serving in Bomber Command. Over the next two years they 'got to know each other very well', and Una was happy, but, having assumed this was the beginning of a lasting, permanent relationship, was to be wretchedly disappointed at its demise.[14]

When Dudley Thompson arrived in England in June 1941 he was twenty-four, twelve years younger than Una. A bright and ambitious young man, educated at Mico College, Jamaica, he won a Rhodes scholarship to Oxford where he read law at Merton after the war. RAF duties took him away from London, but during his secondment to the Colonial Office, where he worked as a liaison officer, he was within easier reach of Una. At that time she was flat-sharing in West Hampstead with Linda Edwards. Theirs was not a place renowned for privacy and, as Dudley Thompson saw it, he counted himself as one of many to welcome their congeniality: 'We all came there to entertain her, take her out, dine and wine. ... [It was] more than a club house, less than a family house. She shared her home; she welcomed us all ... Una cooked, but Linda was a better cook.'[15]

Home entertaining apart, Una, displaying a healthy capacity for enjoying a closer relationship, was seeing quite a lot of Dudley. They went to nightclubs, dinner dances at Crystal Palace and the Caribbean club at Piccadilly, and on one occasion to visit a Scottish friend of his, the mother of an ex-gunner who had died in battle. In private Una cut a picture of undiluted femininity: soft, romantic, 'a woman of refinement'.[16] She liked to stretch out on the rug by the fire, reading her own or Countee Cullen's poetry to him; and she read very well. Although she 'never understood money, Una lived like a rich worldly woman, veering towards the extravagant'.[17] She loved to shop locally, had clothes and alterations done for her by a seamstress and bought lots of clothes in the West End, as well as jewellery from a classy Bond Street store. Her taste called for flamboyance, grandeur, richness and loveliness. It was one of the obvious benefits of being in love.

The best way to appreciate Una's love for Dudley would have been to read her many 'long, intimate, love letters planning what we could do together after the war'. Sadly, none has survived. Una sent billets-doux 'almost daily, including poems, many of them unpublished, and written on violet paper, her own personal stationery'.[18] She was very open, delighting him with anecdotes about her work and travels, and sharing her hopes for the future. Dudley was 'not quite as responsive'.

In later life Dudley Thompson became chairman of the People's National Party,[19] the maturation of early political ambitions which, in his view, led to the end of his relationship with Una: 'At that stage of the war, I was preoccupied with the Pan-African movement and I got deeper into its activities. My circle has included Kenyatta, Padmore, Nkrumah ... . I grew away from the literary group.'[20] In July 1944 he married Genevieve Hannah Cezair, a surgeon's daughter, and inevitably, lost contact with Una who he thought had been 'very disappointed that we did not marry'.[21]

Una spun her feelings of disappointment into a cool, classic defiance, warning in the title poem of *Towards the Stars*:

Man must stand
Alone
Firmly planted
in Humanity
and grow
Towards the stars.

Here she contends that the desire to be attached is a sign of cowardice; this was because companionship, her preferred option, no longer seemed feasible. Nevertheless, in this fourth collection, the lonely woman persona has been supplanted. Una's tone is more philosophical, less individualistic, less constricted.

Frozen Winter 1941

The heart of humanity is frozen.
It is too cold for Poets to sing.

Una Marson's dominant image or idea was the need for independence and resilience. It was expressed in varying tones, sometimes ironic, sometimes tragic or sarcastic. 'The test of true culture', she wrote in one verse, 'The Test':

> Is the ability
> To move among men,
> East or West
> North or South
> With ease and confidence
> Radiating the pure light
> Of a kindly humanity.

The lighter side of life in wartime Britain found no place in Una's poetry. She felt she had been dropped like a bomb. She observed instead that ambitious men now 'seek their prey / In darkness', and demonstrated in 'They Also Serve' her alertness to racial politics. Una's attitude to being black in Britain, like Nigerian novelist Buchi Emecheta in *Second Class Citizen* (1974), was that of a disillusioned colonial who had entirely abandoned her belief in an egalitarian England.

Una had written this well-balanced poem, 'Black Burden':

> I am black
> And so I must be
> More clever than white folks
> More wise than white folks
> More discreet than white folks
> More courageous than white folks
>
> I am black
> And I have got to travel
> Even further than white folks
> For time moves on.[22]

It is not strange that Una, appallingly run down in spirits, should have resorted to such harsh verdicts on the human condition, even though her pain was occasionally lifted by other friends. Relationships and friendships may be demanding, but they are also essential. During 1944 Una continued to look to her many West Indian companions for solace and fun; she dropped into nightclubs and dance-halls but they sometimes failed to provide remission from feelings of emptiness, leaving her sharply aware of her mental and spiritual isolation, and longing to see Jamaica again.

Una was now living at 44 Lancaster Gate in Bayswater, west London. She had the top-floor flat in a dingy, untidy block, and just her two cats for permanent company, though servicemen and students frequently dropped by. She was surrounded by people, but as to a faulty magnet they came to her without adhering: every day no fewer than twenty-five West Indians could be seen hanging about her BBC office, and usually on returning home she found others waiting for her there too. She never left the prison of her depression and once on Wednesday 10 August 1944, a summer's day which brought her nervous energy to a pitch, she tried to find comfort in the outside world. That was a day off work. It had been a quiet night with only 'very slight enemy interference', and until midnight she'd been reading Somerset Maugham's latest book, *The Razor's Edge*. It was a mystical tale about an American, Larry Darrell, who goes to India, stays in an ashram and learns the value of non-attachment. It was a salutary tale. Sunlight entering the room caused her to stir and then the kittens, Sabu and Roma, purring loud enough to wake the dead, made their entrance.

Out on the landing, in search of her newspaper, Una hoped that the cleaner, who was busy polishing the tiles downstairs, would bring it up later, at her own convenience. She came back into the flat, listened to the news 'at dictation speed' and decided to walk down the 120 steps to fetch the paper herself, before a modest breakfast; having missed the shops on Saturday, she had no rations but for a little American dried eggs, but

> Sabu and Roma won't eat it however I cook it, so why take the trouble to cook it for myself alone. Ah! there were some prunes I soaked. They'd boil quickly. Well on with the kettle and the prunes. Tea and bread and prunes ... an excellent breakfast and what with the vitamins from the sun.

Settling to read the paper, Una forgot the kettle and the prunes, which had burnt, and had to go out to buy provisions. It was going to be a day of sweet idling. She took the bus across town to her dressmaker's house, and found in the empty workroom the brightly coloured dress fabric she had left to be made up. Rediscovering it, she reflected that marriage might have robbed her of the freedom to wear such gaudy colours: 'God is good', she had told one such impoverished friend, 'He spares me from husbands.' But Una's prayer was showing ambivalence: a moment later her thoughts turned to Rosenstein, her Austrian male friend, and she found herself mollifying her agitated spirit with 'some tempting cakes' from a Viennese cake shop, and the purchase of some 'early chrysanths and coreopsis'.

Although Una professed to dislike smoke, drink and 'the kind of place where people get closely matey', she called at two nightclubs but, finding both closed, spent the early evening strolling:

> There was a strange violence, an unrest, a blind misery deep down in my heart. But the trees seemed to breathe a deeper peace. A brace of bombers returning from a mission flew overhead scarcely distinguishable from a brace of birds, as they soared higher and higher in formation. For a moment all the hate and death and tumult of war held me to the earth in a sharp agony.

Walking past the allotments, all of which were worked by middle-aged people, a story which was said to typify the difference between the English and the French occurred to her. When a middle-aged English woman consulted her doctor, the latter suggested taking up gardening, but a French woman would be advised to take a lover. Una, in her late thirties, judged herself unable to face 'the agony of the one, [or] the patience and peace of the other' and ended this day off typing alone in her west London loft.[23]

It is ironic that Una, who at twenty filled books with poetry of unrequited love, was nearly forty before she knew how it felt. All she could do was to sit in the lap of unhappiness, because a mixture of hurt pride and infantile regression told her there was no way out. She needed a good friend, but since there was no confidante and she was confused, tired and tense, a deepening melancholy was massaging her soul.

The friends who came to Bayswater were appalled by what they saw. The Larsens, visiting Una's new abode, were no less critical of, and baffled by, her taste in decoration. 'She had put up a picture of Jesus which follows you with its eyes' which Egon judged 'the worst painting of kitsch'. Another friend to be taken aback at what she saw as the drab discomfort of Una's room, which contained only the bare necessities, was Mary Treadgold.

Mary made only one visit to Una's Bayswater home. One night, in desperation, Una called Mary to come over. She came with their mutual friend Scott Goddard, the music critic. The flat was dark, cold and dreary. The watchful eyes of Una's guests found plenty to peer at: it was a dark, squalid little room, furnished with only the cheap and rickety bits and pieces the landlord could spare. On the bed lay Una crying out in torment. In pained and slightly blurred voice, Una said she would phone for further help. Mary saw the sick young woman, distraught and near the end of her endurance and in that moment she sensed 'a hint of suicide':

> Una was definitely seeing a psychiatrist because she rang him in my presence, at my urgency, that night I spent with her. ... I think she got rather a dusty answer. I don't know who it was, but I rather gather that he said, 'Well, I'm seeing you in a couple of days, aren't I?' and that wasn't what Una needed. She needed consoling.

Unconsoled, Una tossed and turned all night, muttering to herself, her words unclear, her thoughts disarrayed. At daybreak Scott Goddard and Mary Treadgold left when at last they felt she could be safely left to rest: 'I know we both shivered as we went out into the very cold dawn.' Years later, in recollecting the horror of that night, Mary Treadgold did not find its telling easy. In Jamaica there has been considerable speculation about Una's mental stability; some people have wondered if she were mad. The truth was a little more complicated. Una suffered 'ordinary depression', but it was deep and terrifying. In her loneliness after Dudley's apparent abandonment, a war-time of being emotionally targeted and years of self-doubt, that depression came out of the closet. Una was honest with herself and with her friends. She never shied away from disclosing her depression even in public. It is a paradox and an enchantment that a woman who doubted herself so easily was so frank about what many called her flaws.

Christmas 1944 found her still solitary, homesick and troubled: 'it is the coldest Christmas in 50 years and, perhaps I might add', she told her listeners on *Calling the West Indies*, 'the saddest too'. She was two months away from forty, that mystical middle age, and anxious about her future. Sufficiently herself, nevertheless, to realise what action she had to take, Una started to make plans for 1945. More at ease, in late summer 1945, she reminisced:

> I felt that somehow I must leave London and come to the West Indies. I wanted to get away from the cold and the atmosphere of war, but more than anything else I wanted to come to the West Indies to meet as many people as possible to whom I had been speaking for nearly five years. I asked for permission to come, feeling very definitely that I could not go on broadcasting to you without learning about life in other islands of the West Indies I had not visited before. When permission was granted for me to do so I was overwhelmed with joy.[24]

On 14 July 1945 Una left England for a three-month trip to the West Indies via New York. She was combining a well-earned vacation with a special job for the BBC, wrote the *Daily Gleaner* shortly after her arrival in Jamaica in mid-August. Her major tasks were to research listeners' opinions of the current broadcasts and to scout for new programme ideas for the postwar era.

The crossing between London and New York lasted a fortnight, but Una arrived in the USA feeling 'fit and strong'. Staying a week in New York to visit friends such as the Reverend R. O. C. King, who was about to take up his new post as chaplain to the Archbishop of the West Indies, Una went on to Washington where she had work to do. She took part in a broadcast, on the West Indian Newsreel in which William Harris, known as 'the Vagabond Traveller', was the main presenter. The West Indian programme, while not as highly respected as Una's *Calling the West Indies*, had won approval in the region for training West Indian personnel: assisting Harris was Gerry De Freitas, manager of ZOI in British Guiana. Work also brought her into contact with Dr Eric Williams, secretary of the Research Council of the Anglo-American Caribbean Commission, the organisation sponsoring the training scheme, an exemplary programme which, according to one Guyanese paper, the BBC needed to emulate.

Una felt that travelling in the United States afforded her 'a wonderful opportunity to study Jamaicans in another country among other people'.[25] She had wanted to see the Jamaican farm workers based in Miami, but failed to do so; instead she enjoyed the city and, while awaiting passage home, frequently ambled around the centre which was decorated 'to great advantage' with tropical flowers. Another, more palpable reason for her reinforcing contacts in the United States was the syndication arrangement which she maintained for articles with the Associated Negro Press, the news agency for which she had written during the early 1930s. Now, a decade later, Claude A. Barnett wrote to thank her for articles which she had written for the British Information Services while in London reminding her that 'this channel is always open to you'.[26]

Just as the Second World War was ending, Una arrived in Jamaica on 14 August, after a seven-year absence from the island. She was pleased to be back home since she had come to feel increasingly out of touch with the island's progress, a shortcoming which she had to address given her broadcasting responsibilities. In her absence the political thinkers of the West Indian region had moved towards more open government. Everywhere in the region constitutions were being changed to increase local participation, following the 1930s labour rebellions and the Moyne Commission. Universal adult suffrage was granted to Jamaica in 1944, to Trinidad in 1945; Barbados would follow in 1950 and Guyana in 1953. The leaders of the new trade unions were the incumbent premiers and ministers, Norman Manley and Alexander Bustamente in Jamaica, Eric Williams in Trinidad, Grantley Adams in Barbados. Among these men the idea of a regional federation was, temporarily at least, very attractive both in commercial terms and because the Colonial Office had created several regional organisations. Una's BBC job was similarly shaped. And the last thing that she would have wanted was to find herself out of step with her listeners and broadcasters. She was very well prepared against such an eventuality and had decided to talk to West Indians of every shade of opinion and of every national group, and to procure as much West Indian literature as possible from the entire region for use in future programmes. With the end of the war, broadcasting was to be given a face-lift: message parties and even light musical entertainment could no longer be a staple part of the service.

Family and friends were welcoming, but this was not a private time. Una had become an icon. Everywhere she went, huge crowds gathered as though she were royalty. She was 'given a rousing applause by 100 children at a Save the Children Fund Fair at Bournemouth';[27] at a cocktail party at the Women's Club at Half Way Tree, there were many speeches eulogising her work and her influence on local literature.[28] Almost daily her name was in the papers with reports of her every engagement: 'Una Marson returned in Wednesday's deluge from Portland and last evening was the honour guest [sic] at the Jamaica Press Association club where members gave a cocktail party for her', reported the *Sunday Gleaner* on 2 September. And so on.[29]

The nature of these gatherings was broadly similar; tributes and flowers were followed by Una's own speech in which she always praised the West Indian servicemen, though she once expressed the view that 'more could have been done in giving them support such as the formation of a West Indian Service club'.[30] Everyone wanted to hear about England, her BBC work and the Blitz. Una obliged: she had always put her faith in God and if he wanted her to live she would live and if he wanted her to die she would die, she told people.[31] Terrifying though it was, Una had coped well with the Blitz and even remembered laughing out loud while reading Damon Runyon in her blacked-out apartment one night.

Old friendships and old contacts came together at the end of the war, just as soldiers returned to their families and loves. Una was glad to see Edna Manley, the sculptor wife of Norman, at the Poetry League lunch held in her honour at the South Camp Road Hotel, to chat with Roger Mais, the novelist, and spend time with Edith and Ethel. Una had become sentimental about Jamaica and her devotion stretched to her family: 'I owe a great deal to my home and my parents and ... my father who shaped my poetic thought.'[32] This was the only indication that her father had become a figure in Una's mind who had actively enhanced her chances of freedom and expression. More than thirty years after his death she was uncovering another truth about his strong personality. When the war in Europe was over in May 1945, Una had been far from her people and felt the emotional exhaustion of a discontented exile. She had also felt pride and satisfaction in the way she had behaved: her poise, her calm professionalism. She admitted to foolishly underrating herself, and now, with a more favourable evaluation of her own abilities and power, she was able to give Solomon Marson a fairer farewell.

At the beginning of October her long-planned tour of the islands began when she set off for Trinidad, travelling via Nassau, Bahamas. Here she spent two glorious days, before reaching Port of Spain, by Royal Air Force Command plane on 3 October. Her host in Trinidad, where she stayed nearly a fortnight, was Audrey Jeffers, the President of the Coterie of Social Workers, whom Una had first met back in 1932 in London. Audrey Jeffers, who in 1936 had become the first Trinidadian woman to contest and win a municipal seat, had her chauffeured round the island. Writers, social workers and schoolchildren turned out to greet her at community centres at Siparia, San Fernando, La Brea and Point Fortin. At Princes Town she met poet and songwriter Harold Telemaque who eagerly pressed his manuscripts into Una's hands, and she promised to airmail them to the BBC.

The exchange of views was brilliant for both parties. Telemaque suggested critical commentaries to accompany broadcasts of West Indian poetry, an idea which in time became the standard format on *Caribbean Voices*. Una silenced everyone with talk about the BBC and later talked with the Trinidad Authors and Writers Association run by Ernest Carr. Little had changed for Caribbean writers since she had begun *The Cosmopolitan* nearly twenty years earlier. Carr's house at the edge of some magnificent forest in Belmont was a beehive for Trinidadian authors like George Lamming and Edgar Mittelholzer, whose first novel, *Corentyne Thunder*, had appeared in 1941. One

Saturday afternoon at Audrey Jeffers's house at Sweet Briar Road Una persuaded the group to set up their own little magazine and co-operate with similar West Indian literary groups such as her own Readers and Writers Club. These were seemingly elementary ideas but they indicate how frail the current infrastructure was. That December, two months after Una's visit, a Christmas edition of such a magazine was planned.[33] In this way Una was building bridges among West Indian writers and the broadcast media, though she already doubted that England would give them a positive response.[34]

Una consistently and firmly pressured West Indians to be co-operative and self-reliant. She found Trinidad exhilarating, she told friends, and was preparing for the cut and thrust of conversational debate in British Guiana, where racial segregation was topical and controversial. Once she arrived in Georgetown on 18 October she found herself in the middle of a debate about federation and racialised organisations. Although she found politics, in the narrow sense, boring, she had long advocated a form of West Indian federation. 'Let us have a League of Progressive People and not a League of Coloured Peoples or any one set of peoples. Let us have a League of all progressive people so that in time all who are outside can be deemed to be unprogressive', she told them. Ulric Cross thought it was now a live and practical reality mainly because of

> Miss Marson's tactful leadership and generous hospitality. In her flat in London and by reason of the mysterious chemistry of her personality, West Indians in England from varying islands have been knit together in a common brotherhood in which baser rivalries have yielded place to common aims and objects.[35]

Luckily for Una her West Indies tour continued to draw out not only writers but the region's literary entrepreneurs, cultural societies and British Council people, many of whom were tempted by the bait of an improved service in exchange for their 'poems, short stories and music'.[36] In Georgetown, British Guiana, the poet and editor Arthur J. Seymour, whose journal, *Kyk-over-al*, was launched that year, met her at the airport. *Kyk-over-al*, named after the ruins of a Dutch fort, which form a prominent landmark over the Esssequibo river, was in Seymour's words 'Strange name for stone, a heap of stones, / But a strong name to take imagination'.[37] It was nearly the end of October when Una arrived at Bridgetown, Barbados, where she met the Barbados Arts and Crafts Society, the historian and poet H. A. Vaughn and

Grantley Adams, the Oxford-trained lawyer who became Prime Minister in 1958. She had been on the road for two hard months and welcomed a quiet rest on the quiet beaches.[38] But it was Grenada which she liked the best. Grenada, a small island in the Windward group, was, like Barbados to the west, a part of the British West Indies Una had not expected to visit during this tour. Una stayed at the Douglas Hotel for nearly a week during which she made several guest appearances: at a Society of Arts concert at which all the local dignitaries were present, a speech to the Youth Council and another to the Grenada Boys Secondary School. And on the evening of 1 November the market square was thronging with people who had come to hear the Caribbean celebrity make her farewell speech to the islanders.[39] She liked the architecture of St George's, the capital, its eighteenth-century provincial houses intermingled with fine English Georgian properties and terraces of pale colour-washed houses and the red roofs. As Una looked down on St George's at night from Richmond Hill she recalled a similar vantage point on the Isle of Capri. The steep hills and sparkling blue harbour of St George's were the most beautiful she had seen in her travels.

When she arrived back in Kingston on 19 November, Una confirmed to reporters the trip's success: 'They all seemed to have followed the programmes as I found they knew a lot about the broadcasts.'[40] She felt confident that broadcasting could be reshaped for the Caribbean and, although June Grimble, the daughter of the Governor of the Windward Islands, was deputising for her during her tour, Una assumed that she would resume her normal duties once she returned to London. At the end of the month she was back in England.

In five months Una had travelled more than two thousand miles since she had had to go via Trinidad to reach the smaller islands, zig-zagging across the archipelago several times over. She had made numerous speeches, shaken hands here and there, gathered scripts and made promises to many a hopeful author. The travelling had been tiring. In the Caribbean the sea is more a barrier than a thoroughfare; contact between the islands was poor. Only a missionary-style zeal would have persuaded a traveller to do so much in so short a time. By the time Una returned to the BBC, her energies were already spent.

Her friends, especially the fellow writer Stella Mead who lived out in Wembley, were struck by her tired-looking face and worried about her health. Una's exhaustion was real. She found that work was beyond her. Her heavy schedule and her ill-health only increased

Una's tensions. Melancholy started to descend and this only exacerbated her sense of isolation. No sooner had she settled down at the BBC again than she had to leave once more, retreating to a country nursing home.

The saviour of the day was Stella Mead, to whom Una had dedicated *Towards the Stars*. She saw how unusual Una looked, how her hands shook and how thoughts darted about her mind in a crazy whirl. Una was in the first phase of a paralysing depression which would keep her out of the world's eye for years. The fact that Stella had to arrange for Clare McFarlane, who was visiting England in April 1946, to take Una back to Jamaica is only testament to her broken spirit.[41]

NOTES

1 Quoted by W. J. West in *Orwell: the War Broadcasts* (London, Duckworth and BBC, 1985).
2 *History of the Voice* (London, New Beacon Books, 1984), p. 87.
3 Una Marson, *Sunday Gleaner*, date unknown, c. 1962.
4 'Notes to Mr Maddon about coloured artists from Una Marson' (undated) but c. January 1941.
5 'Convoy', *Newsnotes* no. 67, April 1945, p. 8.
6 *Ibid.*
7 See L. A. G. Strong talks file, BBC written archives, Caversham. Also file 3b for letter.
8 'Dramatic Historical Sketches for Calling the West Indies', Una Marson memo to John Grenfall Williams, 18 March 1942, L. A. G. Strong talks file 3b, BBC written archives, Caversham.
9 Strong, Preface to *Towards the Stars* (London, University of London Press, 1945).
10 Ericka Smilowitz, 'Marson, Rhys and Mansfield', Ph.D. thesis, University of New Mexico, 1984, chapter 4, p. 131.
11 'There Will Come a Time', *Towards the Stars*, pp. 62–3.
12 'Politeness', *Towards the Stars*, p. 44.
13 'Una Marson's Poems Win Praise in UK', quoted in *Sunday Guardian*, Trinidad, 18 November 1945, p. 4.
14 Dudley Thompson interviewed by the author, March 1990, Kingston, Jamaica.
15 *Ibid.*
16 *Ibid.*
17 *Ibid.*
18 *Ibid.*
19 By the 1960s Dudley Thompson had become a distinguished lawyer, politician and diplomat. In 1983 he was chairman of the PNP.
20 Dudley Thompson interview.
21 *Ibid.*

22 'Black Burden', *Towards the Stars*.

23 All quotations from 'A Summer's Day' 10 August 1944, Una Marson papers, Box 1944B, National Library of Jamaica.

24 'Citizens Give Una Marson a Rousing Public Reception', *West Indian*, 5 November 1945, p. 2.

25 'Una Marson on Visit Home', *Daily Gleaner*, 18 August 1945, p. 15.

26 Claude A. Barnett to Una Marson, 17 October 1945, ANP Papers, Chicago Historical Society.

27 See the *Daily Gleaner*, for example 15 September 1945, p. 16, 'Cocktail Party for Miss Una Marson', and 17 September 1945, p. 10, 'Hundred Children Attend Fair at Bournemouth'.

28 'Press Association Pays Tribute to Una Marson', *Daily Gleaner*, 3 September 1945, p. 8. See also 'Poetry League to Honour Miss Marson at Luncheon', *Daily Gleaner*, 6 September 1945, p. 9.

29 *Ibid.*

30 *Daily Gleaner*, 10 September 1945, p. 12.

31 *Ibid.*

32 *Daily Gleaner*, 10 September 1945, p. 12, 'Literary Re-union at South Camp Road Hotel'.

33 'West Indian Literary Magazine Urged', *Sunday Guardian* (Trinidad), 14 October 1945, p. 7. See also 'Authors Group Agree to Print Xmas Magazine', *Sunday Guardian* (Trinidad), 18 November 1945, p. 3.

34 'Authors Group Agree'.

35 *West Indian*, 24 October 1945, leader column, 'Coming Visitor'.

36 *Daily Argosy*, 19 October 1945, 'Brighter BBC Service for West Indies and British Guiana', p. 2.

37 Arthur J. Seymour, *Over Guinea, Clouds* (Georgetown, British Guiana, Demerera Standard, 1954).

38 'West Indian Member of BBC Arrives', *Barbados Advocate*, 29 October 1945, p. 9.

39 'Citizens Give Una Marson a Rousing Public Reception'.

40 'Jamaica's BBC Announcer Back from West Indies Tour', *Daily Gleaner*, 22 November 1945, p. 11. See also 'West Indian RAF Men Find Colonial Office Not as Helpful as They Were Given to Expect', *Daily Gleaner*, 24 November 1945, p. 10.

41 Una Marson work profile, Foreign General file, BBC written archives, Caversham.

16

Silenced and depressed

A T T H E BBC there was some speculation over Una's sudden dis-
appearance. More than two years elapsed before Una wrote a
casual and brief version of events to her former colleague, George
Orwell: 'I suppose that the last you heard of me was that I had
returned to London from my hectic West Indies tour, had a nervous
breakdown and had to return to Jamaica to find rest and recovery.'[1]
Some of those more closely involved with the West Indian service
heard a more outlandish story, as Henry Swanzy, producer of
Caribbean Voices in the 1950s, was to relate:

> She was unwell and she tried to commit suicide. I think so – it may have
> been gossip but I think she was unwell. I remember that when Clare
> McFarlane, a sort of boss man of Jamaican poetry (he was crowned
> with a lignum vitae as a poet laureate, really), came over to take her
> back to Jamaica, but she didn't want to go … . this has some relevance
> but she didn't want to go and so she arrived too late for the boat and
> the boat had sailed from Liverpool and was sailing down the Mersey
> and they got a motor boat or something and brought poor old Una …
> and so she was brought back by Clare McFarlane.[2]

For almost two years, Una Marson, like a discarded war veteran,
was out of public circulation. At first she was just holding on at her sister Etty's house in Kingston. Her friendships slipped into the dark; Una
was unable to emerge from her home. She had taken so much time and
trouble over the job, the tour and her research and it had all come to
nothing. She felt the influence of an unjust world that told her she
could hold on no longer. About a month after her return to Kingston
Una was admitted to Bellevue Mental Hospital for rest and observation. This was a time of relief and release from all her pain. The anger

and resentment which she had stored from her years in England, the ambivalent feelings about her parents long dead and her fear about her own uncertain future, engulfed her. Una's complex grief, her shouts and tears, were mingled with calm and sleep. Ritchie Riley, a trainee psychologist who saw her at Bellevue, would never forget how 'She was quiet, depressive at times, then she'd get noisy, have to have her own way and then she'd quieten down again. We were all sad about that because we knew her from her work and admired her.'[3]

She was unwell for months with a series of aches, pains, depressions and moody days. A diagnosis was not made, and to all intents and purposes she was suffering just depression. There have, nevertheless, been many suggestions about Una's mental state, ranging from the belief that she was a schizophrenic to the notion that she was a manic depressive. No medical records have survived to indicate whether either view is correct. Among those who knew her well there is a consensus that Una was merely depressed.

Una had exhausted herself through overwork, stress and war fatigue. Unfortunately something unfair and frightening had been afoot when she returned to the BBC. She had desperately tried to hold on to her job, but then it seemed her juniors, Mary Treadgold and June Grimble, were flying up beyond her reach. Finally, she had given up hope: no more laughter with her West Indian service pals (they had gone home); no relationship, no secure work, not even the prospect of a publication. Una had been the darling of the West Indian group: Ulric Cross had commented on what wonders she worked among them all with 'the mysterious chemistry of her personality'; but now the potent magic was waning.

Una never did go back to the BBC after the war to put her research into action, nor did she recover the links with the servicemen or writers whose confidence she had won. This change was a measure of how the war had charged up her life and animated her vulnerable spirit and then deserted her, like so many other women, forced to change direction, with her sense of identity in tatters. How was she to recover within the bare walls of Bellevue, without the comfort of personal belongings and close friends, without familiar bits and pieces that for most people signify a sense of security and sense of self? If the physical environment offered no exit, at least her mind, creating its own renaissance, would.

Una's memory, the most precious part of her tired mind, was restimulated by some of the sounds and scents of Jamaica: holidays at

Oracabessa; the wide and white sands by the cascading Dunns River Falls; the smell of freshly baked patties bought on the roadside; the silver-grey mocking bird singing high up in the poinciana tree; the scent of coffee being parched outside the kitchen at Sharon. These sensual thoughts were her salvation, the backcloth to a new scene in her life-story.

When she finally recovered, in early 1948, Una left 'hectic, political and utterly hard'[4] Kingston for the countryside haunts that made her feel happier and rejuvenated. 'I literally drank milk and honey and ate fruit of every kind and swallowed hundreds of vitamin tablets to cure a very aenamic (I don't know how to spell it) condition', reported Una in a letter to George Orwell.[5] In the spring of 1948 her days of isolation, fear and despondency were, for the time being, ended.

Towards the end of the preceding year, 1947, Jamaica's literati had been enthralled by two influential visiting editors: Langston Hughes, the black American poet, was in town in October 1947 meeting all the major writers and prospective candidates for his anthology *Poetry of the Negro 1746–1949*, while a literary speculator from London, Robert Herring, editor of *Life and Letters* and a personal friend of Edna Manley, came in January 1948. In November 1948 Herring published a special Jamaican edition.

Una missed both editors and, though her friend Vivian Virtue compensated by giving Langston Hughes copies of her books, his accounts of the eminent visit failed to eradicate completely the regret over her two-year crisis. In November 1948 she affirmed to Hughes: 'I can only say how truly sorry I am that I was then too ill to see you. I missed seeing you in London too. Still I console myself with the thought that all things come to those who wait if they wait long enough.'[6] Little could dull her enjoyment of Sharon, Santa Cruz, which she hadn't set eyes on for years: 'It was so refreshing. ... I was so emotionally overcome', she wrote remembering the elderly church ladies who had praised her geniality, intelligence and charm.[7] The passing months brought her back to health. She made leisurely visits to St Ann, where the air was so good and early morning walks were a treat; she shopped in the 'lovely clean market and bought all kinds of fruit and liver at 1/- per pound and cooked it myself'. She was excited by the irresistible market stalls with their colourful displays of yellow yams and sweet potatoes, scale and calalu. Jamaica seemed so attractive again: a half-familiar world to be rediscovered. She felt the need to visit different parts of the island, treating herself. She bathed at Discovery Bay, went to Falmouth where the new Knibb Memorial Church was being built in honour of the Baptist missionary, and spent two weeks in 'Port Antonio the beautiful'.[8]

Her ailing confidence received a welcome boost when in summer she learnt that Langston Hughes had chosen two of her poems, 'Nightfall' and 'Hunted', for *Poetry of the Negro*. Nervous at first about how to approach Doubleday, the prestigious American publishing house, after dealing with modest local operations, Una, along with other writers, wrote to ask the meaning of the term 'credit line'. Vivian Virtue, in frequent and effusive contact with Langston Hughes, apologised for 'our ignorance of such matters this end'[9] and said later, when dispatching publicity photographs: 'If the Una Marson picture is not too defaced after the reproducing block is made, and you do not specially want to keep it, I think she would like to have it back as she does not have another copy, and it is her favourite picture.'[10]

Later in the year, as befitted a parson's daughter, Una passed one week at the Calabar Theological College and High School, attending a re-armament conference for Baptist young people, and joined the summer school at Knox College, a new college opened in the hills by 'a very enlightened young Glasgow Presbyterian minister and his wife, Reverend Lewis Davidson'. 'Going to these places and meeting such a fine set of young people (particularly the women) has given me great hopes for our future', Una informed Randall at the BBC towards the end of August.[11] Una did her best to make do with the local cultural scene, but she felt anxious about her career. As the summer months ebbed away, she started to sound out her former boss on the question of survey-listening: 'Please let me know if you want me to go ahead with my regular listening, or survey of news. Of course I don't want to "cramp the style" of Mrs Lindo, who does your publicity but you'll know best.'[12]

Out of sight for two years, away from the island for seven, Una was preparing with an almost regal conviction to resume her place within the island's cultural life. On 2 October she gave a witty speech at the Poetry League's silver jubilee dinner, 'a brilliant affair', wrote Vivian Virtue in a letter to Langston Hughes, who had sent a congratulations telegram. The dinner, held at South Camp Road Hotel, with some fifty-five people attending, including many writers, poets and artists and lasting until the early hours, was a fitting occasion for reminiscing. Her social life was in other ways looking up: Paul Robeson (with the FBI tracking him) came to Kingston in November 1948 and sang to a large appreciative audience at the racecourse: 'It's a great inspiration to us to have him here', Una told Langston Hughes.[13] At a house party the previous weekend Robeson had recited Hughes's 'Freedom Train'.

'I was very thrilled with the poem itself', Una told Langston, 'and with Paul's wonderful presentation of it. Can you send me any of your poems? I haven't any of your publications.'[14] With the triumphs of her peers so luminously evident, Una looked forward to a brighter future for herself; perhaps in two years' time she might be standing before American audiences reading her own poetry. Langston Hughes could have told her what to expect in the United States. The American literary world would have been curious about Una's work, but perhaps no more so than the English. The truth was that Una was desperate to forge ahead with a new venture; entertainment was becoming a sterile option.

Although her BBC career was formally over, Una's former colleagues in London had not written her off. Closer to home her talents were not so fully valued and acknowledged. During her tour of the West Indies in 1945 she had mentioned in Grenada – at a moment of confident anticipation – that she would like to work in Caribbean broadcasting, but this wish never came to fruition. It was rumoured that the Jamaican broadcasting chiefs had retailed several derogatory remarks about her, saying her 'voice wasn't good enough'; this was probably a mark of jealousy.[15] Nevertheless, with her assured grasp of West Indian culture, literature and politics and her experience of broadcasting Una was still prized back at 200 Oxford Street, the BBC's head office. Once he heard of her recovery, John Grenfall Williams wrote asking her to

> send us something for *Caribbean Voices*. I shall also be very glad if from time to time you will let us have your own comments about this programme. It struggles along against great difficulties but I am sure it is worthwhile if only to give West Indian writers an outlet for the talent which undoubtedly does exist.[16]

The debate about the value and function of *Caribbean Voices* during Marson's period and after persists into the 1990s, recurring on the publication of such books as Edward Kamau Brathwaite's study of the oral tradition in Caribbean poetry, *History of the Voice* (1984). Henry Swanzy, producer of the programme during the 1950s, is fairly credited for maintaining and strengthening this sophisticated catalyst for the region's writers. But as critics, researchers and writers continue to exchange memories, facts and opinions, it has become clear how accurately Una Marson, its architect, assessed Caribbean literary promise and how rarely she has been thanked.[17]

NOTES

1   Una Marson to George Orwell, 2 April 1949, George Orwell Archive, University College London.
2   Henry Swanzy interviewed by the author, 7 June 1988, Bishop's Stortford.
3   Ritchie Riley interviewed by the author, 1990.
4   Una Marson to George Orwell, 2 April 1949.
5   *Ibid.*
6   Una Marson to Langston Hughes, 20 November 1948, Langston Hughes papers, Beinecke Rare Book and Manuscript Library, Yale University, New Haven, Connecticut.
7   Una Marson to George Orwell, 2 April 1949.
8   *Ibid.*
9   Vivian Virtue to Langston Hughes, 31 August 1948, Langston Hughes papers, Beinecke Rare Book and Manuscript Library, Yale University, New Haven, Connecticut.
10 Vivian Virtue to Langston Hughes, 14 September 1948, Langston Hughes papers, Beinecke Rare Book and Manuscript Library, Yale University, New Haven, Connecticut.
11 Una Marson to Randall, 28 August 1949, BBC written archives, Caversham.
12 *Ibid.*
13 Una Marson to Langston Hughes, 20 November 1948, Langston Hughes papers, Beinecke Rare Book and Manuscript Library, Yale University, New Haven, Connecticut.
14 *Ibid.*
15 Jenny DaCosta to the author.
16 John Grenfall Williams to Una Marson, 8 August 1948, Foreign General File, Una Marson, BBC written archives, Caversham.
17 See for example *The Penguin Book of Caribbean Verse in English* edited by Paula Burnett (London, Penguin, 1986), in the introduction of which it reads: 'the single most important outlet for Caribbean writers was Henry Swanzy's BBC Caribbean Service programme, *Caribbean Voices*'.

17

Pioneering people

THE YEAR 1949 marked a change in Una Marson's fortunes. With her physical and mental health fully restored, she returned to Kingston in January in search of work, but, finding job prospects bleak, began devising a new project to publish affordable editions of books by Jamaican authors. She logically turned for backing to the *Gleaner* company which had printed her books and where she knew many senior people. Sydney Fletcher, the recently appointed managing director, was not yet among Una's acquaintances, but was strategically 'hypnotised' into the faith. By early February, already assured of the *Gleaner* board's support, Una called a meeting of writers to firm up editorial policy for the project.

Jamaica's literary intelligentsia had scarcely changed in a decade. Among those who gathered on 11 February were Una's Poetry League friends Clare McFarlane and Vivian Virtue, and Philip Sherlock, the historian and critic who had written the preface to *The Moth and the Star*. Apologies came from Edna Manley, who, in addition to her sculpture, was editing a skilfully compiled occasional literary journal, *Focus*, whose second issue was a mere three months old. The committee was conspicuously divided between the old school and the new. McFarlane, revealing a marked lack of interest in modern trends and in the popular poet Louise Bennett, whose work frequently appeared in the *Gleaner*, was pushing the unimaginative Arthur Nicolas and Tom Redcam, while Philip Sherlock illuminated a more exciting way forward by suggesting a reprint of a booklet on Mary Seacole, the nineteenth-century Jamaican 'doctress' who travelled to the Crimea.

Una adopted none of these proposals. She warmed to the idea of the slogan 'Books in every home', and agreed that the little books be priced at between 6*d* and 2*s*, and issued in series of three. The company, it was decided, was to be known as 'The Pioneer Press', with a broad remit to cover Caribbean poetry anthologies and stories for young people, natural history, Jamaican biography and auto-biography.

Pioneer Press was a natural progression for Una's literary work. She saw that the press would enable her to shape the pedigree of Jamaican literature, much as Victor Gollancz had affected English publishing, and, having noticed the paucity of books in homes, schools and even the shops the year before, realised that such work was essential. Her friends agreed that this move into publishing signalled a ripening of her career. John Grenfall Williams wrote that he was

> delighted to get your letter and to hear that you had started work with the new book publishing company. This seems to me to be exactly the sort of work which should help you fulfil yourself completely and I wish you all the good fortune that you so well deserve.[1]

However, Una felt that to some degree she had deserved even more and would have preferred a period of creative freewheeling in which to encourage young writers. These would have been the babies she'd never had. To this end she gathered around her 'large membership of enthusiastic young people' in her resuscitated Readers and Writers Club and, continuing the habits of a lifetime, was serving up encouragement, criticism and confidence. Financial backing from a three-year Colonial Development and Welfare literary scholarship would have enabled her to do this full time for, as she wrote to her BBC colleague, 'there is so much work to be done here which one can't do because one is neither a bird of the air or a lily of the valley. One must have an income.'[2]

The income came from the *Gleaner* company for the Pioneer Press job; Una gave most of her free time to the new writers. Andrew Salkey, a bright teenager just out of school, met Una in 1949 and she became his 'chief literary guide'. In 1988 he wrote from Amherst, Massachusetts, where he is Professor of Creative Writing, that Una Marson had always been

> very generous, gracious and supportive, always finding ample time, in her very busy schedule, as a journalist at *The Daily Gleaner* and as an unpaid, island-wide, crusading cultural worker, to read our manuscripts, and offer us excellent critical comment and encouragement. ... She was a splendid example of the writer who had made a reputation

abroad and yet who was willing to help us with our poems, stories, plays, essays and newspaper articles.[3]

In rebuilding this club, closed since 1940, Una was recapturing the gratification she had experienced during 1937 and 1938, her most fecund period. The writers she gathered around her now were among the most promising but least exposed of their time. Una helped them, wrote Andrew Salkey,

> place poems, stories, drawings and photographs in local magazines and in Herring's *Life and Letters*, arranged public readings of poetry and short stories to vast audiences, in the open air, (sometimes in our parents' backyards), without an admission charge, and directed plays by Roger Mais, Frank Hill and herself ... I actually played a very small part in her musical drama, *Pocomania*.[4]

It is tempting to speculate that Salkey's first novel, *A Quality of Violence* (1959), which depicts the villagers of St Thomas-in-the-East turning to pocomania during the drought of 1900, and the pervasive 'violence' of their rituals, was born of Una's play.

Salkey's career, and those of many young writers, was greatly furthered by Una's ability to bring them into contact with established English writers and publishers. In May 1949 Vera Brittain, Winifred Holtby's biographer, visited Kingston with her husband, George Catlin, and at Una's invitation lectured the club on 25 May at its new home, 'loaned to us by the Extra Mural Department of the University of the West Indies'. Welcoming Vera Brittain to the island, Una told her that the club aimed to 'encourage our young people to read and take literature seriously', adding, 'your presence will be a great source of encouragement to them'.[5] That evening at 58 Brentford Road, over two hundred brown-skinned boys and girls, packed into a small room and verandah, listened attentively to Vera's talk and continued discussion in the stifling heat for over three hours. Among them was the young chairman, Victor Stafford Reid from the editorial staff of the *Daily Gleaner*, who had recently published with Alfred Knopf, and to encouraging reviews, his first novel, *New Day*, which told the story of Jamaica's struggle for independence.[6]

Una Marson felt quite proud at Reid's publishing debut and wrote to friends abroad announcing the book. But for all her pleasure in Reid's success, Kingston failed to give the intellectual stimulus she wanted: 'I feel marooned in the way of things to read', she told George Orwell, 'have pity on me and send me something.'[7] She had received a copy of the *New Statesman* containing a review of his *Animal Farm* and her subscription to the *Saturday Review of Literature* kept her up to date, but available books and magazines seemed few and ancient, making readjustment to life on what seemed like the cultural margins an uphill affair.

Una Marson, at forty-four, had lost none of her former stamina. The time and energy expended on her Readers and Writers Club, taking into account that she was writing features for the *Daily Gleaner* and poems, setting up a publishing company and doing listening surveys for the BBC, was extraordinary. Langston Hughes, who had kindly sent a copy of one of his collections which she was enjoying, received a cross note in May: 'I ... still await a letter from you ... This is to lodge a complaint. My copy of the *Poetry of the Negro* has not yet reached me. I have seen the copy Virtue has but would like a copy to study at leisure.'[8]

Poetry of the Negro brought Una's work, along with that of fifteen other Jamaican poets, before an American audience for the first time. One of the poems Hughes had selected was 'Nightfall':

> Come quickly, wings of night
> The twilight hurts too deep,
> Let darkness wrap the world around
> My pain will go to sleep.

Readers of *Poetry of the Negro* were not given a fair glimpse of Una Marson's poetic range. The same may be said of the *Kyk-over-al* anthology of West Indian poetry compiled by Arthur J. Seymour in 1951. He put in two of Una's poems: an early sonnet, 'The Impossible', and 'Conspiracy', a love poem. But Una was assured her place in the West Indian literary canon when Britain did for her what the Caribbean had not. In the *Penguin Book of Caribbean Poetry* compiled by Paula Burnett and published in 1986 – twenty years after Una's death – there are six poems by Una Marson: 'Kinky Haired Blues', 'Brown Baby Blues', 'Gettin de Spirit', 'Politeness', 'To Wed or Not to Wed' and 'Repose'. This selection shows a generous recognition of her various modes and qualities.

After her fortieth year Una published little new poetry. Being a patron and an icon became a substitute for writing, and she poured her creative energies into the club. In August, when the club was on a sure footing again, she wrote to John Grenfall Williams asking him to send 'any books with which you have finished ... for our library' and engaging his interest in her other plans: 'Have you read *Cry the Beloved Country* that the South African writer Alan Paton wrote? I got a copy of the American edition last year and I wrote to Alan Paton to ask his permission for our amateur actors to perform this work dramatized by me.' Having learnt that the dramatic rights had been sold in America, she was placing her hopes on Jonathan Cape, the English publishers, to whom she was writing, but 'if you could kindly send a note to Jonathan Cape saying you know me and asking for sympathetic consideration of this request I shall be most grateful. We would like to present it just before Christmas.'[9]

Fortunately for Una, at a time when she needed some editorial help with the Pioneer Press, she ran into her former friend from the Readers and Writers Club, Isobel Seaton. They met by chance in downtown Kingston one afternoon and, as Isobel later recounted, Una had not changed much over the years:

> Una was one of those people who was always the same ... as if you had seen them the day before. We ended up in Kincaids, a chemist shop with a refreshment area and we sat there talking for about an hour. Una took everything concerning herself very personally indeed, not that she was seeking the limelight but she would do things as she thought they should be done ... not anticipating failure.[10]

From the beginning of July 1949 Una became, officially, organising secretary at the Pioneer Press. She took on the full responsibility of an editorial director and decided to move into the *Gleaner*'s offices, a ramshackle building down Harbour Street. Life there was not without obstacles in the shape of recurrent battles between Una and her colleagues on grounds which Isobel Seaton was to make clear:

> Una was a law unto herself, but never a breaker of laws. She had no regard for authority and when we had to be out of our office room, she would sometimes go into the editorial department and clear space, removing papers from someone else's desk and sitting me there. Sealy [the editor] used to get annoyed at this and tell Una, but she'd do it again the following week.[11]

None of this was really Una's fault. The *Gleaner* wanted the glory of a book publishing wing, but hadn't planned for accommodating its staff. Una was bullied into camping in the board room with her secretary and had to fight for a couple of suitable chairs and tables to be brought up to them. But any time the board wanted to meet during the day, they decamped and went on forced march downstairs. Though it was the coolest part of the building, the board room, which had to be left tidy, was not suitable for courting would-be writers or reading scripts. Una's own troubles were increased by her complete lack of fastidiousness about money and by her decision to consign all awareness of time management to history. Since Una was still freelancing for the *Gleaner*, Isobel was sometimes called upon to type her articles: 'It was always the morning of the deadlines. She'd come in and say *we* have to drop everything and get this off.'[12]

Una and Isobel became excellent buddies. In the company of such an inspired but erratic boss Isobel could either hate passionately or adore. She chose the latter. Isobel took to visiting Una at her home which she shared with two funny male Italian lodgers, stone workers who had been German prisoners of war before taking refuge in Kingston where they had a business. Una was living in the north of Kingston, at 101 Old Hope Road in Liguanea, a stone's throw away from the spacious lawns and multi-coloured bougainvillaea borders of the Royal Botanical Gardens at Hope. From her window she had a view of the grassy hills. She lived in a charming old wooden house, with old-fashioned shutters. Her own room, carefully arranged and uncluttered, was draped on one side with marvellous, old-style African lappa cloths and her collection of white shells and corals from Port Antonio, which she had visited the year before. On the wall, apart from a framed poem, hung a set of photographs of her African-American greats, performers and writers such as Langston Hughes, Billie Holiday, Marian Anderson and Booker T. Washington, as well as personal framed pictures. Along one wall were shelves of well-thumbed, hardbacked books and beneath these a ceramic vase of cut leaves and fresh flowers.

Isobel enjoyed visiting Una's home, their domestic chatter and the simple pleasure of walking together in the gardens. Getting away from the noise of town was the only way to win Una's concentration because whenever in Kingston they were obliged to stop every five minutes because she was always bumping into someone she knew. Una had an adorable, unpredictable sense of fashion, thought Isobel: she was 'extravagant' and

> rather impractical ... but she would never spend time on her hair, or go into a beauty parlour. There was a certain flamboyance about her choice of fabrics. And now and again she would try a turban effect with a scarf and then say, 'And how do you like this?'[13]

Una loved her clothes to be distinctive, colourful stuff which Aimee Webster Delisser, who was then a gardening expert and writer, thought was 'dreadful'. Una took a great deal of pleasure in naughtiness for its own sake. Once she asked Aimee whether her scarlet dress seemed unsuitably young and bright for her, and when Aimee honestly replied 'yes', Una returned: 'I'm so glad that's how I feel.'[14]

Isobel, with her excited eyes and enthusiastic spirit, smiled at all this. She felt that time had deepened her friendship with Una, though Una still tended to conceal her private life. Gradually she came to accept that privacy was an inherent part of Una's make-up and there were certain things she would never discuss: her bouts of depression and the details of her love life, although she talked about her disappointment over Dudley.

These aspects of her life were perhaps interrelated, but there is not enough evidence to show that lost love alone caused Una's downs. She always worked very hard. Always inclined to take on more commitments than she could effectively complete because of her determination to live out her vision, Una inevitably made some misjudgements. She knew more than beauty, order, cleanliness and discipline, the qualities her parents had instilled in her from the first. Her courageous character afforded her space for chaos, the accretions of dark thoughts as well as the delicacy and poise of solitude. Una's professional life, like her creative work, was uneven. Writing demanded all the pep she could muster, as she revealed in a letter: 'the impulse to write comes like a madness and I write furiously for a couple of months, usually in the spring and then I go to sleep again'.[15]

Friendships also came in spells. Her moods swung violently. from a joyous activity that drew witty companions and friends to a morbid depression which left her unable to cope with even work-a-day affairs. Living with her sister Ethel, it would have been possible to screen herself from the public gaze, but Una chose not to hide her depressive tendency. In articles she openly acknowledged the depressions. Isobel, sympathetic and attentive, saw that Una was 'a very positive person, in spite of her difficult times. Although she had one or two nervous breakdowns, she came to bring to bear some sense of reasoning and pulled herself through them. I didn't see her at those times.'[16]

The first four Pioneer Press publications, a mixture of fiction and poetry, both for young readers, appeared on 2 September 1950: a volume of fourteen Jamaican short stories including the work of Vic Reid, R. L. C. Aarons, Ulric Simmonds, Vera Bell and Ethel Rovere;

Poetry for Children, a beginner's anthology including some of Una's work and that of Lina Salmon; *Anancy Stories and Dialect Verse*, largely the work of Louise Bennett, but with a handful of Una's already published poems and including work by Dorothy Clarke and Una Wilson; and *Maxie Mongoose and other Animal Stories* by Laurie Bird.

Una Marson's only reviewer was the English-born Jamaican Esther Chapman who, in her monthly *West Indian Review*, praised the new publishing venture, calling it 'a landmark in the literary history of Jamaica', and complimenting the designers on the little books' appearance:

> Red and black have been adopted for the general colour scheme, and all four covers are meritorious (although I cannot quite understand the reason for the blank white panel on the back of the cover) particularly the Short story volume. ... The covers do a great credit to the Gleaner's lithographic department and the books are beautifully printed in a new type imported specially for the purpose.[17]

Editorially, Chapman judged the books were 'not all of equal value'. She liked Laurie Bird's carefully constructed tales, but refused to 'join the adulation of Miss Louise Bennett' in the field of dialect verse. Vic Reid and Vera Bell, among the short story writers, were singled out for showing 'great feeling for local atmosphere' and Ethel Rovere for 'writing with professional assurance and finish'. Slightest of all the books, in her view, was the poetry anthology: Lina Salmon and Una Marson were dismissed as contributors of 'charming and artless verse'.[18]

Published in autumn 1950, a little more than a year after Una took up her post, these collections had been brought out at relative speed with a minimum of editing and re-working. *Poetry for Children*, which opens with 'A Child's Prayer' by D. G. Davies and includes 'On the Death of a Mouse' by Una herself, left the critic Vivian Carrington reeling. In 1961 in an article, 'West Indian Literature in Schools', in the *Sunday Gleaner*, he commented:

> Children are not fools and should not be treated as such. Why encourage them to indulge in sickly sentimentality over a mythical incident that lacks any trace of verisimilitude? In 'Mousie' and the 'Prayer' there is little sense, little imagination, little tendency indeed towards any thought.

He found the opening of 'A Child's Prayer' particularly weak:

> Look upon me as I kneel
> Praying in the fading light

Send a cherubim to stay
Close beside me through the night
Please, Baby Jesus

These flaws were not entirely overcome by the second series of three, published in June 1951, which included an American reprint, *Man of Colour* by J. A. Somerville, whose brother R. C. Somerville had helped Una to publish *The Moth and the Star*. This autobiography was welcomed by Esther Chapman as 'a good book, impregnated with sense, tolerance and decency. It was a pity we were not given a wider and deeper human interest by expansion ... I should have liked the book to be three times its length.'[19] Una was not able, even after her wide experience of literature, to reject the writings of some of the dull, old bores on the literary scene. She published the work of Jamaican laureate the late Tom Redcam (pseudonym of Thomas Mcdermot), *Orange Valley and Other Poems*. McFarlane always made a fuss about Redcam's works and they were to appear in all major Jamaican anthologies. Unfortunately they were no good. Una would have done well to have been more discerning.

Some of the poetry in other Pioneer collections was embarrassingly dreary, but to consider the entire series dull because it lacks the virtuosity of later West Indian writing is shortsighted in terms of literary history. Apart from the occasional journal, *Focus*, and newspapers, the Pioneer Press alone filled the urgent need for a local outlet for Jamaican writing, some of which the literati would normally have ignored. The case of Louise Bennett, the marvellous oral poet, is the most striking. Although she had published *Dialect Verse* in 1942, it was not until 1967, when the Oxford-trained critic Mervyn Morris wrote his persuasive essay, 'On Reading Louise Bennet, Seriously', that attitudes towards the vernacular started to change.[20]

Commercial success eluded the Pioneer Press partly because the *Gleaner* company failed to market the books effectively. No advertisements appeared in the *Daily Gleaner*, and it was left to Una herself to editorialise on the importance of 'Books in every home'. Looking overseas for firmer backing she wrote to Edmett at the BBC for help, but Henry Swanzy, producer of *Caribbean Voices*, feeling that Una was getting better treatment than she was prepared to give, saw to it that Edmett didn't help: 'I don't think incidentally we need to be *too* helpful to UM. Her precious Pioneer stories gave no credit to the BBC although 5/12 at least had been used on CV recently.'[21]

NOTES

1 John Grenfall Williams to Una Marson, 8 August 1949, BBC written archives, Caversham.
2 Una Marson to Randall, 22 August 1948, BBC written archives, Caversham.
3 Andrew Salkey to the author, May 1988.
4 *Ibid.*
5 Una Marson to Vera Brittain, 19 May 1949, at McMaster University, Hamilton, Ontario, Canada.
6 Vera Brittain, *Testament of Experience* (London, Fontana, 1980), p. 458.
7 Una Marson to George Orwell, 2 April 1949, George Orwell Archive, University College London.
8 Una Marson to Langston Hughes, 23 May 1949, Hughes papers, Beinecke Rare Book and Manuscript Library, Yale University, New Haven, Connecticut.
9 Una Marson to J. G. Williams, 28 July 1948.
10 Isobel Seaton interviewed by the author, 11 May 1989, Kingston, Jamaica.
11 *Ibid.*
12 *Ibid.*
13 *Ibid.*
14 Aimee Webster, 'What Una Had to Say', *Daily Gleaner*, 9 May 1965, p. 4.
15 Una Marson to James Weldon Johnson, Beinecke Rare Book and Manuscript Library, Yale University, New Haven, Connecticut.
16 Isobel Seaton interviewed by the author, 11 May 1989, Kingston, Jamaica.
17 Esther Chapman, 'Pioneer Books – A Literary Event', *West Indian Review*, vol. 2, no. 20, 16 September 1950, p. 19.
18 *Ibid.*
19 Esther Chapman, 'Some Books of West Indian Interest', *West Indian Review*, 9 June 1951, p. 16.
20 Mervyn Morris, 'On Reading Louise Bennett, Seriously', *Jamaica Journal*, vol. 1, no. 1, December 1967, pp. 67–74.
21 Henry Swanzy to Edmett, 11 November 1950, Bag 138, Una Marson file, BBC written archives, Caversham.

18

What's wrong with Jamaica

A DESIRE to get away from Jamaica preoccupied Una Marson from early 1951. 'To stay here in this depressing confusion is to stagnate and I'm getting on. You promised to let me know about openings. I would go to New York or West Africa to anything definite. I am very fit',[1] she told John Grenfall Williams in January. But he, believing she was unlikely to secure suitable alternative employment elsewhere, questioned the wisdom of leaving the Pioneer Press. In fact one of the main reasons why Una was again keen to leave Jamaica was that she felt constrained as a *Gleaner* employee because Sydney Fletcher, the managing director, denied her the flexibility she craved to be able to divide her time between publishing and broadcasting.

In 1950 the British government had given a broadcasting franchise in Jamaica to the British-based Rediffusion group, and the Jamaican station, ZQI, had become commercial, moves Una publicly deplored. She and Frank Hill argued that Jamaica was taking a superficial, short-term view of broadcasting which ought, instead, to be publicly funded and socially relevant. This was not her only grievance against Jamaica: her dissatisfaction with her country was becoming pervasive. In the months preceding the general elections of 1949 there had been violence and disruption on the streets of Kingston.

> People hundreds of years old are not making a success of Party politics yet, is it any wonder that our baby politicians are most capable in the field of abuse and sensationalism and their followers in mass fighting and stone throwing and dirt slinging. But don't quote me, I am no politician.[2]

She found fault with the Prime Minister, Alexander Bustamente, whose Jamaica Labour Party had been returned in 1949, though with a reduced majority, after defeating Norman Manley's socialist PNP. Una expressed her political stance in *Public Opinion*: her article 'What's Wrong with Jamaica' accused the people of narrow-minded selfishness: 'What's wrong with Jamaica is that a quarter of its population does not regard itself as Jamaican and has eyes and thoughts directed away from Jamaica.'[3]

Another, equally critical piece, 'The Cinema and Our Youth', questioned the social impact of American films, quoting approvingly a series that had appeared in the *Saturday Review of Literature* on Asian communities disoriented by the American mass media. Without adequate liking for the new wave of Hollywood movies, Una cast her mind back to the good old days of Bette Davis and Gloria Swanson, whose hits she had enjoyed in her twenties. Now she felt that people were becoming dangerously passive in their enjoyment of leisure, receiving popular entertainments rather than making their own, listening to hours of canned music instead of singing round the piano or composing their own music as she had done as a girl. People sat goggling at the foreign films instead of going to church and singing hymns; the last traces of her world were receding and cinema, rather than religion, was the heart of a heartless world.

Now that she was in her mid-forties, and still single, Una was criticising film for portraying marriage as the desired goal in women's lives and for condoning anti-social behaviour.

> Of course, all films must end at the altar to placate the departures from the moral code that may have been used to arouse the audience to admiration. The end justifies the means – and so the young lady gets the idea that life is one long manhunt from the cradle to the grave. She must get her man by fair means or foul.[4]

Increasingly perceived as a prejudiced old woman failing to move with the times, Una Marson now attracted mockery. She explained in the same article: 'I do not write as a prude or as one who would like to see pleasure curtailed. Heaven knows life is drab enough and depressing enough today.' What depressed her, she said, was hooliganism, ostentation and the many 'who would like to rewrite the social history of Jamaica to prove that they have no Negro blood in their veins'.

The *Daily Gleaner*'s obituary of Una Marson in a leader on 6 May 1965 was to characterise her as an interwar intellectual, 'one of those who sought here and abroad, new guiding principles, new stars to steer by'. But while the mid-1930s had been her nadir, the postwar period did not 'place her in a position of new significance' and she was said to be out of touch with the younger generation who found her work 'as remote as Beowulf and just about as West Indian'. This same leader continues:

> Before World War II, the concept of a national literature, the ideal of national solidarity, the aspiration towards justice for all races, were not popular, and anyone who stood by these principles had to expect trouble. After World War II, they became accepted; they were at one and the same time advanced to the position of guiding principles of the society and degraded to catchwords. Miss Marson found herself isolated; it was difficult for her to establish contact with the younger generation; and she was frequently obsessed with a sense of futility.

Much of this is fair. Una Marson's sense of futility sprung from a conviction that Jamaican politics had been reduced to slogans. She had no place among the recently appointed academics of the infant University College of the West Indies who 'preferred merely to inherit the new social comforts created out of the struggle of the 1940s rather than to continue that struggle',[5] nor was she given a role within the Jamaican broadcasting field. From her twenties onwards Una's career had been uniformly successful, with advances and changes coming with relative frequency. The linchpin of her career progress in Jamaica was her long period of 'exile' in Europe, but that foreign asset now carried a deflated value.

Conversely there were always English visitors to help and entertain. In 1951 the photographer Erica Koch was making plans to leave London for a working trip to Jamaica. In April she wrote to Una, who wished her an enjoyable stay: 'Please come in to see me here [at the Pioneer Press] when you are in Kingston on Tuesday and if you can spare the time have lunch with me.' Erica was a friend of Egon Larsen, who had recommended her to

> ask Una to get you in touch with the Jamaica Government Press (or Public Relations) Officer; they're bound to have such a man. Tell him that your pictures will be published all over the world, and it's in the interest of the Jamaican authorities to give you every help you need (which includes transport).

That was a month after she and Una first met in Kingston. Una invited Erica to Hope Road for tea and a chat, but that afternoon, which ended with a photography session, Una was frequently distracted by the little ants which kept wandering into her ceramic sugar bowl. Una looked to Erica like 'a powerful and determined person who when she talked knew exactly what she wanted'. She was not sure, however, whether to take Una seriously when she suggested that Erica's hosts, the wealthy family who owned the Great House in Williamsfield, might like to adopt her as their offspring. She was over forty. Una had unlocked in their mutual friends, the Larsens, an indulgence that smacked of parenthood: Egon had written 'Una ... hasn't written yet which I expected but ... please pester her to write and tell her we still think she's one of the sweetest old girls in the world.' Besides, he had a growing store of children's books which might have interested her.

Erica told her about her various ideas for a photographic essay on Jamaica, which was eventually published in the *Geographical Magazine* in April and May 1952. She wanted to cover sugar, the Botanic Gardens, the university, homes rich and poor and the leading politicians, Norman Manley and Bustamente. Una was able to fix up appointments with Edna and Norman Manley, who had an open day once a week, and she arranged for a journalist to accompany Erica to market to take the colourful local shots, typical of the island, but that left the problem of reaching Bustamente, the Prime Minister, whom Egon Larsen had said 'was very vain and publicity minded and should be delighted to get photographed'.

The very day that Una had arranged to take Erica to see Bustamente at his farm in Clarendon, the wind tore over the island, ripping up farms and rattling rooftops. From dawn the air, stifling, hot and humid, sucked away the slight breeze. At 6.30 a.m. Una, in Kingston, called Erica to confirm there had been a hurricane warning and promised to call again soon: the hurricane was approaching Jamaica's south coast, increasing in speed as it travelled, she informed her. The heat intensified. People, making ready for the worst, began nailing down windows, closing shutters and finding candles since the electricity was bound to fail. The Great House in Williamsfield where Erica was staying was built on arches; underneath were dungeons, hideouts from slavery days – down there she and her host tied up the little calves and hid away the baby chicks.

The last news broadcast came on the radio in the middle of the evening: Sir Hugh Foot, the Governor, counselled the people. Then silence fell again. Only crickets and frogs could be heard; a wilder breeze came up, leaves rustled. And the lights went out. Everything shook, rain fell, water gushed through houses, the tins of roofs flew about. Glass was smashed and huge wooden planks went soaring through the air. Erica, watching nature go wild, rolled up carpets, kept her cameras close by and dragged a mattress behind her, searching for a dry spot to sleep. Toby, the family pet, stayed by her side and finally settled, pressing his wet nose against her face. Gradually the noise and the howling wind ceased. But rain still poured upon the devastated country.

In the morning light cows, pigs, chickens and goats, bewildered and drenched, looked strange. Dampness made aching limbs more weary, but the people went about their business, climbing over fallen trees, to rescue their possessions and go to market. In time the tropical sun began to dry up the mischief of the night before. There were newspapers, but no wireless. Over a hundred people had been killed, thousands were homeless. Una telegrammed Erica to come to Kingston, and late that afternoon they met up at the *Gleaner* office, down Harbour Street, strewn with debris.

Kingston was dismal. Telephone lines were down and electricity still off. Broken glass, bits of roof and bricks lay all about. But Una persevered with her friend's project, promising to track down Bustamente the next morning. The following dawn the two women started out early and travelled into town. First they called at the Jamaican Agricultural Society, then they tried the House of Representatives, only to discover that the House was not sitting that day. No luck at Bustamente's trade union office, nor at the Red Cross Station, where they learnt from a friendly, fat policeman that the Prime Minister had just left. Una and Erica, worn out in the heat on this endless trail, picked their way over the rubble lying on Kingston's streets, before deciding to take a taxi. They drove to the South Camp Hotel, where he was known to drink; they tried his house near the Spanish Town Road and finally they called on his secretary, who promised to fix the meeting for the Tuesday morning, the day of Erica's departure.

And so Erica met Bustamente. He seemed very kind and human: 'He really was most interesting', wrote Erica later, 'and wore a lovely colourful shirt, just right for photographs with the mass of grey hair framing a very classic face.' For a while Una stood with Bustamente, talking about their devastated country while Erica took some last shots of the battered buildings before leaving for England on the SS *Bayano*. It was hard to look upon Jamaica, torn down by the hurricane, without grieving a little.

Una continued to feel that she too wanted out of this troubled land which, after a hurricane such as this, would have to begin again its surge towards modernisation and development. But, as she had written twenty years before, Jamaica was precious simply because it was 'our own'. She believed Jamaica could not yet fulfil its whole potential because of severe damage and serious social impairment, but when, the following spring, 1952, Henry Swanzy of the BBC came on a visit, she asked him to join her on a tour of the island, warts and all.

Late one evening she and her cousin Wesley took Swanzy to the Buccaneer nightclub on Springfield Pond. He observed that during the drive there 'Una was morose' partly because her cousin had made them late, but by the time they left Una was in a more mellow mood and showed Swanzy the stars of the Southern Cross. On another occasion she hired a taxi, at a hefty sum, for a day trip across the island over hairpin roads and through the deep green valleys luxuriant with plantain and bananas to Montego Bay. The outing was connected in Swanzy's mind with the social inequality in evidence everywhere. Packing cases marked 'Harrod's', probably discarded by Noël Coward, who lived at Golden Isle, had been transformed into makeshift homes. Lunch at the lavish new Tower Island Hotel was, by contrast, 'a sumptuous affair, consisting of an incredible buffet, champagne and goodness knows what else all for $5 at the time'. The setting was magnificent. The coral reef protected the white sandy beach from sharks, and a cool wind blew from the sapphire waves. On green-tiled verandahs American tourists lounged about, shielded from the sun by orange-tinted blinds. Una and Henry settled in, but noted that the manager was not too pleased to see them in this exclusive paradise. Black people were a rare feature there, but Una, apparently unperturbed, made a point of pushing her Pioneer Press books at the bookstall, before she made her departure. Their taxi took them on to the Seven Seas at Aracabessa where they had drinks and Henry was relieved to note that more black people were drinking at the bar.

During their long conversations Henry Swanzy saw clearly that Una had suffered and was very tense; she told him she was 'coming back into life'.[6] By September she was fully revitalised: 'This is just a note to tell you what I consider terrific news', she wrote to Claude Barnett at the Associated Negro Press in Chicago. 'I have actually got three months' leave and I am coming to America early next month. I plan to visit New York, Washington and Chicago. I am very excited about this as it really the first time I am going to stay in America.'[7] She had cousins in New York, but no relatives or friends in Washington. She intended to visit the Bureau of West Indian Farm Workers and make contact with Barnett's representative in Washington, presumably with a view to writing articles for the agency. Her relationship with the Associated Negro Press was on even surer ground now since Barnett and his wife Etta Moten, a distinguished singer, had visited Jamaica that May on a Caribbean tour with a group of doctors, and met Una socially. She had enjoyed their company at a grand house party at Shaklefords on Old Hope Road and at the seaside cottage at Seven Miles of Mrs Tavernier, a well-known Chicagoan; Barnett also admired Una and respected her work: 'It was certainly fine having an opportunity to meet you after hearing about you and carrying BS [British Information Service] stories about you all these years. Your energy and zeal live up to all of the previous reports about you.'[8] Similar friendly notes were exchanged after the Barnetts' departure for home. When he heard about Una's decision to visit America, Barnett was again encouraging: 'It is indeed good news to know that you are coming to America. One of your mental vigor and resolute determination to succeed will enjoy a visit here, I feel.'[9]

NOTES

1 Una Marson to John Grenfall Williams, 6 January 1951, Una Marson file, BBC written archives, Caversham.
2 Una Marson to George Orwell, 2 April 1949, George Orwell Archives, University College London.
3 Una Marson, 'What's Wrong with Jamaica', *Public Opinion*, 17 February 1951, p. 4.
4 'The Cinema and Our Youth', *Public Opinion*, 10 March 1951, p. 6.
5 Gordon Lewis in *The Making of the Modern West Indies* (New York, Monthly Review Press, 1968), p. 189.
6 Henry Swanzy interviewed by the author, 7 June 1988.
7 Una Marson to Claude A. Barnett, 25 September 1952, Claude Barnett papers, Chicago Historical Society.
8 Claude A. Barnett to Una Marson, 24 May 1952, Claude Barnett papers, Chicago Historical Society.
9 Claude A. Barnett to Una Marson 4 October 1952, Claude Barnett papers, Chicago Historical Society.

19

America

'A MERICANS are so careful about not wasting food', Una concluded after a short stay in New York – 'three in the family, three lamb chops.'[1]

Una was enjoying her food. She loved eating. Consuming, it appears, had become the prime injunction of her early fifties; after more than five years at home in Jamaica, she had grown accustomed to munching through generous servings. What a shock it was to discover American domestic thrift! Such small portions and, by contrast, a vast range of tempting, mouthwatering, fattening foods in many shops and restaurants. She tut-tutted:

> The ease with which one is lured into eating ice cream and lovely cakes and pies that abound are not conducive to keeping a respectable waistline. As soon as people talk about food, they talk about calories. There seems to be a vast movement in America for keeping weight down. Certainly the restaurants are no help.[2]

Weight gain had become the major burden for Una since her recovery from depression in 1948. Appearance, not health, was the issue: 'I'm ashamed to say I'm a great cow weighing 152 [pounds] instead of my usual 128', she'd had to confess in a letter to Orwell in 1949.[3] Now approaching fifty, unemployed and at leisure, she was rapidly growing plump. References to food popped up everywhere like unwelcome relatives: one day while touring around Bunche Park, a poor, black area of Washington with low-roofed housing, her eyes alighted on corn bread and southern fried chicken, and Dunbar's 'When de co'n pone's hot' came to mind:

> When de chittlin's is a sputter'n'
> So's to show you whah dey's at;

...
When you mammy says de blessin'
An de co'n pone's hot

Was she, Una wondered, wanting to pinch herself, 'in the land of Uncle Remus stories'?[4]

When she first arrived in the USA (the exact date is uncertain), Una dutifully went to see her cousins in Brooklyn, New York, where there were so many West Indians that it was much like being at home in Jamaica, but Una didn't like it. The brownstone houses were 'all one uniform red-brown stone. All with high massive stone stoops and black iron-grill fences staving off the sun.'[5] Una hardly knew anyone and besides, as her cousin was in bed with a fever, she didn't get the attention she'd been looking forward to – good home cooking and a chance to catch up on gossip. Their home was noisy, so she went by train journey to see her friends on the other side of the city – an hour and a half's journey.

When she arrived at her friends' house, they too were busy. Everyone in New York was extremely busy all the time. Life went on until midnight. Women worked all day and spent all evening on housework. They didn't have proper mealtimes. They chewed gum for relaxation. They weren't elegant: not as stylish as Paris or London. When they invited you out in the evening they said, 'Just wear anything.' Una found such casual manners strange and disconcerting.

Una also found that the performing and literary arts could not be relied upon to cheer her up. While she adored Toscanini's flamboyant conducting at Carnegie Hall, she thought theatre prices ridiculously high and not such good value for money as London's West End. She was so familiar with the music of *Porgy and Bess* that she judged it essential viewing, but it turned out to be 'the best produced show I had seen in years and the most revolting as a slice of typical negro life in America'.[6] It was nice to meet the staff of the *Saturday Review of Literature* to which she had subscribed for years, but for all this her most pleasant memory was

> sitting on a bench on an esplanade in Brooklyn Heights from which I could see the wonderful Brooklyn Bridge, the city, the Hudson River and the ferry boat going and coming from Stratton Island and the Statue of Liberty. If I had to choose, I would choose to live within sight of such a scene.[7]

After a short stay in Miami Una tried Washington, where she stayed at the Quaker International Student House which 'reminded me of some lovely English homes I had known, and how I shared a room with an Italian sculptor [in Istanbul]'. But Una did not enjoy Washington. On her train journey into that city she had struck up a conversation with the head Pullman porter who offered to take her to a ball game that night with bands and all. Una was tempted, but, fearful the Quakers might disapprove of a man turning up for her on her first night, she declined with regret, not least because the racial segregation she then found in Washington was so painful.

Restaurants and cafés which would serve her were hard to find, and one day as the manager of an Italian restaurant came to ask her to leave she found herself 'torn between anger and confusion and hot tears burnt my cheeks as I walked away'.[8] Other forms of entertainment seemed no easier to come by: Una gave up cinemagoing after she had been refused entrance to *Hiawatha* and *Salome*. She liked the inter-racial ecumenical centre, the Church of our Saviour in Washington: the irony of segregated church never ceased to disturb Una – 'Christianity and democracy cannot exist hand in hand with vigorous race prejudice and the existence of second-class citizens.'[9]

Howard, Washington's prestigious black university, also failed to provide a much-needed relief from this racial strain. One evening Una saw a play there about a black soldier returning from war to face discrimination at home which made her cry and depressed her for days. A poetry group at the Cochran Library was the kindest and most hospitable milieu; one evening the Irish poet and playwright Padraic Colum, whose *Collected Poems* came out in 1953, addressed the group and on another occasion she attended a memorial meeting for Dylan Thomas, a former BBC contact, who had died that year.

In autumn 1952 Una began to write a series of travel articles about America. These were never published. As a young exile in England her psychology had been deeply affected by relations between Mother Country and colony, black and white people; but now in middle age her view of emigrant life was tamer, less pained. She restricted herself to narrating anecdotes and commenting on the lifestyle without the spills of blood and angst which had typified the British writings.

Una decided to make her home in Washington, and found an apartment at 1707–19 Street NW. Now at last she could put Jamaica behind her. The Pioneer Press was in the capable hands of Adolphe Roberts, a poet and historian, who that year published his own fine *Six Great Jamaicans* and *Tales of Old Jamaica* by a young friend of Una's, Clinton

Black. Later, very successfully, Roberts brought out S. A. G. Taylor's novel *The Capture of Jamaica*, which went into four impressions and sold over ten thousand copies.[10] It was never Una's style to be an organisational type: she relished the early days of a project, but once it was off the ground she abandoned it to more steady temperaments.

Her own writing was a different matter. Although she couldn't muster any poetry these days, Una was 'struggling', she admitted to Langston Hughes, with a 'semi-autobiographical work', *Everyday Life in Jamaica*. This unwieldy project, with years of source material to condense and now in its third year of research, was Una's attempt to explore social development under eighteen chapter headings, including history, religion, social work, education, industries and government.[11]

She was trying to be a 'good girl' and placate her publishers, Knopf, who, alert to the postwar changes in the colonial world, saw such a tome as commercially viable. Una was already a little bored with the idea and had her eye on something more exciting. She wrote to the Larsens back in London:

> Africa is still on the horizon – who knows it may be my next port of call. I tried to get Knopf interested in a book about West Africa, but they wanted me to do one about the West Indies. I may slave at that for a year and they say if it's a success they will help me with the African venture which as you know is my dream.[12]

Cash would have come in handy, but more than that Una needed the confidence boost and recognition that a publication would bring. The BBC, her one full-time professional employer, had let her down. Now on much firmer ground under Henry Swanzy's direction, *Caribbean Voices* had assured a wider audience for the region's poetry and short stories, while the *Kyk-over-al Anthology of West Indian Poetry*, which included some of Una's work, had demonstrated what could be done locally. But where was Una in all this? Having put in so much time and effort, from the early days with *The Cosmopolitan* to the postwar era with Pioneer Press, she had no tangible evidence of her considerable contribution to West Indian letters, little proof that she had done it all before.

Una was alive to an unrealised opportunity, and considered compiling 'an anthology of Caribbean poetry covering 1900 to the present day' because 'now that our people are getting appreciative of their own literature, they need to have the best we have produced repeated time and again'.[13] Sadly, this idea never went beyond the early stages either.

A feel for the importance of literary history led her to champion the virtually neglected poets of her day: where, she wondered was 'the poetry of the renaissance of the 1920s … where is Claude McKay, Countee Cullen, James Weldon Johnson, Paul Lawrence Dunbar to name but a few. I don't see their books around.'[14] But creatively Una had stalled. Several unpublished poems date, as best as can be determined, from this period. Most are nature poems. One, 'Emergence', expresses an optimistic sense of rebirth or release from suffering:

> Over bare rocks
>   the soft green moss
> Over deep wounds
>   a healing balm
> Through the stifling aid
>   a freshning [*sic*] breeze;
> A lightening [*sic*] flash
>   the soul is freed.

When T. S. Eliot was in Washington in 1955, principally to see Ezra Pound, who was being kept in St Elizabeth asylum, Una sent a welcoming poem to his hotel to which he responded. Neither side of the correspondence in which they recalled their first meeting at the BBC has survived, but Una guarded favourable thoughts of Eliot. Although she had seen *Murder in the Cathedral* in London in the 1930s, and had read and re-read *The Waste Land*, Una professed to be 'not really familiar with his work' – a sign of what high standards she set herself. She whiled away many hours at home watching television, having treated herself to a set for Christmas 1955. She liked to spend Saturday afternoons watching ice hockey. Usually she tuned in to the Perry Como and Ed Sullivan shows or *The Wide World* series presented by Dave Garroway. Although she did not have a full-time job Una was sometimes engaged in social work:

> When I was resident in Koinonia in Baltimore some members of our group joined with students from Morgan State University and went down to do manual work in the slums of Baltimore. A weekend project might be to paint rooms of a dirty and overcrowded tenement house. We slept there in sleeping bags on the floor so that work might be started at daylight. It was astonishing to see what could be done between Friday and Sunday evening.[15]

Around this time Una was finding a degree of freedom in education. She had received no formal education or training since

Hampton, and was feeling uncertain of her ability to progress without qualifications, now that Jamaica had its own university college. In autumn 1958 and again the following year Una took courses in writing for children at George Washington University's college of General Studies, after which she attended a summer course at the Catholic University Drama School in writing for theatre and television. Her subsequent approaches to children's magazines were sometimes successful: 'Harvest Thanksgiving Festival' set in Sharon, Jamaica, was published,[16] and 'Christmas on Poinsettia Island', another descriptive piece set in Jamaica, appeared in the December 1960 edition of *American Junior Red Cross News*, with illustrations by James Ponter. It combined two features Una had explored in her earlier work: details of Jamaican flora and fauna and an account of an aspect the island's folk culture.[17]

Later Una's eight-year residence in Washington from 1952 to 1960 was scarcely ever discussed with friends, or mentioned in her powerfully autobiographical articles, nor indeed in 1964 when the Consulate of Israel prepared a detailed résumé of her life did these years even appear. It is difficult to convey the peculiar aura of secrecy that this part of her life-story has, but its themes can be best summed up as marital and mental.

In 1960, aged fifty-five, Una decided it was time to settle down and marry. Her husband-to-be was Peter Staples, a black American dentist, also resident in Washington, a widower with two grown-up daughters.

How they met is unknown, but the wedding (I have been unable to trace the date) was a small affair: few guests congregated in a Washington house with the minimum of fuss. Una looked spectacular for her special day. She wore a deep blue velvet coat, fastened with a gold brooch, over a long, flared, midi-length, white silk dress, with white gloves, gold strap sandals and finely worked gold jewellery. Her hair was pinned up with flowers. This classic, flattering outfit was enhanced by her mature, rather plump, frame. She looked pretty.

As Una came up the spiral staircase with her fiancé, the guests waiting in the lounge could see they were roughly the same height. The smiling couple were both a little stocky; Peter was in a pin-striped, double-breasted grey suit which accentuated his broad build. Standing beside Una, whose bright lipstick looked glossy, Peter looked serious in his dark-rimmed spectacles. But he was a good-looking, moustached man with a kind face and small dark eyes. At the end of the ceremony Una and Peter's friends came forward to kiss the bride. And she, standing by the white lace curtains, pouted her lips and offered her cheek for the welcome felicitations.

The couple lived in a comfortable, if not luxurious, apartment, according to Hugh Morrison, a Jamaican who, while on a three-month fellowship for the US Department of Agriculture, was invited to dine with them. Staples seemed to Morrison to be a self-effacing husband, prepared to allow Una to do as she pleased. Yet even if that was true it did not lead to lasting happiness. After a little more than a year Una and Peter Staples separated.

Una's attitude to marriage had undergone several changes over the years. In *Tropic Reveries* she had shown how the independent woman is still prey to the contradictions of sexual and emotional life. But in her mid-fifties she gave short shrift to the radical feminist ideals within marriage. In a fretful article entitled 'Have Married Women Taken the Wrong Turning?', written after a Business Women's conference, Una concluded that 'in the hot pursuit of happiness' women probably had taken the wrong turning.[18] Turning from a lifetime of promoting feminist sexual politics, she argued against gender equality in marriage, child-rearing and sexual practices. A mother's place, if she had children under ten, was home; she shouldn't work full-time, except in exceptional circumstances, and single women should have preferential treatment in the job market. Marriage, she wrote, 'is a career or should be'.[19]

Becoming old-fashioned herself, Una revealed a lack of confidence in her own sexuality and distaste at sexual pleasure and sexual liberalism a few years before Betty Friedan's *The Feminine Mystique* and at a time when a new women's liberation movement was stirring:

> All the writing about sex has been defended by the explanation that human beings will be happier if they understand how sex works. But sex is such an individual thing that no generalities help ... the real joy has gone out of sex because of vulgar exposure and prostitution of its roots ... the sensationalism and thrills and excitement has taken hold so that every co-ed thinks that life has cheated him or her if from 14 the petting parties are not on the way to mount thrill upon thrill. And later one wonders at the dissatisfaction with life.[20]

Her own 'dissatisfaction with life' was probably now of a sexual nature. With desires and needs between husband and wife neither understood nor met, so much was probably being repressed. The marriage itself was a closely guarded secret even among Una's closer friends and associates in Jamaica. Some people have suggested that Peter Staples required a stabilising influence from his second wife: Una could not, or perhaps would not, accommodate his needs.

Marriage destabilised Una. No sooner had the wedding ring become a part of her attire then depression took hold and consumed several years of her life. The Staples family have been graciously reticent in discussing Una's mental distress. In the early 1980s Erika Smilowitz had access to Peter Staples and his family when she wrote her doctoral dissertation 'Marson, Rhys and Mansfield'. It is only from her reports that the family's feelings about Una's illness can be deduced. Annie Staples, Una's sister-in-law, claimed to have 'put' Una in St Elizabeth Hospital, the mental institution in Washington where Ezra Pound was confined. Peter Staples himself, 'by then very old and sick and in a nursing home', could scarcely recall Una:

> He didn't remember Una at all at first and didn't seem to have any recognition at all but then at the end yelled (he was very deaf) that I should try Jamaica – so something clicked in his mind at least. Another family member, possibly another sister-in-law, asked that I 'let things alone'. She said it with such sadness that I didn't have the heart to try to find out more.[21]

If Una's illness was by this time more than ordinary depression, neither she nor her family wanted that truth to be known.

Before the curtain could be drawn on the marriage, Una hoped for some settlement from her husband. It was not to be forthcoming. On 30 October 1961 Peter Staples wrote from Washington to his estranged wife then back in Kingston.

> Dear Una
> Thank you very much for your most recent letter and the others that I have neglected to answer, due to the reason that I have been very sick, with heart ailment and low blood pressure, the reaction from too much past worry. The reason for my non-appearance in Jamaica was due to my illness, however, I have still been promoting the tours and when the opportunity presents itself I shall be there.
> All of your belongings have been packed and are now being shipped to you, they should arrive in the very near future.
> About your returning to the States right away, as far as I can see, that would only create a lot of unnecessary problems with regard to my health and with all due respects you have got to agree with me that I have to protect my health.
> I'll agree that I have been slow about supporting you but you must agree that I have had a lot of expenses from which I have only now

begun to see daylight. In my next letter you will receive something.
Have to close this now.
Peter
Best regards to all.[22]

Even if in private Una longed for Peter Staples to claim her as his wife, in her casual exchanges with Jamaican friends she struck a particularly breezy note. 'I met her a few times with father down Kings Street', remembered John Aarons, 'and he said "Married? What's the name?" and she said "Oh, don't worry about that".'[23]

NOTES

1 'The America I Have Discovered', Una Marson papers, Box 1944A National Library of Jamaica.

2 *Ibid.*

3 Una Marson to George Orwell, 2 May 1949, George Orwell Archive, University College London.

4 'The America I Have Discovered'.

5 Paule Marshall, *Brown Girl, Brownstones* (London, Virago Press, 1982), p. 3.

6 'What I Have Discovered in America', Autumn 1952, p. 5, Una Marson papers, Box 1944A, National Library of Jamaica.

7 *Ibid.*

8 'The America I Have Discovered'.

9 *Ibid.*

10 Peter Abrahams, *Jamaica: an Island Mosaic* (London, HMSO, 1957).

11 Una Marson to Langston Hughes, October 1953, Langston Hughes papers, Beinecke Rare Book and Manuscript Library, Yale University, New Haven, Connecticut.

12 Una Marson to Egon Larsen, 9 December 1952. Larsen papers, in the possession of Ursula Larsen, London.

13 Una Marson to John Grenfall Williams, 20 November 1948, West Indies: Jamaica file E1/1303, BBC written archives, Caversham.

14 'The America I Have Discovered'.

15 'The Rehabilitation of Western Kingston', *Daily Gleaner*, no date, c. 1962.

16 A note in Una Marson's papers suggests that this story was published. Magazine unknown.

17 For a full description of *jonkonnu* see Sylvia Wynter, 'Jonkonnu in Jamaica: Towards the Interpretation of Folk Dance as a Cultural Process', *Jamaica Journal*, June 1970, pp. 34–48.

18 The National Federation of Business and Professional Women's Clubs 12th biennial convention.

19 'Have Married Women Taken the Wrong Turning?', no date, Una Marson papers, Box 1944B, National Library of Jamaica.

20 'Discovering America', no date, Una Marson papers, Box 1944B, National Library of Jamaica.

21 Erika Smilowitz in a letter to the author, January 1989.

22 Fragment in Una Marson papers, National Library of Jamaica.

23 John Aarons interviewed by the author, Kingston, Jamaica, April 1990.

20

Independence

THROUGHOUT the early 1960s Una worked hard in social develop-ment, rejoining Jamsave which she had left in its infancy, back in 1938. Since the mid-1940s this organisation, a boon to working-class mothers, had spread its wings, building three play centres at North Street, in Jones Town and at Spanish Town Road, which together catered for more than five hundred children. Una, as the new execu-tive secretary, took pride in the biggest venture to date, the opening of the Jebb Memorial Play Centre where over two hundred children enjoyed a full range of amenities: 'pictures, books, crayons, slates, blackboards, toys, musical instruments and swings'.[1] She no longer saw herself as a mere administrator but, as her writings make clear, was taking a more scholarly interest in social work. In one article, 'Save the Children Fund Needs You', she endorsed the view of a senior lecturer in education at the University College of the West Indies who wrote that

> Very few young children in Jamaica get … basic training. The Ministry of Education supports 30 infant schools or Departments for children aged 4 or 5 to 7 and 800 Primary Schools where children enter at an average age of 7 so that Infant education is provided for less than 4% of Jamaica's children.[2]

Una was distressed by the continued discrimination against the Rastafarians, whose appalling dwellings, often mere 'shacks, dreadful, nasty little structures – a cluster of cardboard, barrel sides, old cod fish boxes, flattened tar drums and timber scraps', stretched from beyond the main market.[3] Periodically the police burned down this 'cardboard city' otherwise known as the dungle, and ejected the inhabitants, who were then compelled to live as best they could among the charred remains. Others had also started to take notice of this. In 1960 the Jamaican sociologists M. G. Smith, Roy Augier and Rex Nettleford had published a research paper, *Rastafarian Movement in Kingston*, which called for improved educational facilities, housing and employment, an end to police harassment and an uncompromising recognition from the general public that 'the great majority of Ras Tafari brethren are peaceful citizens'. Una took action and set up the Foreshore Road Infant Centre for Rastafarian children. She looked wearily upon her social worker colleagues:

> I must say I find myself getting a bit impatient with people who need to research for seven months to find out what is obvious. I suppose getting to know the area and winning people over is important but when one starts with the knowledge of urgent needs, the planning and persuasion should not be too long drawn out.[4]

With a lifetime of social work experience behind her, Una was ready to praise excellence where she found it, but her congratulations were frequently temperate. She bore no grudges about Jamaica Welfare now, and was glad to see a project into which she had added her 'little quota of ideas' flourishing: 'I have watched its growth and development with interest', she wrote.[5]

But as a social work pioneer she was as energetic now in her late fifties as she had been at thirty. Deep down she felt a sense of urgency to change society and eradicate injustice, which some of her younger colleagues did not share. So while she wrote favourable accounts of the YMCA or the Polio Rehabilitation Centre, her chief object was to stress how much hard work still lay ahead. In July 1961, before attending the week-long Social Development Conference organised by the University and the Council for Voluntary Social Services, Una wrote about the need for partnerships between the commercial sector and welfare organisations: to 'end the belief of the masses that nothing is being done in their interest'.[6] And she asked the landowners of the United Manchester Association to cater for their needs rather than their wants, as a means of stemming the economic imbalances in the country.[7] She had become sick of the great divide between the haves and have-nots and, refusing to allow the ideal of equality to become a vanishing dream, covered a great deal of paper scrutinising trade unions, party politicians and the establishment. The following extract on the 'Rehabilitation of Western Kingston' written under her recently acquired pen-name, 'The Torch', was not untypical:

When London's social workers awoke to the squalor of East End London plans were made for the rehabilitation of the whole area. Last year I talked with an outstanding British social worker who was visiting Jamaica. We talked about London's East End. She explained that the area had been thoroughly worked over and was no longer a centre for visitors and workers who were interested in social problems. We talked about the late Sir Whyndam Deedes who lived among the underprivileged in this area for many years. I had visited with him there and was very moved by his devotion to the needy. Several other workers actually lived there at Settlement House so they understand better the problems of the people among whom they were working. ...

There is nothing that brings you so close to the needy as doing manual labour among them. This brings down the class partition.

At her comfortable home, 43 Hopefield Road, Kingston, the house she shared with her sister Ethel, Una continued to fill notebooks with poems, though only a few, such as 'For Bishop Mary Cloore', a eulogy to the Bishop of City Missions, are known to have been published. She was working on a semi-autobiographical book now, having failed to have the original published, and was putting in a substantial amount about social issues. Una, in her late fifties, was putting on weight and, as a result of this, suffered from high blood pressure, but walking kept her fit and in touch:

I have no car. I walk about and have to breathe in the dust the cars rushing behind leave behind. But I have something these drivers haven't got. I smile with and have a conversation with people I meet at the bus stops, in the shops ... I talk with the higgler and the man pushing the wheelbarrow.[8]

Ethel kept herself busy working on a biography of George Goode, the classical musician who had been her boss at the Department of Agriculture and the focus of her adult life. She had been a member of his Kingston Glee Singers and secretary of his Diocesan Festival Choir. She and George Goode were, recalls Goode's son Coleridge, 'very close and very fond of each other. She was the right person to write the biography and she did a great job.'[9] Ethel sent a copy of the biography to Coleridge, a jazz musician based in London since the 1930s. Ethel's biography demonstrated how 'very conscientious' Goode was. 'Ethel points out how hard he studied – he was completely self-taught. Anything he did was 100% concentration. He read a lot. He was a genius', he remembered.[10] Sadly Ethel shied away from describing the man and his impact upon her own life. She rationed the personal in a way which would have been inconceivable for Una and in her Author's Note wrote:

> This account of the life and work of George Davis Goode, drawn mainly from published records, has been compiled by the writer as a tribute to this worthy Jamaican and in the belief that this record will bring back to some pleasurable recollections and be to many a source of pride and inspiration.[11]

However, it was a detailed and well-researched little book, illustrated with several photographs, including one taken in 1925 of the Kingston Glee Singers: Ethel, demure and solemn, was seated in the front row.

The Jamaica in which the Marson women now lived was governed by new codes. In September 1961 Jamaica had withdrawn from the West Indian Federation and sought independent status. In February 1962 a government delegation, led by Alexander Bustamente, flew to London for discussions with the Secretary of State for the Colonies and within a fortnight reached an agreement that Jamaica would become independent on 6 August 1962. The Jamaica Labour Party was returned in the April elections and preparations began for Independence. The three-hundred-year-old coat of arms was to be retained, but a new motto, a reminder of the island's ethnic mix – 'Out of Many, One People' – was adopted.

Una was disappointed that the PNP, Norman Manley's party, lost the general election. With Alexander Bustamente, the maverick but charismatic labour leader, back in power, what, she asked would national leadership and independence really mean? 'It will be a long time before all the people of this young nation will fully understand and succeed in living up to the implications of independence', she wrote.[12] Would the old-fashioned values of hard work, good manners, social conscience and fair pay still count?

The Marson women stuck to what they knew. Edith, after many years at Jamaica College, was teaching at De Carteret, the prep school in Mandeville, though officially she had retired. She was like a grandmother to her nine-year-old boarders, telling them bedtime stories and tucking them in; she did a marvellous rendition of 'Toad of Toad Hall', recalled John Aarons, whose father R. L. C. was Una's friend. Edith, stout though a little frail now, had lost none of the assets of her Hampton education: she taught Latin skilfully and played chapel piano with a flourish. Sometimes she invited John to take tea at her house and there on occasion he met Una, who was touchingly introduced as the most distinguished of the Marson sisters.

Meanwhile the clever youngest sister was experiencing some professional setbacks; the *Gleaner* was put off by the tone and content of some of her unsolicited articles: 'The Startling Increase in Brothels' and 'Denuding Jamaica', among many others, came back with rejection slips. But the *Sunday Gleaner*, with its cultural bias, published several lively pieces on the arts, including a testy little piece on Jamaican poetry:

> Mr Vivian Carrington, a Barbadian, first reduced us to the status of versifiers and [called] the verse produced 'precious, vapid and inane.' What was said of the novelists can be left to the novelists to consider. It is the matter of poetry and poets with which I am concerned ... and this in the context of this gloomy prediction that 'it will be a long time before West Indian Literature becomes of sufficient significance for serious study in schools'.[13]

Una expatiated on the strength of West Indian literature, her work at the BBC, Clare McFarlane's achievements and her own collections, all of which had been used in schools: 'I get requests for copies from time to time from teachers who want to use certain poems but they are out of print. It is no unusual thing to go to a school and hear Jamaican poetry recited with much more understanding that those about unknown lands and unknown ways of life.'[14]

She was not wrong, but anyone could see that she was clutching at straws. In 1962 Clare McFarlane died; Adolphe Roberts, the poet and historian also died; George Goode was dead. The quaint literary world fashioned by these pioneers was finished. Amateur writers' groups had been displaced by PEN, a professional outfit run by Mrs Orsmby Marshall; but it was dreary and meetings were sparsely attended. Una took the changes in her stride. Attention had turned, and rightly so, she affirmed, to the younger writers, most of whom were now abroad: she had written in December 1961,

> Andrew Salkey and John Hearne, two of Jamaica's expatriate novelists, visited their homeland this year. There are now 52 West Indian novelists resident in London. They have been successful and are likely making a better living than they would in Jamaica if they were published here, or in any other island of the Caribbean.[15]

Una was also able in these late articles to promote her concern for children's fiction and women's writing. She maintained that the *Inde-*

pendence Anthology of Jamaican Literature edited by poet A. L. Hendricks and his cousin, Cedric Gale Lindo, should be accessible to a wide audience including children and she championed the 'Women Poets of Jamaica':

> It is of national importance when a columnist has the effrontery to deplore the fact that this year poems from more women than men have been chosen from which selections are to be made in the speech competition in the 1964 Jamaica Festival. He doubts if this is a good thing for our youngsters to set their standards low but will instil in them a lifelong conviction that poetry is something written by women. Verse speaking competitions have been presented in Jamaica for the best of twenty years. Jamaican children have been learning poetry by a majority of men all their lives. It just happens that this year whoever selected the poems knew that Jamaica had ten women poets with a collection worthy of choice for this occasion. I have no reason to believe that the poems were selected for any other reason but that they seemed worthy of the occasion … . This anti-feminist diatribe is shocking.[16]

Having anthologised Louise Bennett in 1950, Una, whose literary tastes were wide, had been puzzled by McFarlane's decision not to include the 'well-established and beloved writer of dialect verses', folklorist, and champion of Jamaican language, Louise Bennett, in his critical work *A Literature in the Making* of 1956. Now she concluded that 'for reasons best known to himself' he had made this serious omission.[17]

In May 1964 Una was depressed by the death of her older cousin, Angie. It was a keen reminder that she was now the 'older generation'. Before that Una had started to compose a series of pieces, published in the *Daily Gleaner*, that were to form something of a memoir. The character of rural Jamaica had greatly deteriorated since her youth: Malvern, once a charming town, had no electricity, the public phone rarely worked, and Clacken Produce Shop, the joy of her schoolgirl trips, was old and dilapidated:

> I sat in a car and watched a couple of bare-footed children walking along the gravel which must have been most unkind to the soles of their little feet.
> Instead of a gas station of which there are so many beautiful ones in Kingston, there is a lone gas pump by which cars can pump and groan along the gravel and raise a dust which is most disagreeable. The shabbiness of the Post Office is mercifully hidden by climbing vines and flowers.[18]

Behind such displays of irritation was her sense of being of another,

gentler world. Away from the Jamaican countryside, visiting community centres, social organisations and clubs, her strong social conscience struck people as endearing and rare. But in Kingston her
conservative views increasingly marked her as out of step with the
times.

In mid-October 1964, while at work at Jamsave, Una received a telephone call from the Israeli consul-general in Kingston, who had an
invitation for her from Golda Meir, Israel's Foreign Minister, to attend
a seminar for women leaders at the Mount Carmel International Training Centre for Community Services in Haifa and later a three-day
conference in Jerusalem on *The Role of Women in the Struggle for
Peace and Development*. Una was delighted: 'I could hardly believe my
eyes.'[19]

Aaron Matalon, at the Israel Consulate in Jamaica, had written her
an excellent testimonial, saying that Una was 'one of the outstanding
women of my country in this particular field and would be able to
continue this work irrespective of which political party is entrusted
with the running of the affairs of the country'.[20] He added this post-
script: 'Despite her age she is very youthful and energetic and enjoys
the best of health.' Una was fifty-nine, though her age was given as
fifty-eight.

NOTES

1   'Save the Children Fund Needs You', *Sunday Gleaner*, 25 June 1961, p. 5.
2   *Ibid.*
3   Orlando Patterson, *The Children of Sisyphus* (London, Longman, 1982), p. 7.
4   'The Rehabilitation of Western Kingston', *Daily Gleaner*, no date, c. 1962.
5   'Social Welfare Takes a New Look', *Sunday Gleaner*, 16 July 1961, p. 10.
6   *Ibid.*
7   *Daily Gleaner*, 25 February 1961, p. 1.
8   'Give the Worker a Better Deal if …', *Sunday Gleaner*, 17 December 1961, p. 9.
9   Coleridge Goode interviewed by the author, London, 1992.
10 *Ibid.*
11 Ethel Marson, *George Davis Goode* (Jamaica, published by the author, 1964).
12 'The Foundations of Independence', *Daily Gleaner*, 1 August 1964, p. 3.
13 'Jamaican Poetry – There Will Come Another Time', extract in Una Marson
     papers, 10 December 1961, p. 4.
14 *Ibid.*
15 *Ibid.*
16 'Women Poets of Jamaica', *Sunday Gleaner*, 2 August 1964, p. 28.
17 *Ibid.*
18 'Malvern: the Glory has Departed', *Daily Gleaner*, 29 August 1964.

19 'Una Marson Tells of an Unusual Visit to the Holy Land' (BBC Home Service), December 1964, Mount Carmel International Training Centre papers, Haifa, Israel.

20 Aaron Matalon to Eliashiv Ben Horin, Embassy of Israel, Caracas, 24 September 1964.

21

Haifa and London revisited

On Sunday 8 November 1964 Una 'stood in line at the Kingston airport, weak kneed and exhausted, but with a loving push from a few relatives and friends' she climbed aboard the aircraft for Tel-Aviv, a two-day journey with stops at New York, London and Rome. 'I had always said', Una later recounted, 'that if ever I reached the Holy Land, I would bow down and kiss the earth, and I did too. I had no idea what would happen in the month ahead, but I was in the Holy Land and it was sure to be good.'[1]

The Haifa seminar on 'Social and Cultural Integration in Urban Areas' had attracted nearly fifty delegates from Africa, Asia, Latin America and the Caribbean principally to discuss migration from rural to urban areas in terms of health, education, housing and problems faced by young people and women. The seminar had come about through the work of Golda Meir. During 1960, while touring West Africa, she had been asked to assist in development programmes for women. Following an initial conference in 1961 with over sixty delegates from Africa, Asia and the Mediterranean countries, Golda Meir had decided to expand and continue the international forum for women social workers, nurses, teachers, and MPs. The Mount Carmel Training Centre was founded that year as 'a permanent education centre for women'.[2]

On the first morning of the conference someone came to wake Una to breakfast: 'I ... went down for a cup of tea and saw through bleary eyes a huge hall with thirty delegates seated, each with the name and flag of her country indicating her place, saw the Jamaican flag and Jamaica in bold letters staring at me.'[3] Many of the African countries were unfamiliar to her, and yet the similarities among developing countries was striking: 'this was further emphasised as each delegate presented a paper on the problems facing her newly independent country'.[4] Una was yanked back into nostalgia. It had been so long since she had been able to enjoy such a vast, international gathering of professional women: memories of Lady Astor, Mrs Corbett Ashby, Mrs Rama Rau in Istanbul went rushing through her mind and she smiled at the recollection of her young inexperienced self. It really was a lifetime away.[5]

The conference was a successful one, and, though there was serious work to be done, there was ample time for leisure. The delegates entertained themselves with concerts, songs, folklore, dances and sketches; they went to the theatre to see the Israeli Dance Group. Una was overjoyed to be able to visit Nazareth, Upper Galilee, Beer-Shaba and the Dead Sea in the Negev. On 29 November Una left Haifa for the three-day international Conference in Jerusalem on the role of women in the struggle for peace and development. This gathering, like the Haifa seminar, was distinguished for the number of 'Third World' delegates present. Una was the only West Indian, but from Africa came Margaret Kenyatta from Kenya, Desta Gebrou from Ethiopia, Dorothy Atabong from Cameroon, Patience Hamilton from Sierra Leone and many others. Eighty-four women from forty-nine countries debated the sharing of responsibilities in political, economic and social spheres, the fulfilment of education and women in the vanguard of peace. Una spoke in the last debate and presented a ten-point plan of how women in the home, at work and within their countries could help bring about international peace. After the conference Una left for London.

It was a grey December morning in December 1964 when Una arrived back in London. It 'seemed so peaceful and quiet that I just sat back and let the solid peace and security of this lovely old city sink again into my heart. I couldn't see a single crater or damaged building. Here and there I saw a new moderate skyscraper which didn't seem to upset the landscape too much.'[6] Stella Mead came to Victoria Station to meet her and they taxied out to her cottage in Wembley Park, where Una had spent many happy days during the 1940s.

Later in the week she slipped into one of her old haunts, the busy Lyons Corner House by Trafalgar Square. It was 'much smarter inside and the prices a great deal higher, but the atmosphere the same. At dinner time people still crowded in to hear the orchestra playing the same old melodious tunes.'[7] But in other ways London was very different; there were familiar faces from 'back home', West Indians now living in Brixton, Camden Town and the whole borough of Paddington and in cheap rooms in Ladbrooke Grove, warmed by cheap oil burners. During the day they washed cups at £5 a week at the Lyons Corner House or spent hours, enclosed in the narrow confines of the tube carriage or the dark alleyways, underground. They had come to the 'Mother Country' in search of a better life, but many of them wondered what was better about bitter cold, basement flats and sharing the nervousness of the foreigner.

One chilly afternoon Una made a trip to Brixton market in south London. There she bought some ardoe bread, just one of the foodstuffs West Indians were picking up; the stocks of things they liked – saltfish, red beans by the pound, pig's foot and hot pepper sauce – were all ways to make the new home homely. Una loved the market's bustle and the music shop where ska, reggae and the wicked calypsos of Mighty Sparrow were for sale. Ska was coming from this Trinidadian shop that day.

Una spent a few days with the Larsens, her German friends, who were living in Kilburn, and met Erica Koch, the photographer. The Larsens were delighted to see Una after so many years. She kept on talking about her need to diet, and then moments later was spied eating a great deal of cheese. She knew she shouldn't. Her high blood pressure was troubling her and she had 'grown very fat' during the years in Washington.[8]

Una heard on the radio of the death of T. S. Eliot, to whom she had written while in Washington in 1955. She and Stella Mead decided to attend his funeral at St Stephen's Church in Gloucester Road, but before the funeral Una borrowed some Eliot from Stella's library and they read it together. Though she found his work difficult Una understood why younger poets 'in many countries have singled him out for special attention … His poetry was neither warm nor passionate … [it was] … hard-going but rewarding.'[9] Eliot had made an impact on some Caribbean poets; in particular, Edward Kamau Brathwaite was to note many years later that Eliot had introduced his generation to 'the notion of the speaking voice, the conversational tone. That is what attracted us to Eliot.'[10] Eliot had written for his sleeve note to *Four Quartets*: 'What a recording of a poem by its author can and should preserve, is the way that poem sounded to the author when he had finished it … . The chief value of the author's record … is the guide to the *rhythms*.'[11] Una had been on the same wavelength when, back in 1935, she listened to James Weldon Johnson's reading of 'Creation'. Sound, by radio, tape or record, had been within her lifetime the chief guide to extending literary knowledge.

Her own broadcasting career was not over yet. She recorded an interview with Andrew Salkey for the West Indies, but her last broadcast was to be on the prominent *Woman's Hour* on the Home Service in which she talked about the Mount Carmel Training Centre and its work for women in developing countries. It was pre-recorded on New Year's Day 1965, and transmitted on 18 February. The producer was Doreen Forsyth. The excitement didn't stop at Christmas: Una had friends to visit and went to the department stores down Oxford Street. The atmosphere of the West End, with cars careening around in the bright lights of Piccadilly Circus, lifted her spirits.

When it came, Christmas morning was mild and pleasantly crisp. Una attended service at St Martin-in-the-Fields led by the Reverend Austin Williams and enjoyed it, then she took a bus to Holland Park for lunch with Andrew Salkey, his wife, Pat, 'their lovely children'[12] and family friends. It turned into a glorious day of witty, amusing conversation with George Lamming, the well-known Barbadian novelist who at thirty-three already had five books to his credit, and other West Indian writers. She was happy to be with people who were engaging seriously with literature, new ideas and race politics. Only when she spent an evening with fellow poet Vivian Virtue, who threw a party in her honour, did she fully grasp how things had moved on: there were so many other West Indian writers to meet. A familiar friendly face from years back was Vera Murphy, who had played Sister Kate in *Pocomania* in 1938.

Caribbean artists and writers were now doing really well in London. A new generation of Caribbean poets, novelists and artists were taking over and beginning to form themselves into what two years later would be the Caribbean Artists Movement, an aid to developing their own cultural aesthetic. The young names associated with the group were Edward Kamau Brathwaite, John La Rose, Andrew Salkey, Orlando Patterson, Wilson Harris, Ronald Moody, Kenneth Ramchand and Gordon Rholehr. They were, in general, male, young and well-educated. The writers had profited from the first decade of *Caribbean Voices* as listeners, and then as contributors; they had lived through the Second World War without having to fight in it and they had the benefit of being the bright youth of newly independent nations. Students, teachers, university-educated, scholarship men, all were products of the interwar Caribbean colonies. As teenage boys they had watched their fathers strike for better pay and now they were impatient with European cultural domination, minority status, artistic isolation and obscurity. Una met them, liked them and respected them, and they her. She especially admired the initiative of one group which included her older friends Vivian Virtue and Rudolph Dunbar who, in response to the conditions of life for Britain's new immigrants, had decided to launch a weekly paper, *New Magnet*, on 9 February with the Guyanese actor-writer Jan Carew as editor.

December 1964 was the month of Martin Luther King's short visit to London on his way to Oslo to receive the Nobel Peace Prize. Una missed his speech at Africa Unity House in Collingham Gardens where he had met David (later Lord) Pitt, Claudia Jones, Edric and Pearl Connor, all leading West Indian political activists. Quite by chance, however, she learnt that Learie Constantine, the cricketer who was 'one of the best loved and respected West Indians in Britain', who had also met Luther King, was living round the corner from the Larsens, and immediately went round to see him and catch up on the important visit.[13] Then she met David Pitt, the Grenadan doctor who had been in England for twelve years and was a London County Council member. By December 1964 the grubbiness of postwar British attitudes towards the new immigrants was beginning to show. She was annoyed to hear how the Labour government had responded, and she cheered up only when she caught C. L. R. James debating the issues in a topical BBC series.

Nevertheless it was an engrossing and flattering experience to be drawn into the debate about CARD, the Campaign Against Racial Discrimination, instigated by Martin Luther King. CARD members were trying to formulate anti-discrimination laws and to repeal the 1962 Commonwealth Immigrants Act.[14] 'We can only hope', she wrote, 'that inter-racial relations will be improved by the formation of CARD and that wisdom, tact and patience will temper their anxiety to bring about better conditions for all coloured immigrants.'[15] Radical measures were not the answer for Una. She remained a little outmoded in the context of 1960s London where youth's screams, mods and rockers slid on to the scene.

Her heart was in the right place; nevertheless, her political caution pointed up one of the signs of age. Una called at the headquarters of the Save the Children Fund in Camberwell to bring the staff up to date with progress in Jamaica. Jamsave was to receive the proceeds of a Christmas matinée at St Martin-in-the-Fields for the Foreshore Road

Infant Centre where real progress had been made for Rastafarian children: 'They are all anxious to co-operate in the administration of food, clothing and the regular infant school work.'[16] Finance was still precarious: the government allowed £12 a term for fruit, subscribers gave 10s a year and Jamsave held a 'Month and TAG Day' to raise funds but money was still tight. Una didn't like begging, but she had to do a lot of it, simply to get 'soap, toilet paper, school books and pencils beads, and sugar for the powdered milk'.[17]

The Save the Children Fund show at St Martin-in-the-Fields was fun; Una and Stella Mead enjoyed 'scenes from "Camelot" in which Laurence Harvey sings in the leading role; a short nativity play; ballet scenes; and the singing of carols with the large cast of Camelot led by Laurence Harvey'. In the *Daily Gleaner* Una wrote enthusiastically about London's West End, citing as evidence the difficulty she had in acquiring tickets for ballet, opera and theatre. But most of what she did see thrilled her and reminded her why London was always her first love. In a spate of theatre going she and Stella caught *The Nutcracker Suite* at the New Victoria and, having just come from Israel, she was 'very interested to see the magnificent film *Lawrence of Arabia*', and enjoyed *Beckett*, the French version of *Murder in the Cathedral*. Her most 'unforgettable memory of the season's theatre', however, was Ibsen's *The Master Builder* with Laurence Olivier playing the lead. 'It is many years since I have seen such excellent theatre.'[18]

In spite of the surface jollity, Una was deeply concerned about her future. She couldn't face the thought of returning to Jamaica. A bolt-hole was essential. Una thought of returning to Israel to work at the Mount Carmel Training Centre as a House Mother. Mina Ben-Zwi, the director, who liked Una deeply and felt that she was more a visionary than a practical worker, was concerned about Una's health and asked her to give the matter 'serious consideration … the job requires quite a bit of physical strain', she wrote on 27 December, 'staying up late at night, attending to the sick and those in need of special help, and various other small duties which you may not have thought about. Please also consider the climate and your health. Except for room and board, the remuneration for this job is rather small.'[19] Her concern did not end there; she went on: 'Dear Miss Marson, as much as I would like to see you with us, I would not like you to be disappointed. If, however, you feel that you are indeed keen and are physically capable of undertaking this job, we shall be very happy to welcome you for a period of three months.'[20]

Una, even in better health, should not have taken this job. Her friend Mina knew it was too much and had said so as sensitively as she could. But Una did not like the feelings she had of rootlessness and displacement, and she clung to the last moments of happiness she had experienced. Haifa it would be. She replied point by point to Mina Ben-Zwi's anxieties, and with superfluous reassurances: 'I have seen the doctor here and my pressure is down. I am physically fit and really quite strong.' Una had never earned a big salary and was not put off by the 'rather small' one on offer: 'I have never had a great concern about money. There are a few obligations I have to meet at home but I live very simply.'[21] The letter was one of her more excruciating revelations of melancholy.

On 24 January 1965, Una flew back to Haifa, ready to face a busy period. Her contract was for three months. Una continued to write articles for the *Daily Gleaner* and did occasional work for the BBC. At the Mount Carmel Training Centre all seemed to be well at first. Una was popular among the participants and Mina became especially fond of her, but Una was still suffering from high blood pressure and the pace of her life never slowed.

Una found Israel's cultural life much to her taste, enjoyed the Israel Symphony Orchestra and hoped that, one day, they would tour Jamaica. Early one morning Una took a bus to the world centre of the Baha'i faith in Haifa:

> The dome glistened in the sunlight and the abundance of pine trees that shaded the paths and flower beds gave one a feeling of joy, peace and serenity. There were few people about though I learned later that on a summer's day last year there had been a thousand visitors in one day. As I walked up the path to the shrine I discovered how wise the pioneers had been in selecting this spot with its fifty acres. Looking over the lower buildings of the city one had the most magnificent view of the Mediterranean and the Haifa harbour that was to be seen from any spot in Haifa. On this lovely day the sky and the sea seemed to be competing to present the most attractive shade of blue. I couldn't [help] feeling that a plain slab over the remains of the Bab here on the spot where I stood would have been shrine enough for any saint. ... Two women stood at the entrance. The older, with greying hair, was conversing with an American tourist. The other came up to me and said I could go in but first take off my shoes. As I walked into the flower decked candle-lighted square hall on the lovely Persian rugs I saw good reason, in addition to reverence, to approach shoeless. A magnificent chandelier hung from the low ceiling, a thin transparent veil protected the shrine.

There was an abundance of fresh flowers artistically arranged. Two exquisite tapestries hung from the walls. That was all.[22]

In March Una was awarded a British Council scholarship to do research into social development in Jamaica over the past fifty years. This was to be her last major work. Una had discussed the project in London with a publisher and 'had been thinking it would be wonderful to end it with my experiences in Israel', but it was not to be.[23] Towards the end of March she began to suffer from a melancholy that aroused Mina's loving concern. Mina tried to coax her into co-operating with the doctors. But Una, ill, frightened and exhausted, took refuge in fantasy. For one thing, she did not want to return to Jamaica. She was afraid of going home, perhaps feeling that there would be nothing there for her. She dismissed her sense of panic by insisting that she would fly to London and continue with her writing. Mina thought not.

As far as the outside world was concerned, Una was suffering only from high blood pressure. She was hoping to complete her Jamaican book and Penguin, it seemed, might have published it. But she, the self-styled diplomat, who had always so ably represented others, was now herself the subject of urgent, confidential conferences. At her wits' end, Mina tried to decide what to do.

Una had to be persuaded to return to Jamaica. Mina must have sensed that she would not live much longer. In any case, work of any kind was out of the question. The physician said she would need constant care until she recovered, Mina later wrote: 'You surely understand that in our set-up as a training centre, it was impossible, neither could we think of placing her in a hospital. She is too intelligent to cause her such distress. ... According to medical advice, it was best for her to return home and be with her relatives.'[24]

On 10 April Una flew home. Mina telegrammed to Ethel, and to Matalon, the honorary consul in Jamaica: 'Una Marson left today via New York, arriving Kingston Monday Pan American 221. Please meet and encourage, letter follows.'[25] On the plane to New York Una was taken care of. The Israeli consulate in New York looked after her and encouraged her until she boarded the plane for Jamaica. Homecoming for Una had so often resulted from pain and distress.

Back in Kingston Una's reliance on Ethel's comforting nursing skills resumed. She was frantic and afraid. Day by day she grew worse until after about ten days at home she was admitted to Kingston Hospital. Ethel wrote to Mina-Ben Zwi, 'Una went very reluctantly to Hospital where she would have more complete rest and care.'[26] Even in a state of severe depression and physical weakness, Una retained her sensitivity to others. On 3 May Ethel was able to spend some time with her and found that she had regained her consciousness: 'She asked me to write to thank you for forwarding her two suitcases and the painting which arrived safely', she told Mina. 'She asked me to enclose $30 in Israeli money towards the cost of this.' Una had been embarrassed about her depression: 'She wanted you to know how desperately sorry she was about the confusion caused at the end. I told her not to worry about it and when she felt well enough she could write to you herself about it.'[27]

She had written her own obituary in her early thirties: 'Confession' of a troubled soul, which said: 'I regret nothing / I have lived / I have loved', ends:

> Why should I
> Sorrowing go?
> Have I not lived?

After ten days in hospital Una 'collapsed and her heart gave out'. She had suffered a heart attack and died on 6 May 1965.

NOTES

1 'Una Marson Tells of an Unusual Visit to the Holy Land' (BBC Home Service), December 1964.
2 Mount Carmel Training Centre, 1981 brochure.
3 'Una Marson Tells'.
4 *Ibid.*
5 *Ibid.*
6 'London Revisited', *Daily Gleaner*, 28 February 1965.
7 *Ibid.*
8 Ursula Larsen interviewed by the author, 1989, London.
9 'After Thoughts on London', unpublished article, Una Marson papers, Box 1944C, National Library of Jamaica.
10 Edward Kamau Brathwaite, *History of the Voice* (London, New Beacon Books, 1984), p. 31.
11 *Ibid.*
12 'London Revisited'.
13 'After Thoughts on London'.
14 *Ibid.* The 1962 Commonwealth Immigrants Act restricted entry for those without dependents already resident in Britain.
15 'After Thoughts on London'.
16 Save the Children Fund publicity.

17 *The World's Children*, vol. 45, no. 1, March 1965, p. 7.

18 'London Revisited'.

19 Mina Ben-Zwi to Una Marson, Mount Carmel Training Centre papers, Haifa, Israel, no date.

20 *Ibid.*

21 Una Marson to Mina Ben-Zwi, Mount Carmel Training Centre papers, Marson file, Haifa, Israel.

22 Una Marson, 'Newsletter from Haifa, Israel', recorded 15 February 1965. Date of transmission unknown. BBC written archives, Caversham.

23 Una Marson to Mina Ben-Zwi, no date but December 1964 or January 1965, Mount Carmel Training Centre papers, Marson file, Haifa, Israel.

24 Mina Ben-Zwi to Aaron Matalon, Mount Carmel Training Centre papers, Marson file, Haifa, Israel.

25 Telegram from Mina Ben-Zwi to Ethel Marson, Mount Carmel Training Centre papers, Marson file, Haifa, Israel.

26 Ethel Marson to Mina Ben-Zwi, May 1965, Mount Carmel Training Centre papers, Marson file, Haifa, Israel.

27 *Ibid.*

22

Epilogue

'I HAVE lost a friend who, though I knew her a short time, has won a special place in my heart', Mina Ben-Zwi wrote to Stella Mead, later that May.

In Jamaica tributes from the Save the Children Fund, the YWCA, the Jamaica Teachers Association, fellow writers, R. L. C. Aarons, Archie Lindo, Aimee Webster and a younger woman of letters, Sylvia Wynter, appeared in the *Gleaner* and the *Jamaica Times*.

Cecil Browne, one-time secretary of the Readers and Writers Club, recalled meeting her in North America when she was 'not in the best of health' and in recent months when

> she had complained of being tired, yet on hearing where I intended to take a special bus, she insisted on accompanying me. I protested but she would not be put off. We talked of many topics, not all serious … as I boarded the bus and waved to Miss Marson, I thought how uncommonly gracious was this woman who had walked with the mighty yet who generously saw me board my bus and faced the walk back alone.[1]

Regret and anger were expressed by Vera Murphy, who had seen Una on her way to Haifa:

> Observing her keenly as we chatted, I could not help a feeling of sorrow which overwhelmed me, for here was a great Jamaican woman going away from her native land – a land striving to establish much of what this great woman had to offer – and here she was going further and further away, not anchored to anywhere, anything or anyone.[1]

A recital in her memory was planned for early July to be held at Kingston Parish Church to help raise funds for a memorial project in St Elizabeth. A memorial fund for a 'Una Marson Memorial Infant Centre' at Trench Town was started by the Jamaica Save the Children Fund.

In London Una's death was briefly noted in the press: references were made to her BBC work during the war and to her poetry.

In Haifa the Mount Carmel Training Centre decided to award a scholarship for a Jamaican young woman to the annual leaders' seminar. This was something, Ethel wrote, that Una would have liked. 'You have all been very kind in your tributes to Una and I am very grateful to you. Una and I were very attached to one another and it will be a long time before the effects of the shock of her sudden passing leave me.'[2] Ethel became Una's executor. She had died intestate, leaving an estate of £1,320.

She was buried at St Andrew's Parish church in Kingston on 10 May. The funeral cortège went on for miles. A simple service was conducted by the Reverend Carnegie. He said Una had lived a full, rich life, incredible in its scope even to those who had known her from her childhood. The church was packed.

Today no headstone marks Una Marson's grave; the ground is covered with 'Rice and Peas', small, pink Jamaican flowers, growing wild.

NOTES

1 Letter, *Daily Gleaner*, 19 May 1965.
2 'Una Marson – Expressions of Love, Now that She's Gone', *The Star*, 14 May 1965. Among the Una Marson papers are many other press tributes.
3 Ethel Marson to Mrs Naayan, 11 October 1965, Mount Carmel Training Centre papers, Marson file, Haifa, Israel.

Selected bibliography

PRIMARY SOURCES

PERSONAL TESTIMONY

Interviews conducted by Delia Jarrett-Macauley:

John Aarons, Amy Bailey, Frank Cameron, Stuart Hall, Cedric Lindo, Ulric Cross, Richard Hart, Aimee Webster Delisser, the late C. L. R. James, Philip Sherlock, Constance Cummings John, Christine Moody, Sylvia Lowe, Wycliffe Bennett, Margaret Ingledew, Hugh Morrison, Egon Larsen, Ursula Larsen, Henry Swanzy, Mary Treadgold, Stephen Hill, Clifton Neita, Carmen Lusan, T. I. Campbell, Archie Lindo, Jenny Goffe, Calvin Boyne, Dudley Thompson, Cecil Baugh, Olive Baxter, Winston White, Vivien Carrington, (Ms) Wesley Gammon, Isobel Seaton, Myra Stedman, Theodore Sealy, Robert Wellesley Cole, Connie Mark

Written testimony sent to the author by:

Emmanuel Abraham, Sibthorpe Beckett, Andrew Salkey, Mary Treadgold, Aimee Webster, Sylvia Vietzen

COLLECTIONS OF PAPERS

Una Marson papers, National Library of Jamaica, Kingston, Jamaica

Women's International League for Peace and Freedom, London School of Economics, London

Claude A. Barnett papers, Chicago Historical Society, Chicago

Caribbean Service: BBC written archives, Caversham Park, Reading

Winifred Holtby Archives, Kingston upon Hull Central Library, Hull

J .E. Clare McFarlane papers, National Library of Jamaica, Kingston

W. M. Macmillan papers, in the private possession of Mrs Mona Macmillan

Nancy Cunard papers, Chicago Historical Society, Chicago

T. S. Eliot papers, in the possession of Mrs Valerie Eliot

Langston Hughes papers, Beinecke Rare Book and Manuscript Library, Yale University, New Haven, Connecticut

James Weldon Johnson papers, Beinecke Rare Book and Manuscript Library, Yale University, New Haven, Connecticut

Larsen papers, in the possession of Ursula Larsen, London

George Orwell Archive, University College London

MINUTES, ANNUAL REPORTS AND ORGANISATIONAL PAPERS

The YMCA Kingston, Jamaica

The British Commonwealth League, Sadd Brown Collection, Fawcett Library, Guildhall, London

The Fabian Colonial Bureau, Rhodes House, Oxford

The Jamaica Save the Children Fund

The League of Coloured Peoples: *The Keys* and *Newsnotes*

The Mount Carmel International Training Centre for Community Development, Haifa, Israel

The Salvation Army, London

The Save the Children Fund, London

NEWSPAPERS AND PERIODICALS

Barbados Advocate; *Baptist Missionary Herald*; *Jamaica Critic*; *The Cosmopolitan*, *New Cosmopolitan*; *Jamaica Times*; *Daily Gleaner*; *Daily Argosy*; *Jamaica Review*; *News Chronicle*; *The Times*; *Times Literary Supplement*; *Manchester Guardian*; *Trinidadian Guardian*; *Port of Spain Guardian*; *Public Opinion* (Jamaica); *World's Children*; *Jamaica Standard*; *The Keys*; *Newsnotes*; *The Blackman*; *WASU*; *West Africa*; *West Indian*; *American Junior Red Cross News*; *Daily Herald*; *Saturday Review of Jamaica*; *The Friend*

OTHER PRIMARY SOURCES

Birth certificate of Una Marson at the Public Record Office, Spanish Town, Jamaica

Tape of Una Marson reading and discussing the work of James Weldon Johnson in the possession of the author

BBC sound archives c/o British Library: interview by Una Marson of Ken Johnson taking part in Christmas broadcast

Pictures held in private collections of Egon and Ursula Larsen and of Mona Macmillan; in BBC photographic unit, London; in the archives of the National Library of Jamaica collections

Performance:

Una Marson, *Pocomania*, Stockwell, London, November 1990

Films:

West Indies Calling, Paul Rotha Productions for the Ministry of Information, directed by John Page. Speakers: Una Marson, Learie Constantine, Ulric Cross and Carlton Fairweather. 1943

Hello West Indies, Paul Rotha Productions for the Ministry of Information, directed by John Page with Una Marson as hostess, 1943

Miss Amy and Miss May, Sistren Theatre Company in association with Jamaican Broadcasting Company, 1990

THE WORKS OF UNA MARSON

Tropic Reveries (Kingston Jamaica, published by the author, 1930)

Heights and Depths (Kingston, Jamaica, published by the author, 1931)

'At What a Price' (unpublished playscript, 1932, British Library)

The Moth and the Star (Kingston, Jamaica, published by the author, 1937)

'Pocomania' (unpublished manuscript, Kingston, Jamaica, 1938)

Towards the Stars (London, University of London Press, 1945)

Short stories:

'Sojourn', *The Cosmopolitan*, February 1931

'Christmas on Poinsettia Island', *American Junior Red Cross News*, vol. 42, no. 3, December 1960

SECONDARY SOURCES

SELECTED BIOGRAPHIES AND AUTOBIOGRAPHIES

Brittain, V., *Testament of Experience* (London, Fontana, 1980)

Brittain, V., *Testament of Friendship* (London, Virago Press, 1980)

Brown, W., *Edna Manley, the Private Years: 1900–1938* (London, André Deutsch, 1975)

Buhle, Paul, *C. L. R. James: the Artist as Revolutionary* (London, Verso, 1988)

Dubermann, Martin, *Paul Robeson* (London, Bodley Head, 1989)

Ford Smith, Honor, *Una Marson: Black Nationalist and Feminist Writer* (Kingston, Jamaica, Sistren Publications, 1986)

Hemenway, Robert, *Zora Neale Hurston: a Literary Biography* (London, Camden Press, 1986)

Hill, Frank, *Bustamente and His Letters* (Kingston, Jamaica, Kingston Publishers Ltd, 1976)

Hurston, Zora Neale, *Tell my Horse* (New York, Harper Row, 1990)

Lord Kinross, *Ataturk: the Rebirth of a Nation* (London, Weidenfeld and Nicolson, 1964)

Lewis, R., *Marcus Garvey: Anti-Colonial Champion* (London, Karia Press, 1987)

Makin, William, *Caribbean Nights* (London, Robert Hale, 1939)

Manley, Rachel, *The Diaries of Edna Manley* (London, André Deutsch, 1990)

Marks, Shula, *Not Either an Experimental Doll* (London, Women's Press, 1985)

Rampersad, A., *A Life of Langston Hughes* (New York, Oxford University Press, 1989)

Sherlock, Philip, *Norman Manley* (London, Macmillan, 1980)

Somerville, J. A., *Man of Colour* (Kingston, Jamaica, Pioneer Press, 1951)

Vaughan, David, *Negro Victory: the Life Story of Dr Harold Moody* (London, Independent Press, 1950)

West, W. J., *Orwell: the War Broadcasts* (London, Duckworth and BBC, 1985)

West, W. J., *Orwell: the War Commentaries* (London, Duckworth and BBC, 1985)

Who's Who in Jamaica and Why (Kingston, Jamaica, Institute of Jamaica, 1951)

GENERAL HISTORIES AND CRITICISM

Baxter, Ivy, *Arts of an Island* (Chicago, Scarecrow Press, 1970)

Brathwaite, Edward Kaumau, *Contradictory Omens* (Kingston, Jamaica, Savacou Publications, 1974)

Brathwaite, Edward Kamau, *History of the Voice* (London, New Beacon Books, 1984)

Bryan, Patrick, *The Jamaican People: 1880–1902* (London, Macmillan, 1991)

Cudjoe, S. (ed.), *Caribbean Women Writers: Essays from the First International Conference* (Wellesley, Mass., Calaloux Publications, 1990)

Fryer, Peter, *Staying Power* (London, Pluto Press, 1984)

Hart, R., *Rise and Organise* (London, Karia Press, 1989)

James, Louis, *The Islands in Between: Essays on West Indian Literature* (London, Oxford University Press, 1968)

Jayawardena, Kumari, *Feminism and Nationalism in the Third World* (London, Zed Books, 1985)

Johnson, James Weldon, *Black Manhattan* (New York, Da Capo, 1991)

Lamming, George, *Pleasures of Exile* (London, Allison and Busby, 1984)

Lewis, Arthur, *Labour in the West Indies* (London, New Beacon, 1977)

McFarlane, Clare, *A Literature in the Making* (Kingston, Jamaica, Pioneer Press, 1956)

Mathieson, Margaret and Schreiber, Adele, *Journey Towards Freedom: Written for the Golden Jubilee of the International Alliance of Women* (Copenhagen, IAWSEC, 1955)

Nasta, Shusheila (ed.), *Motherlands* (London, Women's Press, 1991)

Omotoso, Kole, *The Theatrical into Theatre* (London, New Beacon Books, 1982)

Owusu, Kwesi, *The Struggle for Black Arts in Britain* (London, Commedia, 1986)

Post, Ken, *Arise Ye Starvelings: the Jamaica Labour Rebellion of 1938 and its Aftermath* (The Hague, Institute of Social Studies, 1978)

Ramchand, Kenneth, *Introduction to the Study of West Indian Literature* (Sunbury-on-Thames, Middlesex, Nelson, 1976)

Sherlock, P., *The West Indies* (London, Thames and Hudson, 1966)

Sherlock, Parry and Maingot, Anthony, *A Short History of the West Indies* (New York, St Martin's Press, 1987)

Sherwood, M., *Many Struggles: West Indian Workers and Service Personnel* (London, Karia Press, 1985)

Walmesley, Anne, *The Caribbean Arts Movement – 1966–1972* (London, New Beacon Books, 1992)

ARTICLES

Bennett, W., 'The Jamaican Theatre: a Preliminary Overview', *Jamaica Journal*, vol. 8, nos 2 and 3 (summer 1974)

Cobham-Sander, R., 'The Caribbean Voices Programme and the Development of West Indian Short Fiction: 1945–1958', in *The Story Must be Told: Short Narrative Prose in New English Literatures*, ed. Peter O. Stummer (Bayreuth, Koningshausen & Newmann, 1986)

Fowler, H., 'A History of Theatre in Jamaica', *Jamaica Journal*, vol. 2, no. 1 (March 1968), pp. 53–9

Gradussov, A., 'Thoughts about the Theatre in Jamaica', *Jamaica Journal*, vol. 4 (March 1970), pp. 50ff.

Gray, C., 'Folk Themes in West Indian Drama: an Analysis', *Caribbean Quarterly* vol. 14, nos 1 and 2 (1968), pp. 102–9

Morris, M., 'On Reading Louise Bennett, Seriously', *Jamaica Journal*, vol. 1, no. 1 (December 1967), pp. 67–74

Nettleford, R., 'Pocomania in Dance-Theatre', *Jamaica Journal*, vol. 3 (June 1969), pp. 21–4

Seaga, E., 'Revival Cults in Jamaica: Notes towards a Sociology of Religion', *Jamaica Journal*, vol. 3 (June 1969), pp. 3–13

Tuchman, B., 'Biography as a Prism of History', in *Practising History* (London, Macmillan, 1985)

Warner-Lewis, Maureen, 'The Nkuyu: Spirit Messengers of the Kumina', *Caribbean Woman*, Savacou 13, Kingston, Jamaica, 1981

NOVELS, POETRY AND PLAYS

Bennett, Louise, *Jamaican Dialect Poems* (Kingston, Jamaica, Gleaner, 1948)

Cobham-Sander, R. and Collins, Merle, *Watchers and Seekers* (London, Women's Press, 1987)

Delisser, Herbert G., *Jane's Career*, (London, Methuen, 1914)

Emecheta, Buchi, *Second Class Citizen* (London, Fontana, 1973)

Figueroa, John (ed.), *The Blue Horizons: Caribbean Voices Volume 2* (London, Evans, 1970)

Honey, Maureen (ed.), *Shadowed Dreams: Women's Poetry of the Harlem Renaissance* (New Brunswick, Rutgers University Press, 1989)

Hughes, Langston, *Selected Poems* (London, Pluto Press, 1986)

Hughes, Langston, *The Ways of White Folks* (New York, Random House, 1990)

Lamming, George, *In the Castle of my Skin* (London, Longman, 1970)

Lamming, George, *The Emigrants* (London, Allison and Busby, 1982)

Marshall, Paule, *Brown Girl, Brownstones* (London, Virago Press, 1982)

Paton, Alan, *Cry, the Beloved Country* (London, Penguin, 1987)

Patterson, Orlando, *The Children of Sisyphus* (London, Longman, 1982)

Reid, Vic, *New Day* (New York and London, Heinemann, 1987)

Reid, Vic, *14 Jamaican Short Stories* (Kingston, Jamaica, Pioneer Press, 1952)

St Vincent Millay, E., *Collected Sonnets* (New York, Harper Row, 1988)

Selvon, Samuel, *The Lonely Londoners* (London, Longman, 1972)

Sistren, *Lionheart Gal'* (London, Women's Press, 1987)

Walker, Alice, *In Search of Our Mothers' Gardens* (London, Women's Press, 1984)

UNPUBLISHED RESEARCH PAPERS

Cobham-Sander, R., 'The Writer in Jamaican Society 1900–1950', Ph.D. thesis, University of St Andrews, 1982

French, J., 'Colonial Policy towards Women after the 1938 Uprising: the Case of Jamaica', presented to the Conference of the Caribbean Studies Association, Caracas, Venezuela, May 1986.

French, J. and Ford-Smith, H., 'Women and Organisation in Jamaica 1900–1944', Women and Development Studies, Institute of Social and Economic Research, The Hague

Smilowitz, E., 'Marson, Rhys and Mansfield', Ph.D. thesis, University of New Mexico, 1984

Index